BEYOND THE NORTH-SOUTH STALEMATE

Roger D. Hansen

1980s Project/Council on Foreign Relations

McGRAW-HILL BOOK COMPANY
New York   St. Louis   San Francisco
Auckland   Bogotá   Düsseldorf   Johannesburg   London   Madrid
Mexico   Montreal   New Delhi   Panama   Paris   São Paulo
Singapore   Sydney   Tokyo   Toronto

The Council on Foreign Relations, Inc., is a nonprofit and nonpartisan organization devoted to promoting improved understanding of international affairs through the free exchange of ideas. Its membership of about 1,700 persons throughout the United States is made up of individuals with special interest and experience in international affairs. The Council has no affiliation with and receives no funding from the United States government.

The Council publishes the journal *Foreign Affairs* and, from time to time, books and monographs which in the judgment of the Council's Committee on Studies are responsible treatments of significant international topics worthy of presentation to the public. The 1980s Project is a research effort of the Council; as such, 1980s Project Studies have been similarly reviewed through procedures of the Committee on Studies. As in the case of all Council publications, statements of fact and expressions of opinion contained in 1980s Project Studies are the sole responsibility of their authors.

Lucy Despard was the editor of this book for the Council on Foreign Relations. Thomas Quinn and Michael Hennelly were the editors for McGraw-Hill Book Company. Christopher Simon was the designer. Teresa Leaden supervised the production. It was set in Caledonia by Offset Composition Services, Inc., and printed and bound by R. R. Donnelley & Sons, Inc.

Library of Congress Cataloging in Publication Data

Hansen, Roger D.
Beyond the North-South stalemate.

(1980s project/Council on Foreign Relations)
Includes index.
1. International relations.   2.   Underdeveloped
areas—Foreign relations.   I.   Title.   II.   Series:
Council on Foreign Relations.   1980s project/Council
on Foreign Relations.
JX1395.H324   327'.09172'4   78-10607
ISBN 0-07-026048-6
ISBN 0-07-026049-4 pbk.

1 2 3 4 5 6 7 8 9 D O D O 7 9 4 3 2 1 0 9

To the memory of my Father

Contents

Part V CONCLUSION

Foreword: The 1980s Project

Two central rifts mark international relations: the North-South division between rich states and poor, and the East-West division, which derives from security concerns and differing conceptions about *the management of society*. Neither division is today hard and fast. Both have undergone rapid and dramatic change in the period since World War II. As one looks to the future, the picture becomes even more complicated—with many states fitting less easily into prevailing categories and many global problems cross-cutting conventional patterns of world politics. A major aim in the future should clearly be to facilitate continuing change in ways that reduce tensions and injustices among and within societies.

Several volumes that have been published by the 1980s Project of the Council on Foreign Relations have addressed aspects of the broad cluster of problems that today come under the heading of North-South relations. Only in the last decade have these problems become a central feature of international relations, as power has been diffused more broadly—albeit unevenly—throughout the international system; as developing countries have sought to mobilize their collective strength in pursuit of a new international order; and as industrialized countries have increasingly become the purchasers of critical raw materials and competitive manufactured goods from economies that they are ever less able to control.

In essence, the cluster of North-South problems exemplifies the fundamental questions of all politics—who commands and who benefits. The developing countries have made the case that they have neither an adequate voice nor a fair share of the benefits that

stem from participation in the international system. In making this
case, they have brought the issue of equity to the center of international politics. The debate on equity among nations has, in turn,
drawn attention to the persistence of absolute poverty and the wide
disparities of income and wealth within developing states. And there
is now growing consensus that there must be some reform in the
international system to better reflect diverse interests and to reduce
global inequities both within and among states. There is little
agreement, however, on the shape that reform should take.

In this context the work of the 1980s Project on North-South
relations has sought primarily to identify norms, goals, and principles that should guide change in political and economic relations
between rich and poor nations. Three issues are at the center of this
aspect of Project work. First is the question of prospects for changing
the structure of relations between rich and poor states, and the
impact of alternative reforms on the competing demands of equity,
efficiency, autonomy, and order. Second, Project work on North-
South relations poses questions about the capacity, and the obligation, of the international community to bring about internal
change—especially regarding conditions of absolute poverty and
egregious violations of human rights. The third issue is the impact of
the evolving "South" on the management of international economic
and security problems which range from the supply of natural
resources to the proliferation of nuclear weapons.*

Roger Hansen, a former member of the Project staff, helped to
design much of this work, which suggests ways to improve economic
relations among rich and poor nations and enhance prospects for

---

*Other volumes in the 1980s Project that deal with major problems at issue in
relations between rich and poor states include: *Rich and Poor Nations in the World
Economy* by Albert Fishlow, Carlos Diaz-Alejandro, Richard R. Fagen, and Roger D.
Hansen; *Reducing Global Inequities* by W. Howard Wriggins and Gunnar Adler-
Karlsson; *Sharing Global Resources* by Ruth W. Arad and Uzi B. Arad, Rachel
McCulloch and Jose Piñera, and Ann L. Hollick; and a forthcoming study with
essays by John Williamson and Larry Sjaastad on improved international methods
for long-term financing of development. In addition to these studies the Project has
published a series of studies on the political and economic forces of change in each of
the five major regions of the developing world—Africa, Latin America, Middle East
and North Africa, South Asia, and Southeast Asia—as well as related studies on
control of conventional arms trade and human rights.

growth and development in "the South." In this volume, which is one of several core studies written by members of the Project staff, he not only brings together many of the themes that run through earlier Project studies but also gives his own analysis of the attitudes and interests that have bred today's tensions between North and South. In the latter part of his study he pushes beyond this analysis to suggest ways in which Northern goals, strategies, and policies—in particular those of the United States—should be reformulated to move beyond what he characterizes as today's "stalemate" system to more fruitful, durable, and just relationships.

Professor Hansen's study and other work of the 1980s Project reflect the widely held recognition that many of the assumptions, policies, and institutions that have characterized international relations during the past 30 years are inadequate to the demands of today and the foreseeable demands of the next few decades. Indeed the Project is based on the view that over the course of the next decade, substantial adaptation of institutions and behavior will be needed to respond to changing circumstances. The Project has thus sought to identify future conditions and the kinds of adaptations they might require. More specifically, the Project has sought since its inception to examine means by which governments can resolve their conflicts through orderly processes so that violence will become decreasingly a recourse for the settlement of disputes. It has explored a range of measures to bring about greater equity—among and within nations—in the distribution of income and wealth. And it has suggested ways to enable governments and individuals to gain a greater sense of participation in determining conditions affecting their future.

The principal challenge of Project work has been to identify directions of change that reconcile the three major objectives of moderation, greater equity, and participation—with each other and with the perceived interests of states whose ideologies and levels of income differ. In this pursuit a time horizon of ten to twenty years has been used to free analysis from the constraints of day-to-day decision making and from the short-term perspective from which foreign policy is usually formulated without, however, pushing analysis so far into the future that prescriptions become utopian or irrelevant. In addition the Project has encouraged the examination of political and economic problems not in isolation but in relation to one another. Each Project study that is being published is thus designed to stand on its own; at the same time it has been shaped by a broader perspective.

The 1980s Project is thus both a series of separate attacks upon a number of urgent and potentially urgent international problems and also a collective effort, involving a substantial number of persons in the United States and abroad, to bring those separate approaches to bear upon one another and to suggest the kinds of choices that might be made among them. The Project has involved more than 300 participants. A small central staff and a steering Coordinating Group have worked to define the questions and to assess the compatibility of policy prescriptions. Nearly 100 authors, from more than a dozen countries, have contributed separate studies. Ten working groups of specialists and generalists were convened over the course of two years to subject these studies to critical scrutiny and to help in the process of identifying interrelationships among them.

The 1980s Project is the largest single research and studies effort the Council on Foreign Relations has undertaken in its 55-year history, comparable in conception only to a major study of the postwar world, the War and Peace Studies, undertaken by the Council during the Second World War. At that time, the impetus to the effort was the discontinuity caused by worldwide conflict and the visible and inescapable need to rethink, replace, and supplement many of the features of the international system that had prevailed before the war. The discontinuities in today's world are less obvious and, even when occasionally quite visible—as in the abandonment of gold convertibility and fixed monetary parities—only erratically command the spotlight of public attention. The tendency is to improvise rather than to undertake a basic analysis of the problems that lie before us and of the demands that those problems will place upon all nations.

The 1980s Project has proceeded on the belief that serious effort and integrated forethought can contribute—indeed, are indispensable—to progress in the next decade toward a more humane, peaceful, productive, and just world. And it rests upon the hope that participants in its deliberations and readers of Project publications—whether or not they agree with an author's point of view—may be helped to think more informedly about the opportunities and the dangers that lie ahead and the consequences of various possible courses of future action.

The 1980s Project has been made possible by generous grants from the Ford Foundation, the Lilly Endowment, the Andrew W. Mellon Foundation, the Rockefeller Foundation, and the German Marshall Fund of the United States. Neither the Council on Foreign Relations nor any of those foundations is responsible for statements of fact and expressions of opinion contained in publications of the 1980s Project; they are the sole responsibility of the individual authors under whose names they appear. But the Council on Foreign Relations and the staff of the 1980s Project take great pleasure in placing those publications before a wide readership both in the United States and abroad.

Preface

The final draft of this book was completed in December, 1977. No attempt has been made during the many stages of the publication process to update any of the material contained in it. If the general trends in international relations and particularly in the politics of North-South interaction have been properly identified, updating should not be necessary; if those trends that will affect the "policy space" for the evolution of North-South relations over the coming decade have been improperly identified or their direction misread, no amount of updating can salvage the manuscript.

It is a pleasure to thank all those who provided me with valuable insights and criticism in the writing and revising of this book. The assistance of all those who served on the Staff of the 1980s Project is gratefully acknowledged, with particular gratitude to Edward L. Morse and Catherine Gwin for their exhaustive and perceptive critiques of the first draft. I would also like to thank all my colleagues at the Overseas Development Council, an institution where I was also working while many of the ideas developed in the book were germinating.

A very special debt of gratitude is owed to Peter J. Katzenstein and Robert O. Keohane, whose incisive critiques of the first draft were extremely valuable and deeply appreciated.

Finally, I would like to dedicate this book to the memory of my father, Clarence E. Hansen, who typically did far more than he should have to relieve me of family responsibilities during the months of research that preceded the writing of the manuscript. The other debts I hope to repay; this last and most touching one I cannot.

Roger D. Hansen
Washington, D.C.
July 1978

1980s PROJECT WORKING GROUPS

During 1975 and 1976, ten Working Groups met to explore major international issues and to subject initial drafts of 1980s Project studies to critical review. Those who chaired Project Working Groups were:

Cyrus R. Vance, Working Group on Nuclear Weapons and Other Weapons of Mass Destruction

Leslie H. Gelb, Working Group on Armed Conflict

Roger Fisher, Working Group on Transnational Violence and Subversion

Rev. Theodore M. Hesburgh, Working Group on Human Rights

Joseph S. Nye, Jr., Working Group on the Political Economy of North-South Relations

Harold Van B. Cleveland, Working Group on Macroeconomic Policies and International Monetary Relations

Lawrence C. McQuade, Working Group on Principles of International Trade

William Diebold, Jr., Working Group on Multinational Enterprises

Eugene B. Skolnikoff, Working Groups on the Environment, the Global Commons, and Economic Growth

Miriam Camps, Working Group on Industrial Policy

1980s PROJECT STAFF

Persons who have held senior professional positions on the staff of the 1980s Project for all or part of its duration are:

Miriam Camps	*Catherine Gwin*
William Diebold, Jr.	*Roger D. Hansen*
Tom J. Farer	*Edward L. Morse*
David C. Gompert	*Richard H. Ullman*

Richard H. Ullman was Director of the 1980s Project from its inception in 1974 until July 1977, when he became Chairman of the Project Coordinating Group. Edward L. Morse was Executive Director from July 1977 until June 1978. At that time, Catherine Gwin, 1980s Project Fellow since 1976, took over as Executive Director.

PROJECT COORDINATING GROUP

The Coordinating Group of the 1980s Project had a central advisory role in the work of the Project. Its members as of June 30, 1978, were:

Carlos F. Diaz-Alejandro   *Bayless Manning*
Richard A. Falk   *Theodore R. Marmor*
Tom J. Farer   *Ali Mazrui*
Edward K. Hamilton   *Michael O'Neill*
Stanley Hoffmann   *Stephen Stamas*
Gordon J. MacDonald   *Fritz Stern*
Bruce K. MacLaury   *Allen S. Whiting*

Until they entered government service, other members included:

W. Michael Blumenthal   *Joseph S. Nye, Jr.*
Richard N. Cooper   *Marshall D. Shulman*
Samuel P. Huntington

COMMITTEE ON STUDIES

The Committee on Studies of the Board of Directors of the Council on Foreign Relations is the governing body of the 1980s Project. The Committee's members as of June 30, 1978, were:

Barry E. Carter   *Robert E. Osgood*
Robert A. Charpie   *Stephen Stamas*
Stanley Hoffmann   *Paul A. Volcker*
Henry A. Kissinger   *Marina v. N. Whitman*
Walter J. Levy
                James A. Perkins (Chairman)

Part I
INTRODUCTION

Chapter 1
Thinking about North-South Relations in the 1980s

Is it necessary to devote an entire book to the subject of "North-South" relations in the 1980s? The answer is not as obvious to some observers of world politics as it is to others. While many scholars and policymakers have argued since the late 1960s that relations between the world's industrially developed nations of the North and the developing nations of the South were soon likely to become one of the globe's "relationships of major tension," others have been less concerned by such predictions. As recently as the summer of 1977, Daniel Bell observed that "whether this is a useful conceptualization, or as vague and tendentious as the phrase 'the Third World,' is moot."[1]

There are many reasons why analysts can differ over the nature and importance of the North-South relationship in world affairs. Perhaps the most salient reason involves often sharply differing interpretations of the structure and functioning of world politics in today's international system. Some continue to view the system in pure realpolitik terms; others have almost totally embraced the "global village" concept of interdependence which leaves little, if any, room for traditional forms of statecraft.

1

Bell's observation suggests that some analysts question the value of thinking in North-South terms. Others, looking at what evidence is available, feel that the concepts of North and South, properly qualified, are valid and helpful elements in an understanding of contemporary international relations. Simply stated, if over 110 developing countries time and again, in forum after forum, act as a diplomatic unit, they would seem to merit analysis as a potential actor of major importance in the international system. The same rationale applies to the study of developed-country behavior and to consequent North-South diplomatic interaction.

Some observers focus empirically on such global issues as population control, food production, and the need for a new regime to govern uses of the ocean; each issue is viewed as a technical problem for which an optimal answer can be found. Each is a "functional" problem that, if isolated from "politics," can be resolved for the good of all. Others, looking at the same set of issues, focus not on the functional but on the political content that infuses each problem. The empirical evidence of interest to them inheres in the patterns of international diplomacy—with a very heavy North-South content—that to a great extent control the manner in which such issues almost automatically become "politicized" and generally produce disappointingly suboptimal responses to the management of these global problems.

Additionally, there are strong normative reasons why opinions differ substantially on the seriousness of any growing tensions in North-South relations. Many observers are increasingly sensitive to perceived "inequities" in today's international system that appear to reinforce the gap between rich and poor nations. Others are less concerned with the "gap problem" internationally than they are with the levels of "absolute poverty" at which approximately 1 billion persons within the developing countries are now living. On the other hand, those who continue to emphasize the traditional security-oriented issues of statecraft and traditional norms and patterns of nation-state behavior are less concerned with such "equity" problems and therefore less inclined to grant increased attention to North-South issues for this set of reasons.

As the preceding juxtapositions suggest, one of the crucial ingredients in any analysis of North-South issues will be a degree of precision that sharply limits the "vague and tendentious" potential inherent in the very concept. Throughout this book an attempt will be made to achieve that degree of precision, for the concept of North-South relations is deserving of a far more searching examination than it has thus far received. Few readers will agree with all the analysis, interpretations of empirical data, normative judgments, or policy conclusions offered in this book. But such agreement should not be expected, nor should it be necessary in order to convince one of the seriousness of the global issues linked to the concept of North-South relations. Indeed, it is impossible to imagine a moderate international system a decade or two hence—defined as a system that enhances national, group, and personal security, welfare, and identity—that does not recognize the growing magnitude of present and projected North-South issues and begin to implement international and domestic policies to cope with those problems.

Each successive chapter will attempt to refine the essence of North-South issues in international relations for the coming decade, based on past, present, and likely future trends within the North, the South, and the interactions between the two blocs in a rapidly changing global arena. The remainder of this chapter is devoted to four preliminary issues and a brief exposition of the structure of the succeeding chapters.

I

The first issue is one of definition. In this book the term *North* is used as a shorthand description for the world's rich, industrialized noncommunist states. Included are most Western European countries, the United States, Canada, Japan, Australia, and New Zealand. Average per capita income in these countries in the latter 1970s exceeded $6,000. Most of these countries are members of the one international organization clearly associated with the North, the Organization for Economic Cooperation and Development (OECD). The terms *North* and *the OECD countries* are often used interchangeably in the following chapters.

The term *South* is used as shorthand for the world's less developed or developing states. They range from the suddenly rich but yet-to-industrialize oil states of the Middle East to the so-called Fourth World states, the poorest countries of the globe, located for the most part on the Indian subcontinent, in sub-Saharan Africa, and in the Caribbean region. Most of the population of this poorest stratum of countries is located in India, Pakistan, Bangladesh, and Sri Lanka, where upwards of three-quarters of the people have per capita incomes of less than $100 per year. Average annual per capita incomes in the Fourth World as a whole were estimated at $150 (in 1975 dollars) in the mid-1970s.

Between the Fourth World and suddenly wealthy oil countries is found the so-called Third World, encompassing most South American countries and others from Asia and a few from Africa. A great many of these states are semi-industrialized, are now exporting manufactured products at a rapidly increasing rate, and have average per capita incomes of close to $1,000 (1975 dollars).

It should be noted that these two groupings of countries of the *North* and *South* reflect the empirical *process* of international politics at its present stage of evolution and not some analytical approach based on levels of economic development. It is because the heterogeneous countries encompassed by the term *South* have forcefully coalesced over the past decade as a diplomatic unit that we examine them as an actor in global politics. Likewise, it is in direct response to the diplomatic activity of this group that the developed countries of the North have institutionalized norms of bargaining behavior vis-à-vis the developing countries, thus solidifying the second diplomatic unit of central concern to this study.[2] How long the present degrees of cohesion that make these two groups of states serious international actors will hold is an empirical question examined in detail in coming chapters. For now it is enough to say that the study focuses on these two diplomatic units, their interaction, and the consequences for global politics because "they are there."

The second preliminary issue, linked to the first one, concerns the extremely limited degree of attention given to the East (or the communist countries) in this study. At several points in the following analysis it will be crucial to include comments on the potential for triangular interactions involving North, South, and East. This is particularly true of analysis involving security matters, where East-West security problems may have a definite impact upon

Northern (especially United States) policies concerning individual—or blocs of—Southern countries. Nevertheless, the major focus of this study is on relations between North and South as defined above, and the rationale for this focus is entirely empirical. Most of what the South presently desires it desires from the North, not the East. It wants access to Northern capital markets, to Northern commodity markets, to Northern technology. It wants enhanced status and power in Northern institutions (e.g., the International Monetary Fund (IMF), the International Bank for Reconstruction and Development (IBRD), and the Nuclear Supplier's Group).

Since many current Southern demands are economic in content, the following statistics suggest why the East has thus far been able to sit on the sidelines and observe the emergent North-South clash. The developing countries sell less than 5 percent of their exports to the East. Close to three-quarters of non-OPEC developing-country exports are sold to the North. Over two-thirds of all less developed country (LDC)-manufactured exports—which until recently have been growing at over 15 percent per year—are purchased in the North. Less than 5 percent of developing-country manufactured goods that are exported are bought by countries of the East.

As noted in the case of security issues, the North-South dichotomy becomes far more complex in other, noneconomic issue areas. In current Law of the Seas negotiations the United States and the Soviet Union have worked closely and relatively harmoniously in support of several great-power interests, often in joint opposition to developing countries. In other cases—Middle East and African issues in the UN, for example—the East will often join North-South confrontations in support of the South. But so long as trade, technology, capital, access to increased financial assistance from the IMF and the IBRD, and a host of related economic issues remain near the top of the developing-country agenda, there will be an increasing potential for North-South conflict that will remain relatively unaffected by events in the other issue areas of world politics in which the North-South axis loses some—often much—of its salience. Additionally, so long as political leadership in these countries requires perceived external causes to explain domestic difficulties, and so long as foreign "threats" are needed to produce internal cohesion, the (Northern) ex-colonial or "neocolonialist"

powers—not the countries of the East—will in most cases best fill
the role. As further analyzed in Chapter 4, the rich, ex-colonial
powers of the North can neither understand latent Southern hostility nor deal effectively with it unless the historical roots, both
psychocultural and economic, of the present North-South conflict
are comprehended.

It should be noted that both the historical background of East-
South relations, which has not involved much manifest Eastern
colonial activity in the South, and present international economic
structures, which make the North the natural target of Southern
demands, are factors that will undoubtedly prove to be of diminishing importance in Southern perceptions as the years pass. With
regard to East-South political relations, the constant Soviet refrain
that the U.S.S.R. has never been a colonial power and therefore
owes no "reparations" to the South is beginning to wear very thin.
Developing countries that have had direct experience in dealing
with the Soviet Union are often the first to attribute "neocolonial"
designs to it irrespective of previous historical relationships. The
Soviet Union is perceived as a great power attempting to expand
its influence and degree of control in the global arena. In this sense
it is thought of much as the United States is. As the behavioral
patterns of both great powers are perceived as similar within the
South—at least as behavioral similarities vis-à-vis the developing
world are seen to outweigh differences—there will be a growing
tendency for the South to demand that the East also recognize and
contribute to the "just needs" of the developing countries. China,
for many complex cultural, historical, ethnic, and developmental
reasons, will be allowed to sit on the sidelines and observe the
North-South conflict indefinitely; the Soviet Union's days as a
Southern cheerleader without responsibilities would appear to be
numbered.

From the economic-structural perspective the same conclusion
is suggested. Already the developing countries, viewing the Soviet
Union as a "have" power, are increasing their criticism of Soviet
trade and aid policies that are negligible in their effort to assist
Southern economic development. An examination of Southern in-
dictments of "the system" over the past decade, most easily found
in the communiqués of the major Southern organizations analyzed
in this study, reveals a slowly rising trend of criticism of the Soviet

Union for its extremely limited responses to Southern requests for direct economic assistance and more fundamental systemic reform. Within a decade it may well be that no study of North-South issues would limit its analysis of the Eastern problem the way this book does.

A third preliminary issue concerns the audience for whom this book is written. Several readers of an initial draft suggested that it was essentially a Northern book, written for a Northern audience. To a certain extent, of course, this observation is correct. The author's own values, norms, technical training, and policy experience introduce a Northern bias on many of the issues examined and policy suggestions proposed which cannot be avoided. Nevertheless, there are two other factors that may make the following chapters seem to contain a Northern bias when in point of fact they do not. The first concerns an issue of substance and the second, an issue of policy initiative. At the level of substance, the book may seem Northern because of its somewhat unsympathetic handling of some major Southern policy positions, for example, those taken by the South in the analysis and argumentation supporting a New International Economic Order (NIEO) in the spring of 1974. There will also be implicit criticism of LDC bargaining tactics at the Law of the Sea Conference.

Whenever one criticizes Southern bargaining positions and collective demands, one runs the risk of being accused of attempting to undermine Southern unity. This sensitivity has reached the point where the accusation is faced by anyone who simply points out the heterogeneity among the needs and wants of the developing countries that form the South and its two major diplomatic groupings, the Group of 77 (now containing over 110 states) and the Non-Aligned Countries. Thus the very attempt to analyze the strains within the Southern coalition, let alone criticize Southern consensus positions, is equated with a Northern attempt to break present degrees of developing-country unity. Typical of this hypersensitive reaction was the response of the developing countries to Northern analysis that, several years ago, began to disaggregate the South into the Third and Fourth Worlds. For most who engaged in this effort, the point of the exercise was to understand what types of Northern policy initiatives were appropriate for which developing countries. However—and not without some good historical reasons—many Southerners were highly critical of any analysis of such "artificial" distinctions, despite the fact that developing countries themselves made very similar distinctions in UN and UN Conference on Trade and Development (UNCTAD) debates and documents. In these debates and documents one finds repeated references to the "least developed" LDCs, the "most severely affected" LDCs, and other distinctions that many Northern analysts were making with no malevolent intent.

Therefore, both the style of analysis and the treatment of certain Southern policy positions presented in the following chapters will brand the book as a biased Northern product to many Southerners from the outset. Regrettable as this result may be, it may also be inevitable at this particular stage in the global politics of North-South relations. Nevertheless, every attempt has been made in the material that follows to apply the same analytical standards to the examination of both Northern and Southern blocs and bloc cohesion and to the examination of positions taken by both sides to the confrontation throughout the 1970s. The one area in which bias is unavoidable is policy prescription. These prescriptions are wholly imbued with the author's own values and norms, and are most apparent in the final chapter.

At the level of policy initiative, the book may also seem Northern in the sense that the final four chapters focus to a considerable degree on likely Northern responses to existing Southern demands as well as preferred Northern responses to them. But the reason for this emphasis is less a Northern orientation of the book than it is the state of the North-South debate in the late 1970s. Southern demands and desired policy initiatives are already on the bargaining table; indeed, they have been sitting there for several years. Chronologically, psychologically, and diplomatically, it is time for a Northern response—a response that was expected but not produced by the 1975–1977 Conference on International Economic Cooperation (CIEC), which concluded indecisively in Paris in June of 1977.

Furthermore, the lengthy history of North-South friction over major economic (and, increasingly, international status) issues has been one of Southern initiative followed by extremely belated and often ill-conceived Northern responses. These responses are often as inappropriate to the problems of Southern economic growth as the original Southern proposals, and are often delivered with a combination of condescension and arrogance that assures further conflict even if conflict were not built into the very structure of North-South relationships in today's world politics.

Therefore the final four chapters concentrate to a considerable degree on Northerners' perceptions of the issues involved and Northern policy options. But the reason for this concentration is not that this is meant to be a book oriented solely to a Northern audience, but that it is time for the North to make a serious bid for a more constructive set of relationships with the developing countries before the still controlled conflict escalates—perhaps more accurately, degenerates—into a "negative-sum" game in which both sides pay a heavy price for their lost opportunities. And the coming 2 years of planning for the UN's Third Development Decade may provide one of the few major opportunities to channel the present conflict into more positive and mutually beneficial bargaining modes.

The final preliminary issue concerns the nature of the Council on Foreign Relations 1980s Project, of which this book is one product. Two distinct aspects of the Project have heavily influenced the thought process leading to the analysis in the following chapters. The first has been the Project's persistent desire to explore normative and value issues in considering global politics over the next 10–15 years. Complex as this effort has been, the benefits clearly outweigh the costs. In the following analysis and prescription the major goal being sought, at the highest level of generality, is "a moderate international system." Somewhat more concretely, the major ingredients in this "moderate order" are captured in the following diagram:

Figure 1-1

	SECURITY	WELFARE	AUTONOMY/IDENTITY
Nation-states			
Groups (ethnic, communal, religious)			
Individuals			

Ideally, the moderate order being sought would be one in which the goals of security, economic welfare, and autonomy/identity would be steadily increased at three different levels: those of the nation-state, of groups beneath the state level, and of individuals. Can enough by way of shared substantive and procedural values, norms, and goals be developed over the coming decade to produce an international system that not only allows but also actively induces increased levels of physical security, economic welfare/security, and autonomy/identity at the state, communal group, and individual levels?

The answer may well be no. Many analysts and practitioners continue to view international relations as a subject that has little or no room—analytically or normatively—for the consideration of individuals or subnational groups except as they may destabilize or otherwise significantly influence interstate relations. Such analysts are concerned almost exclusively with the first row in the above matrix. Others may confine their interests even more narrowly to one box within that row—that which encompasses security issues for nation-states.

But the introduction of a normative framework together with the second distinctive aspect of the Project, a 10–15 year time frame, draws the analyst's attention all the way from the upper left corner of the matrix to the lower right corner and to all the combinations along the way. What are the purposes of national security? Surely one of the most salient purposes is to promote "life, liberty, and the pursuit of happiness" on the part of individuals and groups constituting the nation-state. Thus the moderate-international-system goal informing the prescriptive elements in the following chapters—and specifically focused on North-South relations—is one that would induce improvements, however difficult the measurement of such "improvements" might prove to be, in each of the nine boxes of the above matrix.

Admittedly it is far easier to highlight the potential incompatibilities inherent in the matrix than to design internally consistent policies to produce the desired result. Do not priorities have to be established? Will not the security of the nation-state always take precedence over that of the individual? If so, will not issues associated with row 1 always take precedence over those associated with rows 2 and 3? Will not the conflict between state identity and group identity be a classic and predominant problem for many developing countries—particularly in sub-Saharan Africa—in the 1980s? And will not concerns for state identity prevail?

Will not the economic welfare of the state be viewed as prior to that of groups and individuals, therefore influencing choice of development strategies and international economic reforms in favor of those that emphasize high-technology industrialization and the growth of gross national product (GNP) rather than its distribution among groups and individuals? Does not this issue already lie close to the center of the economic development debate of the mid-1970s and probably close to the center of any potential North-South "accommodation" in the 1980s?

Additionally, will not East-West issues of state security intervene at least enough to make all the other goals in the matrix "fifth-order" issues for the United States—by necessity if not by choice? Will not all the fine Northern policy pronouncements relating to all the other boxes pale when challenged by perceptions of threats to the East-West strategic balance? How soon after President Carter's initial human rights pronouncements were "security exceptions" being made? How soon after his arms sales limitation pronouncements was his administration trying to convince Congress of the need to sell the most sophisticated conventional military hardware imaginable to Iran and Saudi Arabia?

While many other examples could be given, those noted above are chosen because they are of particular importance to the major themes of this book. On the one hand, throughout much of the developing world but particularly in sub-Saharan Africa, stable nation-states are still but a gleam in the eyes of certain leadership groups. Under these conditions, the rank ordering introduced in the nine potential goals of the above matrix by an African leader is likely to be substantially different—at the very least, the weighting of the goals will be far different—from that introduced by a typical Northern policymaker. The spectrum of viewpoints may be similar, but the rank orderings among Southern leadership views will most probably not tend to correlate very well with those of Northern leadership views. And on the other hand, despite an apparent United States concern for the broader array of goals suggested by the matrix, the United States' ultimate role in maintaining the present global strategic balance may severely limit the nature and duration of support it attempts to give to those less conventional goals and concerns of international politics.

Despite the obvious difficulties in extending the scope of this study beyond the more traditional limits of the international relations discipline, the attempt is made in the following chapters for three reasons. First, as noted, the nature of the 1980s Project invited a broader, less traditional approach to the subject matter. Second and of ultimately far more significance, a less traditional approach is dictated by the changing nature of today's international system. This issue will be analyzed in some detail in Chapters 2 and 3. Finally, implicit in many of the succeeding chapters and explicit in Chapters 8 and 9 is the view that any successful resolution of North-South conflicts and tensions—and by resolution, I mean no more than the capacity to manage within a "moderate" system a relationship that will for decades remain conflicted for reasons of colonial history, realpolitik, relative deprivation, and so on—will depend upon the striking of bargains and the implementation of policies that of necessity will reach beyond the boundaries of traditional statecraft and are intimately related to some of the more novel elements in the above matrix.[3] The more one thinks about North-South relations at the present stage of world politics the more difficult it is to imagine satisfactory resolutions to the issues plaguing those relations which limit themselves to matters of physical security and economic welfare at the nation-state level.

II

Part II of the book focuses on the dramatic emergence of the North-South axis in world politics since the early 1970s and the resulting problems posed for a moderate international system in the 1980s and beyond. Chapter 2 examines the events of the 1970s that have suddenly given such prominence to the North-South issue, particularly those major events that were triggered by the Arab-Israeli War of 1973 and the subsequent oil-price actions of the Arab members of the Organization of Petroleum Exporting Countries (OPEC). The chapter then analyzes the changing nature of world politics, which helps to account for these actions and to explain the nature of the North-South problem from an international systemic point of view.

Chapter 3 analyzes the major perspectives on North-South relations that have emerged in the face of this apparently sudden Southern challenge to the international status quo. An examination of these Northern and Southern perspectives illuminates both the large number and the fundamental importance of many global issues likely to be influenced by the course of North-South relations in the coming decade.

The analysis in Chapter 2 attempts to develop a more abstract, "systemic" explanation of the essence of the North-South problem; the focus of Chapter 3 is on partial aspects of the problem as perceived by actors in the system rather than by analysts of the system. But the two chapters are closely linked and should be read as such, since actor perceptions, both analytical and normative, are one of the major factors accounting for the changing nature of the international system.

Part III is devoted to a much more detailed examination of the North and the South as diplomatic entities and of the domestic determinants of their present and future capacity to act as cohesive units. Considering the South, for example, how can close to 120 states act with the degree of unity that has characterized Southern multilateral diplomacy over the past 5 years? Given the present and projected degrees of differentiation within these countries, how long can such cohesion be expected to last?

Part III also analyzes the major trends within Northern and Southern societies which are most likely to affect North-South relations in the 1980s. What effects are trends concerning authoritarian regimes and domestic instability in the South likely to have on North-South relations? Similarly, what effects on these relations are suggested by contemporary problems within Northern societies captured by such current aphorisms as "the social limits to growth," "the cultural contradictions of capitalism," and "the crisis of democracy"?[4]

Part III is included to assure that the normative sections of the study will take into account the "real-world" constraints that will have to be faced in North-South relations in the 1980s. This exposition of the likely evolution of Northern and Southern states in the coming decade should help to optimize the progress that can be made by suggesting policy directions that are likely to avoid the most obvious problems and take advantage of more promising "policy space."

Part IV examines three "modal" sets of Northern policy responses to present developing-country demands, analyzing their potential costs and benefits and measuring their potential for combination into a much broader "strategy" for producing more constructive North-South relations in the coming decade. The first set of policy responses examined in Chapter 6 would be viewed as a minimal rejoinder to developing-country demands from the aggregate Southern point of view if it were adopted in isolation from the other two. The second (Chapter 7) would come closer to some of the systemic change desires of many Southern states as expressed in the NIEO demands, but a major emphasis would be on those changes that would improve the capacity of the international economic system to manage the global challenges of the 1980s—emphasizing (but not exclusively devoted to) North-South areas of conflict. The third approach focuses on the subject of "basic human needs" and a strategy to eliminate what has come to be called "absolute poverty" in the coming two decades.

Part IV of the book is likely to seem the most Northern, in that it focuses more, though certainly not exclusively, on Northern initiatives and cost-benefit calculations than it does on Southern equivalents. The reasons for this emphasis have been noted above. I hope that these reasons and the critiques of each of the sets of policy responses presented in Chapter 6–8 will provide the reader with an adequate representation of all major issues and points of view.

Finally, Part V presents a very idiosyncratic view of the goals, strategies, and policies that should form the major ingredients of North-South relations for the 1980s. Some of the ingredients are procedural; others are substantive. The appropriate balance between substantive and procedural norms is itself likely to be one of the crucial determinants of success or failure in moving toward more constructive North-South relations in the coming decade. There is much room for improvement in procedures to overcome many North-South differences, especially in areas where status is a major (if latent) concern. In other areas there would seem to be no substitute for agreements on substantive issues.[5] This problem is analyzed in the final two chapters.

It is very unlikely that any reader will agree in all specifics with the policies proposed in Chapter 9 or even that most readers will agree with the general approach encompassed by those policy suggestions. However, it is hoped that the chapter pulls together the major North-South issues of global politics in a manner that will fulfill a primary goal of the 1980s Project—that of beginning serious normative thinking about a major set of issues that the international system of the 1980s should not (and in all probability cannot) avoid.

NOTES

[1] Daniel Bell, "The Future World Disorder," *Foreign Policy*, no. 27, Summer 1977, p. 112.

[2] The North had, of course, formed a wide range of institutions in response to a broad spectrum of perceived needs that had little or nothing to do with the developing countries. Some of these institutions, such as NATO, were developed in response to security needs; others, such as the OECD and its predecessor, the OEEC, were developed primarily to manage issues of economic interdependence among the industrialized countries of the world. When in the mid-to-late 1960s Southern solidarity began to strengthen considerably, Northern states sought to use the OECD as their "secretariat" and coordinating body as they were slowly forced to develop responses to Southern reform demands presented through the UN system—primarily through the United Nations Conference on Trade and Development (UNCTAD). The evolution of this process in the 1970s is analyzed in chaps. 2 and 4.

[3] The elements, of course, are not novel. The novelty lies in their growing importance in the practice of interstate politics and in the understanding of contemporary international relations.

[4] See the following books for a stimulating examination of these issues: Fred Hirsch, *Social Limits to Growth* (Cambridge: Harvard University Press, 1976); Daniel Bell, *The Cultural Contradictions of Capitalism* (New York: Basic Books, Inc., 1976); and Samuel P. Huntington et al., *The Crisis of Democracy* (New York: New York University Press, 1975).

[5] The degree to which the attempt to establish international procedural norms in North-South relations should take precedence over attempts to reach agreement

on more substantive issues dividing North and South is a matter of considerable concern to many analysts of international relations. Particularly interesting discussions of this issue can be found in the writings of Stanley Hoffmann, Ernst Haas, and John Ruggie. Of particular interest are the following three works: Stanley Hoffmann, "No Choice, No Illusions," *Foreign Policy*, no. 25, Winter 1976–77; Ernst B. Haas, "Is There a Hole in the Whole? Knowledge, Technology, Interdependence and the Construction of International Regimes," *International Organization*, vol. 29, no. 3, Summer 1975, pp. 827–876; and John Gerard Ruggie and Ernst B. Haas, "Environmental and Resource Interdependencies: Reorganizing for the Evolution of International Regimes," *Commission on the Organization of the Government for the Conduct of Foreign Policy*, Appendix vol. 1, pp. 218–230 (Washington, D.C.: U.S. Government Printing Office, 1975).

Part II
THE EMERGING NORTH-SOUTH AXIS IN WORLD POLITICS

Chapter 2
The North-South Problem: A Systemic Perspective

The nature of the North-South problem continues to evade consensus. Each analyst, practitioner of statecraft, or casual observer concentrates attention on that part of the relationship that most preoccupies him. Generally, definitions of the problem reflect the idiosyncratic view of world politics the observer brings to the issue of North-South relations. As the next chapter will indicate, within the North at least five major sets of responses to this definitional issue have evolved over the past several years. Quite clearly these responses reflect deep-seated value judgments as well as (if not more than) dispassionate analysis of the question: What is the essence of the North-South problem?

In attempting an answer to this crucial question, Chapter 2 will first examine the leading manifestations of the problem that have appeared since 1973, when the North-South issue suddenly became a prominent concern in global politics. Then, using this initial examination as background, an answer to the definitional question posed above will be suggested.

I

The fourth conference of the heads of state of the Non-Aligned Countries, which met in Algeria in early September of 1973, might well have passed unnoticed had it not been for the series of dramatic events that soon followed it: the Arab-Israeli War of 1973, the Arab oil embargo, the quadrupling of OPEC oil prices, the Sixth and Seventh Special Sessions of the UN General Assembly, and the Paris CIEC meetings (1975–1977). But these subsequent events force any analysis of North-South problems back to the 1973 Algeria meeting of what had been until that year the *political voice* of the developing countries when speaking as a unit: the Non-Aligned Countries (NAC).

The origins of the group, which will be examined in some detail in Chapter 4, date back to the 1950s. But throughout the middle and late 1960s the Non-Aligned Countries grew in number and cohesion; by the time of the fourth Non-Aligned Country summit, 75 member states were in attendance, eight others sent official observers, three countries were present as guests of the conference, and one regional and one international organization were also represented.

In its early years the major themes preoccupying the Non-Aligned Countries were neutralism and nonalignment with the great powers during the period of the cold war; increasingly during the 1960s the theme of anticolonialism came to dominate the debates and work program of the organization. Until the 1970s, however, economic issues were almost entirely ignored, leaving analysis and the formulation of policy proposals in the economic area to the *economic voice* of the South when it acted as a unit: the so-called Group of 77 (G-77) developing countries, which became institutionalized during the first UNCTAD meeting in 1964. Thus the Non-Aligned Countries as an organization paid little attention to the first three UNCTAD conferences (Geneva, 1964; New Delhi, 1968; Santiago, 1972), at which the demands of the developing countries for changes in existing international economic structures, rules, and norms of behavior were constantly being advanced with slowly increasing coherence and background documentation.

The 1973 Algiers summit, hosted and in many ways guided by the Algerian government, witnessed a dramatic shift of interest and emphasis toward UNCTAD's economic agenda. And with that shift both organizational embodiments of "Southern unity," the Non-Aligned Countries and the G-77 coalesced in support of a single set of international economic reforms that would become the touchstone of Southern unity for the indefinite future. This convergence of goals, strategies, and work programs between the Non-Aligned Countries and the G-77 was in and of itself bound to increase the organizational and institutional capacity of the South to press its demands for economic (and associated institutional and political) reforms in the plethora of international and regional organizations and specialized agencies to which most developing countries belong and in which they have a major voice. The greater the unity, the stronger the voice.

By the time the Algiers conference adjourned it had adopted an "Economic Declaration" and an "Action Programme for Economic Cooperation," called for establishment of "a new international economic order," called for the convening of a conference of developing countries to analyze commodity (raw materials) issues, and decided that the UN Secretary-General should be invited to convene a special session of the General Assembly to be devoted exclusively to a consideration of the role of the UN system in helping to overcome the hurdles to economic development. As we shall have cause to observe, each of these resolutions contained portents of highly significant developments in North-South relations in the following 4 years.

The second manifestation of the emerging North-South problem worthy of attention is the Arab-Israeli War of October 1973, the subsequent Arab actions on oil (including both embargoes and pricing), and, for our purposes, the manner in which this set of issues influenced the growing North-South conflict.

The first point of interest is that most OPEC nations embargoed oil shipments to several Northern states without challenge, military or otherwise. A second point is that many Northern states either were very cautious in giving any form of support to Israel during and immediately after the war or quickly became decidedly pro-Arab in their public pronouncements. A final observation deals with the Northern reaction to OPEC pricing action, which quadrupled the price of oil over the year following the war. Except for a few muffled warnings from the United States about the potential for hostile actions in the event of "economic strangulation," no Northern words were uttered or actions taken that might have suggested that the use of armed force against the Arab countries was even contemplated. Quite the contrary. Arab leaders were courted throughout Europe, invited to attend high-level European Community diplomatic sessions, and offered a plethora of bilateral trade, technical assistance, and industrial development packages in an effort to assure individual Northern countries access to needed supplies of petroleum. And despite its disgruntlement and occasional shrill words, the United States joined in the search for strengthened bilateral ties; before the end of 1974 it had entered into an intensive bilateral relationship with the biggest catch of all, Saudi Arabia.

In summary, the Northern response to the challenge to the present international political and economic order raised by the Arab oil embargo and the quadrupling of oil prices by OPEC was one that caused considerable dissension within the North itself (both within the European Community and between the EC on the one hand and the United States on the other). The challenge apparently never led any Northern country to consider seriously the use of force (or even a serious threat to use force); it led to a short period of intense competition for special bilateral relationships which further threatened Northern cohesion in the face of OPEC actions; and it demonstrated a very limited Northern capacity to take coordinated actions of a nonmilitary nature to deal with the energy problem and the inherent economic strains that the quadrupling of oil prices entailed for the United States and other Northern countries.

Southern responses to the Arab and OPEC actions were equally revealing in their illumination of the potential for North-South conflict. The short-term response was best captured by a prominent African scholar who noted that

from the point of view of millions of Asians and Africans, the Arab oil sanctions against select Western countries will probably rank in history alongside Japan's victory over Russia in 1905—as milestones in the story of how Asians and Africans discovered their own potential power against Caucasian might . . . as a lever against the rich certain Third World resources will become the equivalent of organized labor in the history of the industrialized countries—as a basis for collective bargaining.[1]

The longer-term response of the rest of the South to OPEC price actions is even more revealing of the psychological depth of the North-South conflict. For despite the very significant economic stress these price increases induced in almost all developing countries—both directly, through increased petroleum (and petroleum derivative) costs, and indirectly, by the oil price contribution to global stagflation and LDC debt-servicing problems—almost no criticism of OPEC pricing actions was forthcoming from other developing countries over the following 4 years. Most LDC spokesmen have instead continued to praise OPEC actions for reversing years of "Northern injustice."

Has this paucity of public criticism from the South been based on the fear of OPEC retaliation, on the as yet unsubstantiated hope that substantial OPEC aid flows will ease the financial burdens of the most affected Southern countries, or on a latent hostility toward the world's rich countries that enables the South to place a premium on the psychic rewards of seeing Europe and Japan in a panic that outweighs their own suffering? If it is one or a combination of the first two possibilities—fear and/or hope—Southern solidarity with OPEC may prove to be a function of the degree to which OPEC aid flows ease the growing financial problems of other developing countries. If the third possibility—hostility toward the North keyed to the historical colonial relationship between the North and much of the South and to the emerging "global equity" issue—is closest to the mark, any substantial Southern criticism of OPEC may be withheld indefinitely.

The remaining major manifestations of the North-South problem are revealed in the series of international conferences that grew out of the context of the Algiers Non-Aligned conference and the aftermath of the Arab-Israeli War.

The first major conference was the Sixth Special Session of the UN General Assembly (UNGA), held in the late spring of 1974. Algeria, as chairman of the Non-Aligned Countries, called for the session, a call that was very quickly endorsed by the requisite number of member countries of the UN. The Special Session, called

to study the problems of raw materials and development, was a
direct Southern counter to the United States–sponsored oil consumers'conference held in Washington to elaborate a common approach to the oil crisis in February 1974.[2] The latter conference,
attended by 13 Northern countries, eventually led to the formation
of the International Energy Agency (IEA).

The Southern counterconference, the Sixth Special Session of
the UNGA, produced the now well-known "Declaration on the
Establishment of a New International Economic Order" (NIEO)
and the accompanying "Program of Action." While little substantive
progress has been made toward the achievement of the NIEO goals,
the ideas expressed in the program have, for better or worse,
dominated all UN and UN-related agendas ever since 1974.

A detailed discussion of the Southern demands contained in the
NIEO proposals will be found in Chapter 4; no substantive analysis
of them is required here. For purposes of this chapter, the most
important aspect of the proposals is that their endorsement by the
Sixth Special Session represented the symbolic culmination of 20
years of growing Southern criticism of various aspects of the present
international economic system and its political foundations. The
Sixth Special Session, without a dissenting vote, endorsed the view
that major changes in existing regimes for trade, aid, investment,
technology, and international finance were required to reduce the
"inequities" inherent in the international economic system of the
1970s. Most of the NIEO proposals would directly or indirectly
increase the North-South flow of resource transfers and would require a rapid restructuring of Northern economies to allow for much
higher levels of Southern production of manufactured goods.

Continued discussion of the NIEO issues dominated the 1974
regular session of the General Assembly, which in its final days
overwhelmingly endorsed the Charter of Economic Rights and
Duties of States, a document that was fully consonant with the
NIEO philosophy concerning the "inequities" of the present international economic system. At the request of the developing
countries, this document had been under consideration by the UN
for several years. The United States, West Germany, the United
Kingdom, Belgium, Denmark, and Luxembourg were the only UN
members to vote against the Charter's adoption. Two leading North-

ern concerns were that the Charter would greatly increase the probabilities of expropriation of foreign direct investment without compensation and would encourage the formation of "producer associations" to increase the price of raw materials.

Following these initial essays in manifesto writing, the developing countries held a further series of Southern conferences—most notably at Dakar in February of 1975—where they reached a consensus on concrete proposals for transforming the NIEO from rhetoric to reality through specific reforms of the rules and norms of the existing international economic system.[3] Most of these proposals were subsequently incorporated (with only the United States casting a negative vote) into the Lima Declaration issued by the Second General Conference of the UN Industrial Development Organization (UNIDO) in Peru in March of 1975.

The following month the United States failed in its lengthy attempt to align LDC oil-importing countries with the North against OPEC. Instead, the Paris meeting of oil consumer and producer countries of April 1975 further solidified OPEC-LDC bonds, isolated the North, and produced a turning point in United States policy toward the South in general and toward the energy question in particular. In the fall of 1975 Secretary of State Kissinger's speech to the Seventh Special Session of the UN (the Session called for at the Non-Aligned Country Algiers summit) opened what has come to be known as the period of "North-South dialogue." In conciliatory tones and marginal (but numerous) programmatic initiatives, the Secretary's speech indicated that the United States was now willing to "turn away from confrontation" and seriously consider the modalities by which the economic needs of the developing countries could be better served by the international economic system. And against this background of apparent change in United States attitude the dialogue was instituted at the first CIEC session in Paris in December of 1975.

Representing the South were 19 developing countries, which soon became known as the G-19. OPEC countries in attendance were Algeria, Indonesia, Iran, Iraq, Nigeria, Saudi Arabia, and Venezuela; representing the other developing countries were Argentina, Brazil, Cameroon, Egypt, India, Jamaica, Mexico, Pakistan, Peru, Yugoslavia, Zaire, and Zambia. The North (soon known as the G-8) was represented by the European Community, the United States, Japan, Canada, Australia, Spain, Sweden, and Switzerland.

The conference terminated in June of 1977 with a singular lack of positive results. For differing reasons almost all members to this North-South dialogue seemed glad to end a conference that was the cause of so much frustration and so little progress. No agreement was reached on a single issue of importance to either set of participants, despite 18 months of stop-go discussions, and optimists were reduced to concluding that "each side understood the other better."[4]

Throughout the mid-to-late 1970s Southern attempts to achieve some of the NIEO goals through bargaining at the Third UN Law of the Sea Conference (LOS III) contributed to yet another international deadlock. In this setting certain NIEO demands further complicated the bargaining over the complex issues of a "deep-seabed regime" that would establish rules and regulations for all ocean mining beyond territorial waters and "economic zones" of coastal states. The inability of North and South to find a mutually acceptable compromise to the deep-seabed-mining issue after 5 years of debate threatened the defeat of a decade of efforts to develop and codify an ocean regime appropriate to the technological and political stresses affecting the oceans in the 1970s.

A final manifestation of the North-South problem, one apparent in almost all UN family organizations and institutions, is generally referred to in academic jargon as the "politicization of functional institutions." In the mid-1970s the United Nations Educational, Scientific, and Cultural Organization (UNESCO) and the International Labor Organization (ILO) became the scenes of some of the most publicized aspects of this process. In both organizations the South controlled enough votes to grant membership to the Palestinian Liberation Organization over the strong objection of many Northern countries. In UNESCO the G-77 also managed to expel Israel for 2 years and engaged in a lengthy and bitter struggle to limit Northern press access to the developing countries before the initiative was finally beaten back at the 1976 UNESCO Conference.

II

What do these recent manifestations of the North-South problem suggest about its real nature? The answer is clearly dependent upon the level at which one is analyzing the confrontation. If we are asking how the problem is viewed by most Southern observers, the answer would run somewhat as follows: (1) The present international system in its political and economic rules, norms, and institutions is structured so that day-to-day outcomes favor the designers of the system, i.e., the industrial states; (2) the process of colonialism (and the newer processes of "neocolonialism") have made it impossible for developing countries to compete on equal terms with the North; and therefore (3) systemic changes must be introduced that will right past wrongs and introduce more "equity" into the system, even where the international equivalent of domestic "affirmative action" programs are required to achieve a more egalitarian distribution of wealth, power, and status. This third point is perhaps best exemplified in the LOS III discussions concerning the nature of a deep-seabed regime. Southerners argue that unless developing countries are given access to appropriate technology and the necessary capital, they cannot possibly compete with Northern corporations in mining the ocean floor. Therefore the only "equitable" solution would involve very strict controls over Northern companies and the necessary technology transfer to a deep-seabed authority controlled by the G-77.

Northerners, as the following chaper will indicate, have very divergent views on "the problem" when examined at this level of analysis. A few share in toto the Southern view outlined above; others would disagree with that perspective in its entirety.

For the purpose of this chapter, however, such responses to the question are cast at the wrong level of analysis. They are, in essence, normative views concerning what is "right" and "wrong" about particular process outcomes—almost exclusively of an economic transactional nature—produced by rules and norms of the present international system, rather than views about the more fundamental issue: the structure and functioning of the present international system itself.

An examination of all the manifestations of the North-South conflict noted above suggests the following dilemma. On the one hand, the events of the past half decade highlight growing limitations on traditional assumptions, forms, and guidelines of statecraft in the present international setting. Militarily powerless states embargo the shipment of vital raw materials to great powers and are not challenged. Great powers announce programs to free themselves from such vulnerabilities, but are unable to achieve enough domestic support to undertake such programs. The world's weakest countries from all continents coalesce in a diplomatic bargaining bloc that (1) hires Northern consulting firms to plan strategies and aggregate evidence supportive of new international policy initiatives, (2) controls agendas of most major international organizations to the dismay of great and middle-range powers, and (3) links issues across organizations and agendas in a determined effort to achieve concrete results despite overwhelming relative material weaknesses.

On the other hand, we have not witnessed the profound change in the attitudes of humanity and in the consequent behavior of nation-states that would be required to make obsolete the basic norms of interstate behavior heretofore associated with the processes of international politics. With specific regard to the growing North-South conflict, attitudes and state behavior have not changed to the point that Northern and Southern states can agree in defining the North-South problem as one of reducing existing international inequalities according to mutually acceptable rules and norms.

It is not surprising that agreement of this nature has not been reached. As Robert W. Tucker observed in examining the North-South struggle, "the history of the international system is a history of *inequality* par excellence." A major contributing factor has been "the condition in which its members have existed in the past and *from which they have yet to emerge.* It is the condition of a society marked by the absence of effective collective procedures, competitive rather than cooperative, and lacking in commitment to a common good that has insured that differences in power and wealth will be employed to perpetuate inequality."[5]

Perhaps, then, the North-South problem—and the problem for resolution in the 1980s—is best conceptualized as the absence of a statecraft more congruent with an increasingly novel international system. As the statement of the fundamental dilemma suggests, we seem to have witnessed enough change in the structure and functioning of the international system to weaken the predictive power of the old assumptions and the effectiveness of the old norms of interstate behavior. Each of the manifestations of the growing North-South problem noted above attests both to system change and to a weakening in the effectiveness of traditional diplomatic behavior to achieve its desired outcomes. At the same time we have *not* witnessed enough change to induce many states to reconsider traditional assumptions affecting North-South relations and alter their diplomatic goals and methods accordingly.

The practice of the old statecraft is rapidly breaking down under the novel conditions of the present international setting. Three examples should suffice to illustrate the point, a point that the earlier discussion has already illuminated. The first example concerns Northern reactions to the Arab oil embargo and the subsequent quadrupling of OPEC oil prices. It is difficult to fit the responses of Northern states threatened by these actions into the traditional (or "realist") explanation of world politics. A primary tenet of the realist model is that military force is a usable and effective instrument of policy. As noted, however, the use of force against the Arab states does not appear to have been seriously considered throughout the North, except in the pages of *Commentary* magazine. Furthermore, all the post facto reasons cited for not giving serious consideration to this option lack conviction. "Russian intervention," "guerrilla warfare," "world opinion"—all are unconvincing when closely analyzed *if* the traditional realist mode of statecraft is still the guiding principle of state behavior. For the fact remains that a potentially severe threat to the stability of powerful states posed by several very weak states evoked not threats of forceful retaliation but pursuit of accommodation at almost any cost.[6]

Furthermore, Northern reactions in this instance would also appear to negate the traditional realist assumption that there is a hierarchy of issues in world politics and that the military security issue will dominate all others whenever it is raised. Once again, if this tenet remains operable, Northern reactions to the Arab oil initiative seem entirely disproportionate to the events that were taking place. No matter how Northern inactions were rationalized (country by country, there were endless rationalizations to be heard), the fact remains that these states rather quickly allowed control over a raw material vital to their military security to fall into the hands of a small group of very weak states. And all the erudite observations "explaining" inaction by reference to the heterogeneous diplomatic goals of varying Northern states cannot avoid this conclusion.

A second example of the weakening of the old statecraft can be noted in the evaluation of LOS III. First, one should note the simple fact that the developing countries, working as a bloc through the G-77 apparatus, have prolonged the period of preparation and the conference itself to the point where the conference might well end without resolving any of the major issues on its agenda. For the better part of 5 years no combination of (nonmilitary) threats and compromises on the part of Northern states have proved capable of achieving Southern acquiescence; by 1978 the questions of how long the conference would continue and whether or not it would produce any agreement required hazardous conjectures.

The final observation concerns the entire set of conferences that grew out of the Sixth Special Session of the UN, including particularly the Seventh Special Session and the CIEC meetings. Once again it should be noted that the meetings were all held at the instigation of the South (and generally against the wishes of Northern states), that the agendas for each meeting were dominated by Southern desires and proposals, and that the slow but steady "appeasers" at each conference were the Northern states. As noted earlier, very little was "given" at these conferences; what was given, however, was in almost every instance given by the North. It is interesting in this framework to note that the one quid pro quo the Northern states hoped to achieve above all at the CIEC sessions, the institutionalization of an ongoing energy "dialogue," was denied them by the Group of 19 Southern states. Ignoring Northern threats to break up the conference over this issue, the South rejected the demand. Despite this rejection the G-8 did not disrupt the conference. In fact, Northern leadership spent the waning hours of the conference fighting hard to achieve some sort of consensus, and the final conference results were far more vigorously criticized by the leaders of the G-19 than by those of the G-8.

All these examples are hard to fit into the realist model of world politics. For the North, at least, the old statecraft does not seem to be working—often isn't even tried—in the North-South arena. We could accommodate the facts to the old realist model if we postulated that the Northern power resource base was weakening relative to that of the South, but this postulation would not bear very close scrutiny. OPEC and a few other developing countries aside, the gap in traditonal power resources between Northern and Southern states shows no tendency to narrow. If there is a trend, it may well be in the other direction. An examination of economic, military, technological, and political trends affecting power resources defined in traditional terms would, in the aggregate, overwhelmingly support this judgment.

One could support the argument that the Southern power base was growing relative to that of the North only if one made the further assumption that a strengthening of Southern ties with the Soviet Union was a growing factor in world politics or that the sudden wealth (and therefore power) of the OPEC countries was being devoted to strengthening the South in the North-South balance.

Again, in point of fact, both assumptions are unsupportable. There are no growing diplomatic ties between the Soviet Union and the South in the aggregate. While relations may vary from country to country, no trend in this direction can be demonstrated. In fact, over the past decade a reverse trend is the easier to document. Whether one is looking at Latin America, Africa, the Middle East, South Asia, or Southeast Asia, there is simply no evidence of strengthening East-South relationships in the aggregate (or even with key Southern countries).

As for OPEC support of the South, one must conclude that OPEC actions in the aggregate have thus far been a *major net economic drain* on Southern strength, in the neighborhood of $15 billion to $20 billion per year. OPEC economic aid disbursements have not exceeded 1–1.5 percent of total OPEC GNP, and the great part of this aid flows only to other Arab countries. Furthermore, many OPEC countries appear to be cutting back on present aid levels, arguing that they will need all the resources they can accumulate for their own development. Finally, their excess earnings are generally being invested in Northern—not Southern—countries and financial institutions. Thus, the financial support from OPEC upon which the South had hoped to mount a dual strategy, consisting of "self-reliant" Southern development on the one hand and international "producer power" on the other, that might have narrowed the "power gap" between North and South has not yet materialized.

The actions of Saudi Arabia, Iran, Venezuela, and other OPEC members are in many ways quite consonant with the state behavior the realist model would predict. They, and other Southern countries such as Brazil and Mexico, are countries whose economic base provides them with potential power resources needed to "graduate" into the ranks of those states one step below the two superpowers over the next two to three decades. Given the potential opportunity to achieve the age-old state goals of "power, glory, and idea," they have apparently decided to make the most of the opportunity.

In short, the actions of both Northern and Southern states over the past half decade suggest serious uncertainties about the traditional realist rules of statecraft as they apply to North-South relationships. Is military power usable, or is it not? If it is, are the limitations on its use growing? Are threats of its use of any value? Are Northern and Southern "blocs" cohesive, and are they important? Are resolutions of the UN General Assembly— which can, after all, only recommend, and not enforce—serious matters for international politics, or not? Is the much debated idea of international equity to be a major transnational force shaping international politics in the 1980s, or is it an elitist notion shared by few and destined for early demise? Can the world of the 1980s afford present levels of North-South conflict, which stalemated most efforts at multilateral diplomacy in the 1970s, or will the world face problems that necessitate the evolution of altered and more conciliatory forms of North-South multilateral relations?

Because the answers to these questions are so uncertain, both Northern and Southern governments currently bluff, bluster, and temporize. Their actions are often ambiguous, their public versus their private statements are contradictory, and their objectives lack clear definition. The result has been negative and disappointing for the North and for the South. Of course, some of this result can be explained in terms of traditional statecraft. The entire North-

South conflict can, in oversimplified terms, be characterized as resistance by "status quo" powers to the growing demands of "revisionist" states.

However, traditional statecraft cannot account for enough of the behavior explored thus far. More is needed to explain the present dilemmas of North-South relations, and much of the answer would seem to be contained in the changing structure and functioning of the international system over the past decade, changes not yet internalized in enough leaders and policy makers to produce the necessary degree of congruence between international systemic constraints and day-to-day state behavior. This lag in perception helps considerably to explain the tensions, frustrations, and contradictions now characterizing North-South relations.

III

A recent attempt to analyze this period of "world politics in transition"which focused for the most part on interdependence among developed countries examined several structural and process aspects of present-day international relations that are also very illuminating when applied to the analysis of North-South relations. They included (1) the diminishing role of military force, (2) the increasing constraints on (particularly Northern) state behavior due to the growing domestic demands produced by the "welfare states," (3) the role of international organizations, and (4) the potential for "linkage strategies."[7]

An examination of these issues is revealing in that it suggests the potential in the North-South arena of the international system for an erosion of hierarchy based on military power, a dispersion of "power" on a much wider basis than heretofore experienced, and a growing capacity for Southern countries to use international organizations for the dual purposes of (1) developing linkage strategies that allow them to overcome bargaining weakness in one issue area by linking it to another in which their bargaining position is stronger and (2) cumulatively introducing new norms—for example, those of equity or equality—which, with a time lag, effect changes in the international system. If this potential is, as events of the past 5 years suggest, already in the process of realization, the increased level of North-South tension is much easier to comprehend; so, too, is the necessity to consider attentively a range of reforms that might make North-South relations more congruent with the international political realities upon which they must rest.

The erosion of hierarchy formerly based on military power in North-South relations has several causes. They flow from both growing perceptions within the North of the disutility of force in North-South conflicts and from a growing capacity within the South to withstand the costs such confrontations may entail. Four leading causes are worthy of special mention. The first concerns the Northern weighing of the costs and benefits of the use of force against Southern states in the postcolonial era of emergent Southern states and potentially strong anti-Western feeling. As recently noted, "the limited usefulness of conventional force to control socially mobilized populations has been shown by the United States failure in Vietnam as well as by the rapid decline of colonialism in Africa. Furthermore, employing force on one issue against an independent [Southern] state with which one has a variety of relations is likely to rupture mutually profitable relations on other issues."[8] One might add that, given present degrees of "Southern solidarity" developed through the Non-Aligned Country and G-77 organizations, the potential use of force against one Southern state jeopardizes a series of profitable relationships with well over 100 countries unless that use of force is also perceived by most Southern countries as an appropriate action in a special instance.

Second, there is the issue of the willingness of Northern publics to tolerate, let alone support, such military interventions unless they are very swift and very effective in achieving their objectives. While the reasons for this shifting public view are difficult to disentangle and document, they would seem to include the following elements: the potential conflict between expensive foreign policies and the domestic demands on welfare states, a questioning of the need for "assured access" to Southern states, and the moral issue involved in the use of force in such "unequal" struggles.

As Ernst Haas noted years ago, the great majority of citizens in post–World War II industrialized states no longer seem concerned with or interested in the traditional state pursuits of power, glory, and idea. They are far more concerned with the bread-and-butter issues to which the rise of the welfare state has responded. The primacy of foreign policy is no longer self-evident in the North unless that policy can be demonstrated to involve a fundamental security issue.

Coupled with this development is the growing comprehension within developed countries, relatively more sophisticated in their understanding of economics and in their capacity to manage their economies, that they need not stake exclusive claims to resources and markets in the South. The OPEC oil embargo served as a reminder that this particular change in viewpoint was based on implicit assumptions that included, among others, the existence of a liberal trading system and no resource scarcities. If, as the Bretton Woods system is significantly altered, access to raw materials is greatly impeded and international market uncertainties concerning both exports and imports increase rapidly, some factors that have served to constrain the use of force between North and South may prove less formidable than events of the 1970s suggest.

The third factor is the related issue of the normative aspects of force used against developing countries. Has the Northern world moved close enough to that of the so-called global humanists so that Northern states would find it impossible to use overt force in a developing country unless events in that country (or region) were perceived to have a significantly destabilizing potential for East-West relationships? Clearly the cases of Vietnam and Chile suggest that overt force may still be used (unless indirect methods can prevail, as they did in the latter case) when the East-West syndrome of security issues can be linked to specific LDC situations. Furthermore, the mutterings by President Ford and Secretary of State Kissinger about the possible use of force in the Middle East to avoid "economic strangulation" further emphasized the uncertain strength of the normative constraint examined here.

Finally, the use of force is constrained more generally by the East-West conflict and the present "regime" of nuclear deterrence. This structural element in the present international system affects both the potential for competitive intervention in developing countries and the risk of other forms of East-West escalation of tensions originating in interventions in the South.

The erosion of international hierarchy formerly based upon military power in the North-South context has, together with several other factors, led directly to a dispersion of power that is far more pronounced than heretofore experienced in world politics. This is the case whether we think of power in terms of resources that constitute the basis of traditional military power or in terms of control over outcomes of contested international issues.

To the degree that military power is discounted, other forms of power rise in importance. One of the most widely discussed new elements of power—"asymmetrical interdependence," in academic language—suggests one form in which power has spread. In the asymmetrical interdependence framework, a state that is *relatively* invulnerable to nonmilitary actions of another state but retains the capacity to injure that state has "power." In this sense most countries of the world are now operating under the duress of OPEC power, since most of them are vulnerable to OPEC's control over a large amount of the world's exported petroleum. But the complexities of asymmetrical interdependence also allow for the recognition of the vulnerabilities of the OPEC governments themselves. All desire Northern technology; some perceive the need for Northern military support; and most desire Northern political and financial stability which they perceive to be consonant with their own political, financial, and security interests.

The ambiguities of measuring power via asymmetrical interdependence are numerous, but this characteristic would seem to be a virtue, not a weakness. For it appears to be an accurate reflection of the ambiguous nature of the structure and functioning of the international system itself and of the difficult search for new rules and norms of state behavior which is already in progress. Consider the present case of United States relations with Brazil.

In the mid-1970s an American Secretary of State, aware of the growing limitations on the direct use of force in developing countries but desiring to ensure continued United States influence in and access to South America, signed an agreement with Brazil which clearly established that state as *primus inter pares* in United States–Latin American relationships and promised extensive bilateral consultations as a matter of course from that date forward.

Within the space of two years, relations between the two countries deteriorated seriously as the United States severely criticized and attempted to have revoked a Brazilian–West German nuclear energy arrangement that would substantially increase Brazil's opportunity to become a nuclear power if it so desired and suddenly became equally critical of Brazilian human rights policies. Despite the application of substantial pressure on both Brazil and West Germany, the United States has thus far been unable to alter the nuclear agreement in any fundamental way or to influence Brazilian human rights policies to any noticeable degree. And Brazil, increasingly angered by United States actions on these two issues, eventually refused a $50 million credit for the purchase of United States arms, cancelled a 1952 agreement under which a joint commission supervised Brazil's purchase of American military equipment, and finally nullified four more military pacts with Washington, ending all formal military cooperation between the two countries.

The present ambiguities in this three-player game remind us of the Keohane-Nye observation that

the decline of hierarchy is not so much an erosion of power resources of the dominant states [in this instance, the U.S.], compared with those of other countries, as an erosion of the dominant state's power to *control outcomes* in the international system. The main reason is that the system itself has become more complex. There are more issues and more actors; and the weak assert themselves more. The dominant state still has leverage over others, but it has far less leverage over the whole system. [9]

An examination of the West German perspectives on its nuclear arrangement with Brazil offers an illuminating confirmation of the above observation and a further commentary on the growing potential for substantial change in North-South relations. One major reason the West German government did not relent on its Brazilian nuclear sale despite United States pressures concerned the needs of the West German economy. The Brazilian sale meant jobs in a high-technology sector of German industry. It meant the continued growth of German capacity in what is viewed as a growth industry and, more important, an industry with great export potential in Germany. It was perceived as an essential ingredient of a strengthened capacity to export over the coming decade. And it was thought to guarantee an assured supply (from Brazil) of uranium for West Germany's own power needs. Thus the demands of major domestic pressure groups and the needs of the German economy at the macro-level would have made it extremely costly in domestic political terms for the German government to bow to United States pressures to cancel the agreement with Brazil. In 1967 West Germany's desire to placate the United States for reasons of its own security vis-à-vis the Soviet Union might have led to the cancellation of such an arrangement. In 1977 the same security concerns and the desire to retain the greatest possible United States support were still present, but "the system itself has become more complex." The weakened and uncertain state of Northern economies in the wake of OPEC oil price actions, their need for diversified sources of energy, and their concerns with domestic employment and balance-of-payments problems have all severely complicated perceived power calculations and predictable responses in recent years. With potentially enormous OPEC-induced trade deficits facing Northern countries (unless they allow the deficits to fall upon the South, assuring major damage to the international monetary system and widespread Southern defaults on present debts), with fears of competitive Northern currency devaluations and increasing trade restrictions, and with growing domestic discontent with historically high rates of unemployment and inflation, the demands of the welfare state on Northern governments have become another significant factor that helps to account for the erosion of hierarchy in global politics, the dispersion of power (defined either as asymmetrical interdependence or as control over outcomes), and a growing capacity for the South to use these trends to increase its degree of *influence* in the present international system.

OPEC aside, it has been within international organizations that the developing countries have most successfully developed what capacity they have to alter the international system in directions of interest to them. As noted above, this process has involved the introduction of potential norms of international behavior through an unending series of resolutions for which the G-77 can easily muster automatic majorities. With the assistance of generally sympathetic secretariats, resolutions stressing equity and equality of states and reforms to achieve these goals have been pressed with ever-increasing frequency in all UN and UN-related meetings. As the South used international organizations to develop new norms on the colonial issue in the 1960s, so it is now attempting to use them to introduce new norms in the realm of interstate equity. Slowly the rhetoric has its effect on the norms and values of the international system and North-South relations, if only because constant and adamant opposition can be and often is perceived as reflecting a selfish and self-serving desire to retain "inequitable" rules of the game. And each small victory offers a new starting point for the unending effort to alter the present system.

An added factor that has recently aided the developing countries in their capacity to use international organizations more effectively in their campaign for change is their growing organizational capability to link disparate issues—issues sometimes not even considered by the same international organization—in an effort to achieve their objectives. A classic example of this strategy of issue linkage took place at the CIEC, where the developing countries, aided greatly by the support of the OPEC countries, were able to link and discuss such issues as economic assistance, trade, monetary reform, multinational corporations, technology transfer, energy, and raw materials in a manner they had never before been able to accomplish. Southern gains at the CIEC meetings, as noted above, were marginal at best. But the fact remains that the South for the first time forced a discussion of all its grievances on these issues in the same forum.

Furthermore, the capacity of the Group of 77 to carry the NIEO demands, bag and baggage, into the Third UN Law of the Sea Conference and to enforce a very substantial degree of discipline upon its member states *despite* their extraordinarily disparate interests in the LOS III setting suggests a capacity for continued use of international organizations and conferences for joint policy formulation and pursuit which should not be underrated in the present period of "world politics in transition."

IV

As following chapters will suggest, there is no unanimity supporting the proposition that world politics is really in transition, that the international system is experiencing any fundamental changes in its structure or what Raymond Aron has called the "transnational forces for change" within it. It is probably accurate, however, to say that more observers—both government leaders and scholars—are emphasizing change rather than continuity as the hallmark of present-day world politics.

Even those analysts who are predisposed to deny the existence of significant change are deeply aware of and concerned about the challenge to today's system inherent in the present North-South conflict. Thus the following concluding paragraph to one of the most thought-provoking essays on some central aspects of North-South relations written in the 1970s:

It is banal to conclude that the power structure of the future will evolve in a manner largely independent of our wishes and designs. Yet it is probably no less true for being banal. We can also be reasonably sure that the *challenge to the present system will eventually give rise not so much to a new system but to a new hierarchy.* That the new hierarchy will prove more benign than those of the past can be little more than a profession of hope in a world that seems destined to repeat the cycle of nation-state development we have already witnessed in the West.[10]

Other observers more inclined to accept the proposition that the system is indeed changing are equally skeptical that either the substantive or procedural norms of North-South relations will benefit thereby.

So long as complex interdependence does not encompass all issue areas and relationships among all major states, the remaining role of military force will require sovereign states to maintain military capabilities. Moreover, so long as the world is characterized by enormous inequality of incomes among states—a condition that cannot be changed quickly even on the most optimistic of assumptions about economic growth—citizens are likely to resist the dismantling of national sovereignty. The *increase in complexity and decline of hierarchy may simply result in the absence of any effective leadership in organizing international collective action.*[11]

The evidence examined in this chapter is already highly supportive of the proposition that the international system is in a period of change. The diminishing role of force in North-South relations, the growing constraints on Northern state behavior attributable to growing welfare state demands, the rapid growth in Southern organizational capacity, and Southern use of international organizations and of linkage strategies to achieve goals in bloc diplomatic conflicts all lend both empirical and analytical support to this interpretation. The attitudinal evidence examined in the next chapter—evolving attitudes and normative frameworks that certainly fit into Aron's category of "transnational forces for change"—lends further weight to the view that the international system is in transition. One can easily agree that the case for change (as an empirical fact, not a normative goal) has often been greatly overstated in recent years, yet disagree with the conclusion that the only novelty to result from the present period of North-South conflict will be encompassed by a new hierarchy among states.

From the perspective of the structure and process of present-day global politics taken in this chapter, the North-South problem has seemed best conceptualized as the absence of a statecraft congruent with the emerging constraints of a changing international system. The growing constraints on the old statecraft analyzed in this chapter have magnified—if not caused—most of the ambiguities now inherent in North-South relations, but the constraints have not yet led analysts or policymakers toward any consensus on the appropriate implications for North-South interstate behavior.

If this characterization comes at all close to isolating the problem, then the challenges to North-South relations in the coming decade can be viewed as the necessity to determine (1) how much system change is likely to occur regardless of policy choices by individual states and groups of states and (2) what appropriate objectives and policies affecting North-South relations are potentially congruent with the major alterations in the international system.

As noted above, the past 5 years have witnessed a constant Southern probing of the limits to change and a Northern resistance to almost all such probes. The actions of both sides reveal confusion concerning the nature of the changing international constraints on interstate behavior and uncertainties about appropriate norms of statecraft to accommodate those changes. The period has in many ways been a confirmation of the Keohane-Nye observation that "the increase in complexity and decline of hierarchy may simply result in the absence of any effective leadership in organizing international collective action."

How far beyond this "stalemate system" implicit in North-South interactions during the mid-to-late 1970s can we expect to travel in the 1980s? Much will depend upon the domestic and the international constraints to "organizing international collective action" in the emerging system and upon individual states' responses to those constraints once their implications for the future are better understood.

NOTES

[1]Ali A. Mazrui, "The Arab Oil Boycott and the New Balance of Economic Power: A Third World Response to the Western Energy Crisis," remarks at an Overseas Development Council press briefing, San Francisco, November 28, 1973.

[2]Algeria actually called for what became the Sixth Special Session in response to *two* Northern initiatives: (1) the United States–sponsored Washington consumers' conference and (2) a French call for a UN-sponsored emergency conference on energy.

[3]A detailed listing of these reforms will be found in chap. 4.

[4]One consistently rumored "positive result" of CIEC was "a better understanding"—whatever that may mean—beween OPEC and member countries of the IEA, essentially the North. Two observations are called for. First, this "result" remains undocumented. Second, it is difficult to "credit" such a (possible) result to a conference insisted on by the South in order to play the "oil card" in order to produce Northern payoffs in *other* areas—payoffs that were never made.

[5]Robert W. Tucker, *The Inequality of Nations* (New York: Basic Books, 1977), p. 3.

[6]Given the potential severity of the threat, "world opinion" would have been very heavily discounted in a "realist" analysis. So, too, would guerrilla warfare given the desert terrain involved. Russian intervention would have raised a more serious issue. Nevertheless, it is difficult to deny that this problem could have been minimized and a "balance of interests" favoring the North established if quick and decisive United States action had been taken with full European support.

[7]See Robert O. Keohane and Joseph S. Nye, *Power and Interdependence: World Politics in Transition* (Boston: Little, Brown & Co., 1977).

[8]Ibid., p. 29.

[9]Ibid., p. 228. In the aggregate North-South context, the North's demonstrated capacity to stall endlessly in North-South negotiations suggests a continuing power to "control outcomes." But even at this most aggregate level what we may be witnessing is the weakening power of the *demandeur*—Northern *or* Southern— in a more complex system. For the North cannot get what *it wants* at the LOS III Conference either. This may eventually lead to unilateral Northern actions, but the very *uncertainties* of the chain of events that might follow unilateral action have kept Northern states at the international planning and negotiating tables for close to a decade despite growing levels of frustration reflected in Northern legislative bodies.

[10]Tucker, op. cit., p. 201

[11]Keohane and Nye, op. cit., p. 229.

Chapter 3
Prominent Perspectives on the North-South Split

I

The constraints on collective action to manage North-South problems in the emerging global system will be significantly affected by the ways in which those problems are perceived by both sides and by the "policy space" that mutually compatible Northern and Southern perspectives offer to policy makers in both sets of countries.

The degrees of freedom available to work toward constructive resolution of these problems in the 1980s should not be exaggerated. There will be constraints emerging at the global level reflecting the general distribution of force, "relationships of major tension," and all the other traditional limitations on the policy maker imposed by the state of anarchy characterizing large segments of the international system. Likewise, there will be a broad range of domestic constraints on the formulation of North-South policies. These will receive considerable attention in the following two chapters, which look much more closely at the evolution of "postindustrial" societies of the North and "preindustrial" and industrializing societies of the South.

But there will be room for choice, regardless of these international and domestic constraints. While these constraints set limits to the probable, they are not inflexible parameters. One major reason why they are not inflexible is that North-South relationships are beginning to be analyzed through nontraditional conceptual frameworks and are reflecting changing norms and values even within traditional frameworks.

To take but one introductory example, it is interesting to note how many commentators and how many emerging perspectives on North-South relations rely heavily on imagery and concepts generally foreign to international politics. Southern "solidarity" is spoken of as representing a "trade union" organizing to increase bargaining power vis-à-vis the North. Directorates of international organizations are expected to increase their developing country membership "because they deserve more representation." A "global fairness revolution" requires a third major try (after the League of Nations period and the Bretton Woods period) at world order. Finally, even the quasi-traditionalist plea of Stanley Hoffmann for "world order politics" is made with the explicit recognition that major changes in traditional state behavior would be required which "go against the traditional logic of the international milieu."[1]

These perceptions and others will help to determine whether or not statesmen and scholars will continue to apply the traditional dichotomy between domestic and international politics to questions of North-South relations, with all the policy implications that this dichotomy implies, or whether a significant number of them will begin to question the validity of the dichotomy in present-day global politics. Since these perceptions are likely to prove an important element in the evolution of North-South relations, this chapter is devoted to an examination of the major perspectives now emerging in this arena. The stronger they become, the more they will influence the trends of change in the international system analyzed in the previous chapter.

II

Within the developing countries there are three perspectives that merit analysis. The first, the "international inequity" theme, overwhelms the other two in salience and "legitimacy" in Southern eyes. It is the one that can link Southern countries with per capita incomes of $200 to those at the $10,000 level. Built on the historical evolution of North-South relations in both the pre- and postcolonial periods, this perception provides the cement that binds the otherwise disparate and potentially discordant membership of the Southern bloc. The second and third perspectives, which merit brief note, are those of "Southern self-reliance" and "basic human needs." The second perspective, little debated or criticized, is perhaps unchallenged because it thus far remains a rhetorical posture that has not yet required any implementation costs. As long as it remains essentially rhetorical, it will meet with little Southern resistance. The difficulties for the South that it entails will be exposed only if and when it is taken more seriously than it was in the late 1970s.

The third perspective—a focus on meeting the basic human needs of the so-called absolute poverty population within the developing countries—is not shared by a majority within developing-country governing circles or even academic groups. Often it is viewed as a Trojan horse, a perspective that will undermine the legitimacy of Southern claims against the North under the international inequity theme and the legitimacy of the position of Southern elites within their own societies. Nevertheless, enough governments, technocrats, and intellectuals within the South have endorsed the perspective to give it at least a controversial prominence.

A. The International Inequity Perspective

The international inequity perspective has served as the driving force behind the activities of both Non-Aligned Country and Group of 77 activity since the inception of these organizations. Although the NAC movement was initially inspired by the idea of avoiding involvement in the cold war, it soon became the preeminent international platform for attacks on colonialism, apartheid, neocolonialism, and all other forms of Northern or white domination, imagined or real.

By the early 1970s, as illuminated at the 1973 Algiers conference, political issues—many of them resolved—began to give way to the economic agenda. And here the case for international inequity had been documented for over a decade by the Group of 77 and the UNCTAD Secretariat. Against the backdrop of aggregate per capita income differences measuring approximately 10 to 1 in favor of the developed countries and still widening,[2] five of the most persistent Southern charges concerning the inequity of the international economic system ran as follows:

1.   Efforts at international trade liberalization through the instrument of the General Agreement on Tariffs and Trade (GATT) had been singularly biased in favor of products of interest to developed-country exporters, and the developing countries had therefore gained little from the six rounds of tariff-cutting negotiations that took place between 1947 and 1967. Few economists have disputed this perception, and most attempts to measure the extent of the problem have suggested that Northern levels of protection (through quota restrictions, health and safety regulations, nominal and effective tariff structures, variable levies, internal taxes and price supports, etc.) were costing the South several billion dollars per year in forgone export earnings during the mid-1960s, the most significant portion stemming from agricultural protectionism.

In the late 1970s, despite the potential trade gains to be derived from the Tokyo Round of trade negotiations, the developing countries were more fearful of growing Northern protectionism than they were pleased by GATT negotiating prospects. The growing use of "Orderly Marketing Arrangements" by the United States against LDC manufactures and similar restrictive measures in Europe and Japan seemed all too likely to neutralize a considerable portion of the potential benefits of the Tokyo Round.

2.   The volume and value of foreign aid flowing from North to South have been unjustifiably low whether measured by "absorptive capacity" of funds in Southern development projects or by proclaimed Northern commitments to assist Southern developmental efforts. Again, there has been little Northern disagreement with either premise except by those who have felt that most aid has merely served to support Southern elite groups who were not really committed to equitable development strategies within their own countries. The members of the Development Assistance Com-

mittee (DAC) of the OECD as an aggregate have never approached their often enunciated target of transferring 0.7 percent of their annual GNP to the South in the form of official development assistance (ODA), and the trend—as indicated in Table 3-1—has moved downward rather steadily throughout the past decade. Additionally, the increased tying of aid to purchases of goods within the donor country during the 1960s substantially lowered the real value of most Northern aid transfers.

3.   The North had systematically rejected—or stalled for lengthy periods of time before accepting in altered form—a wide variety of Southern proposals to increase the availability to the South of scarce foreign exchange needed in the development process. The South suggests international commodity agreements to raise and stabilize the prices of its major exports; the North responds by citing the (generally genuine) problems commodity agreements raise and by effectively rejecting the approach in all but a few specific cases. The South suggests a "supplementary financing" mechanism as part of the World Bank's efforts to increase North-South resource flows; the proposal is quietly forestalled by the North. The South requests a system of generalized tariff preferences (GSP) to increase its capacity to export manufactured goods to the North in 1964; in 1974 the U.S. Congress finally adopts legislation granting the President the power to implement a scheme that bears only a pale resemblance to the program requested a decade earlier. This list of examples, which gives rise to the Southern perception of Northern unwillingness to aid the development process through reforms in present trade, financial, and aid mechanisms, could be extended indefinitely. The point is *not* that all Southern schemes have had analytical merit; many decidedly do not. The point is the pattern of request and denial which enhances an a priori feeling of inequity based on the present international distribution of income and wealth, among other things.

4.   Northern multinational corporations have in general restricted their potential contributions to the Southern development process in countless ways. Among the most obvious and widespread have been (a) the limitation on tax liabilities through certain patterns

Table 3-1　Flow of Official Development Assistance from Development Assistance Committee Members Measured as a Percentage of Gross National Product*

	1960	1965	1970	1971	1972	1973	1974	1975	1976	1977	1978	1979	1980
Australia	0.38	0.53	0.59	0.53	0.59	0.44	0.55	0.61	0.42	0.45	0.47	0.48	0.49
Austria		0.11	0.07	0.07	0.09	0.15	0.18	0.17	0.10	0.17	0.18	0.18	0.19
Belgium	0.88	0.60	0.46	0.50	0.55	0.51	0.51	0.59	0.51	0.61	0.64	0.65	0.67
Canada	0.19	0.19	0.42	0.42	0.47	0.43	0.50	0.58	0.48	0.58	0.61	0.64	0.66
Denmark	0.09	0.13	0.38	0.43	0.45	0.48	0.55	0.58	0.58	0.64	0.67	0.70	0.70
Finland†		0.02	0.07	0.12	0.15	0.16	0.17	0.18	0.18	0.17	0.17	0.18	0.20
France	1.38	0.76	0.66	0.66	0.67	0.58	0.59	0.62	0.62	0.62	0.62	0.62	0.63
Germany	0.31	0.40	0.32	0.34	0.31	0.32	0.37	0.40	0.31	0.32	0.32	0.32	0.31
Italy	0.22	0.10	0.16	0.18	0.09	0.14	0.14	0.11	0.16	0.12	0.11	0.10	0.10
Japan	0.24	0.27	0.23	0.23	0.21	0.25	0.25	0.24	0.20	0.26	0.27	0.29	0.30
Netherlands	0.31	0.36	0.61	0.58	0.67	0.54	0.63	0.75	0.82	0.97	1.00	1.02	1.03
New Zealand‡			0.23	0.23	0.25	0.27	0.31	0.52	0.42	0.41	0.45	0.48	0.49
Norway	0.11	0.16	0.32	0.33	0.43	0.43	0.57	0.66	0.71	0.87	0.96	0.97	0.98
Sweden	0.05	0.19	0.38	0.44	0.48	0.56	0.72	0.82	0.82	0.93	0.97	1.00	1.00
Switzerland	0.04	0.09	0.15	0.12	0.21	0.16	0.15	0.18	0.19	0.15	0.16	0.17	0.17
United Kingdom	0.56	0.47	0.37	0.41	0.39	0.34	0.38	0.37	0.38	0.39	0.37	0.38	0.38
United States§	0.53	0.49	0.31	0.32	0.29	0.23	0.24	0.26	0.26	0.26	0.26	0.26	0.26
Grand Total													
ODA ($billion-nominal prices)	4.6	5.9	6.8	7.7	8.5	9.4	11.3	13.6	13.7	16.3	18.8	21.5	24.4
ODA ($billion-constant 1977 prices)	12.2	14.1	14.4	15.5	15.8	14.3	14.2	15.1	14.8	16.3	17.4	18.6	19.7
GNP ($billion-nominal prices)	0.9	1.3	2.0	2.2	2.6	3.1	3.4	3.8	4.1	4.6	5.3	5.9	6.6
ODA as percentage of GNP	0.52	0.44	0.34	0.35	0.33	0.30	0.33	0.36	0.33	0.35	0.35	0.36	0.37
ODA deflator¶	0.38	0.42	0.47	0.50	0.54	0.66	0.80	0.90	0.93	1.00	1.08	1.16	1.24

*Figures for 1975 and earlier years are based on actual data. Figures for 1976 are preliminary actuals. Those for 1977–1980 are based on OECD and World Bank estimates of growth of GNP, on information on budget appropriations for aid, and on aid policy statements by governments. They are projections, not predictions, of what will occur unless action not now planned takes place.

of transfer pricing, (b) the limitations on job creation through the use of capital-intensive production methods and artificial limitations on exports, (c) the exaction of monopoly rents on the corporations' technology, and other, less generalized, forms of corporate behavior. In addition, these companies have on many documented occasions interfered in internal politics of host countries, with or without the support of their home governments. Finally, they and their home governments have been able to limit if not altogether halt other international capital flows to host governments in situations involving serious corporation–host government conflict. [3]

5. The terms of trade have moved consistently against the typical developing-country export basket, and they have done so for reasons that are related structurally to the operations of the Bretton Woods system. (This particular perception continued to exist until the raw material price boom of the early 1970s despite a great deal of conflicting evidence; post-boom price movements revived the faulty perception).

The five general perceptions noted above are not universally shared within the developing world. Indeed, the Bretton Woods years witnessed significant economic progress within many individual countries of the South as well as within the South as an aggregate. It is often forgotten that the growth target for the First Development Decade—5 percent per year—was exceeded and that per capita growth rates averaged 3 percent despite the high rate of Southern population growth (well in excess of 2 percent per year). What the previous paragraphs have tried to capture is not an *analytical assessment* of major Southern complaints about present international economic structures and processes, but rather a de-

†Finland became a member of DAC in January 1975.

‡New Zealand became a member of DAC in 1973. ODA figures for New Zealand are not available for 1960 and 1965.

§In 1949, at the beginning of the Marshall Plan, U.S. Official Development Assistance amounted to 2.79 percent of GNP.

¶Includes the effect of parity changes. Deflators are the same as those for GNP.

Source: Address to the Board of Governors by Robert S. McNamara, President, World Bank, Washington, D.C., September 26, 1977, p. 39.

veloping-country *feeling* about the *equity aspects* of North-South economic relations which has grown over the past two decades.

While the Group of 77, particularly through its chosen organization, UNCTAD, continues the struggle over various aspects of the agenda of economic issues reviewed above, the increasingly troubled years since 1973 have produced some much broader, institutional considerations on the inequity perspective from the South. One of the most integral of the blueprints for a "more equitable" global order was presented in the following language:

There is need to establish a single World Development Authority (WDA) where decisions on international economic issues can be coordinated. This should be under the aegis of the United Nations and have complete jurisdiction over all international economic institutions, old and new. The WDA should be run by a board elected periodically by the U.N. General Assembly, representing the interests of various regional and ideological blocs. Its major tasks should be to:

(a) Regulate short-term international credit;
(b) Provide long-term development finance;
(c) Create a framework for expansion of world trade;
(d) Strike a balance between world population increase and food production; and
(e) In general, act as a global economic planning commission in an advisory role.[4]

Under this plan the following new international institutions would be established: (a) an International Central Bank, (b) an International Development Fund, (c) an International Trade Organization, and (d) a World Food Authority. Each new institution would work to "correct" the inequities of the present international economic system, and each would provide a much larger political role for the developing countries in international economic relations.

While there are major disagreements among the developing countries on the rank ordering of systemic injustices and proposals for change, this general perspective does provide an umbrella for all: OPEC states, the Third World, and the least developed. The second and third Southern perspectives worthy of note are not at all as effective as visions that can be universally shared.

B. The Southern Self-Reliance Perspective

In the early and mid-1970s the phrase "Southern self-reliance" appeared with increasing frequency, particularly in documents prepared for UNCTAD meetings and others sponsored by the G-77 or the Non-Aligned Countries. A close reading of those documents indicates that the phrase almost always incorporated two distinct goals.

The first involved an increased capacity for intra-Southern "self-help" in the development process. This form of Southern self-reliance might include any of the following initiatives: Increased efforts to liberalize trade flows among Southern countries, the development of Southern multinational corporations through joint governmental cooperation and financial support, jointly sponsored and financed technological institutions to enhance autonomous Southern research and development capacity, joint support of Southern producer associations that would attempt to raise and stabilize the prices of raw materials exported in large quantities by developing countries, and, where the political will existed, the creation of Southern regional free trade areas and/or customs unions.

The second major goal implicit in the Southern self-reliance strategy—more political in nature—was to use enhanced Southern unity to bargain more effectively and forcefully with the North for desired changes in the international economic system. Once the OPEC countries successfully raised oil prices, the strategy of Southern self-reliance was increasingly linked to OPEC's new political and economic strength. Other Southern countries immediately looked to OPEC for political support in international bargaining arenas, such as CIEC, and for the financing to support the building of other producer associations. OPEC diplomatic support was generally forthcoming, but within the space of a few years it became clear that the organization had no intention of financing major Southern self-reliance efforts.

Unless the OPEC countries reverse their thinking and contribute substantially to such a strategy, this second perspective will most probably never amount to more than a rhetorical adjunct to the global inequity perspective. Even with OPEC backing this conjecture will probably remain valid for the simple reason that political and economic elites in most developing countries desire greater participation in the OECD-dominated international economic system rather than less participation. Furthermore, as all Southern experiments with regional-integration schemes suggest, it has proved extremely difficult in practice for developing countries to create economic forms of mutual self-reliance. Finally, some of the most developed countries of the South are deeply involved in Northern commodity-market exchange, they borrow heavily from Northern capital markets, and they rely heavily on Northern technology at various stages of their development.

For all these reasons most developing countries would much prefer growing degrees of participation in a more equitable international system to a turn toward Southern self-reliance, particularly if and when the term refers to limiting or breaking linkages to Northern economies and the present international economic system. There are individuals, schools of thought, and a few governments within the South that would prefer the limiting or breaking of those linkages that now exist. But if anything is predictable in the North-South arena it is that this theme will remain a cultural and value-oriented counterpoint to the growing emphasis on creating a "more equitable" international economic system in which North-South linkages can be maintained under rules and norms that are increasingly profitable to the developing countries.[5]

As a psychological counterpoint, the theme of self-reliance will undoubtedly grow. Recent disputes in UNESCO over the role of the Northern media in developing countries, the creation of such intellectual groupings as the Third World Forum, and the establishment of the Third World University in Mexico City in 1976 are all the inevitable products of the changes in the international system discussed in the preceding chapter and the growing intensity of communication among developing countries. As an economic strategy of development, self-reliance will probably remain, with marginal exceptions, a gleam in the eye of leftist intellectuals and a very few governments. And a continuing capacity for Southern bloc unity will determine the future of self-reliance as a political bargaining strategy.

C.   The Basic-Human-Needs Perspective

The final Southern perspective—concerned with meeting the minimal needs of the poorest people within the developing countries—remains a minority view at present.[6] Support for the concept of refocusing development strategies to meet more rapidly and effectively the minimum needs of the poorest strata of society in the developing countries can be found throughout the South, but the actual degree of support would be extremely difficult to measure. Many governing elites oppose changes in development strategies that continue to reward them well; others doubt that a basic-human-needs strategy can actually be made operative; still others fear that support for such domestic reform efforts will draw attention away from the global inequity struggle against the North. For all these reasons, it will remain most difficult to measure levels and degrees of support for a basic-human-needs perspective within the South over the coming decade.

Nevertheless, it should be noted that Southern lip service is almost always given to the perspective in discussions of development strategies within the UN, that workers' and employers' representatives from many "moderate" Southern countries explicitly supported the concept in the final Declaration of Principles of the ILO-sponsored World Employment Conference in 1976, and that the perspective is central to concerns of many Southern intellectual groups, such as the Third World Forum. How fast and how far Southern support for the fulfillment of basic human needs might spread as a "legitimate" perspective on North-South issues will be one of the central concerns of Chapters 8 and 9.

III

The preceding 5 years of intensified North-South conflict have led to serious reconsideration of North-South issues within the developed countries for the first time since the height of the cold war era. While the Southern global inequity perspective has a long history, Northern thinking has been characterized by a virtual lack of any coherent perspective on North-South relations. To the extent that the South was singled out for special consideration, it was either in the context of its tendency toward neutralism during the cold war period or in a general developmental context which envisioned developing countries "graduating" into the ranks of developed societies as LDC development strategies—aided by Northern foreign economic assistance, international investment, and trade liberalization—produced emergent industrial states.

With the birth of UNCTAD in 1964, the emergence of the Group of 77, and the continued outspoken criticism of the North by the Non-Aligned Countries on the issues of colonialism and global economic policies, Northern governments were forced to respond to Southern manifestos and multilateral agendas with increasing frequency in the late 1960s. But the attitude that there were no "serious" problems inherent in growing Southern unity and criticism remained overwhelmingly predominant until the events of 1973 and after. Only in the wake of the OPEC actions, the Sixth and Seventh Special Sessions of the UN, and the collapse of Portugal's African empire did Northern governments and nongovernmental groups begin to reexamine some fundamental premises of Northern policies toward the developing countries.

During the late 1960s and early 1970s most Northerners with the time or interest to explore North-South issues started with the rhetorical question: Does the South really matter? And most analysts felt hard-pressed to demonstrate the importance of the developing countries to "the system" from a national interest point of view. By the mid-1970s, there had been a rather fundamental change in this perception. By then, those who thought that Southern solidarity did not represent a serious diplomatic problem and that developing-country cooperation in resolving problems that were global in nature was of little importance seemed to be in a minority. The issue was no longer whether the South mattered, but rather *what strategy* to adopt to achieve at least the minimum necessary Southern support for Northern foreign policy goals. As the following discussion of emerging Northern perspectives on North-South issues demonstrates, there remained a very broad spectrum of views on the ingredients of a successful strategy. But the fact that the issue posed had changed rather dramatically reveals more about the shifting parameters of international relations and the policy space for North-South relations in the 1980s than do present differences of opinion on which strategies are most appropriate to an increasingly novel international system.

By the mid-1970s the view that the capacity to achieve many Northern foreign policy goals would be substantially influenced by the evolving relationship between developed and increasingly cohesive developing countries seemed obvious for many reasons. In the arena of military security three potential conflict situations within and among developing countries were viewed with concern, particularly for their capacity to engender East-West conflict. The first of these "triggering" challenges to Northern military security involves contests for regional hegemony taking place and likely to continue to do so within the developing world. The very process of economic development produces "leaders" and "laggers"; as in the evolution of the European state system, this process inevitably creates regional tensions as the unevenly expanding capacities for projecting external influence which generally accompany industrial/ technological growth stir expansionist tendencies in some states and create defensive concerns in others.

Whether this source of instability need eventuate in armed conflict is highly uncertain. More certain is that the pace of growth of a Brazil or an Iran ipso facto creates both tendencies toward and fears of bids for regional hegemony. As both leaders and laggers turn to other states for diplomatic and material support, the opportunities for East-West involvement are created. Whether or not the United States and the Soviet Union will be drawn into such conflicts and at what degree of risk to themselves are difficult questions to answer out of context.

A second type of Southern triggering mechanism for potential East-West involvement and confrontation concerns bilateral conflicts of historical origin. Disputes of this nature are to be found on the west coast of South America, in North Africa, on the Indian subcontinent, and in parts of Southeast Asia. The permeability of most of the states involved increases the probability that armed conflict may be used in a number of instances to solidify the position of certain governing elites.

The third trigger, closely related to the second, involves regional ethnic and religious conflicts and the armed clashes that often accompany them. Again related to the softness of the states involved, such conflicts are more likely to spill across national boundaries, assume perceived ideological lines, and invite outside intervention if the degree of instability introduced into a region is interpreted as affecting the East-West strategic balance and the "rules of the game" of détente. Sub-Saharan Africa may be the scene of many conflicts bearing such potential.[7] And again, while there is nothing inevitable about great-power intervention, it is also obvious that each such occasion introduces the possibility of destabilizing East-West relations.

In the arena of Northern economic security, the importance of developments in the South and in the evolution of North-South diplomatic relations was much more direct. At its broadest, economic security would include such ingredients as (1) assured access to all needed raw materials, (2) assured access to all other commodities, (3) assured access to global markets for the sale of domestically produced goods and technology, and (4) protection for foreign investment, direct and indirect. Finally, economic security would call for a global system of rules and norms of behavior that automatically regulated any deviations from the system outlined above so that no sudden and unexpected economic policy changes on the part of individual states participating in the international economic system could undermine the economic security provided by those rules.

The capacity of the developing countries to undermine the goal of economic security is far less contingent than it is with regard to military security. While OPEC actions present the most dramatic example, hints of many others pervaded the international atmosphere in the mid-to-late 1970s. The growing capacity of the developing countries to raise prices rapidly in periods of global boom and to rewrite the rules of foreign direct investment are but two of the examples one might cite from recent evidence. Additionally, careful attention was being paid to the second-order ramifications of the unpredictable behavior thus introduced: wider international cyclical swings in economic activity, more unemployment, higher rates of inflation, less investment in the production of raw materials in developing countries, and a host of others.

OPEC actions aside, these illustrations did not suggest an aggregate loss in Northern power (control over outcomes), but they did suggest a pattern of growing cost to the North to exercise increasingly contested control. Thus observers who examined these issues did not offer them as evidence of Northern vulnerability to Southern economic behavior or of Southern strength in a test of wills with the North. They were focusing on the issue of the sensitivity of Northern states to economic disruptions that could be caused by Southern behavior and on the potential losses to the global economy that could be caused by such actions as those noted above. To cite but one example, an econometric study that attempted to quantify the potential economic benefits to the United States of commodity-price stabilization during the decade 1963–1972 concluded that stabilization could have resulted in "economic gains (the *prevented* unemployment and GNP loss) amounting to a total present discounted value of about $15 billion."[8]

In the arena of what Arnold Wolfers once labeled "milieu goals," it has become increasingly obvious that the North cannot achieve its purpose without more constructive North-South relations. By the mid-1970s two areas in particular illuminated this dilemma. The first concerned the capacity of international institutions and multilateral diplomacy to manage what have come to be labeled "global agenda" issues: nuclear proliferation, population control, food production, pollution, management of the oceans, and other problems that very often require the cooperation of most nations if significant progress toward their resolution is to be made. The 1970s were replete with international failures to make much progress in managing such problems; this record was in large part attributable to the growing North-South confrontational atmosphere, which produced little but rhetoric and deadlock. If Secretary Kissinger was correct in noting that "progress in dealing with our traditional agenda is no longer enough. . . . The problems of energy resources, environment, population, the uses of space and the seas, now rank with questions of military security, ideology, and territorial rivalry which have traditionally made up the diplomatic agenda," and if Southern cooperation were the sine qua non of significant progress on these new issues—particularly in the workings of international institutions and conferences—then the South really did matter if it continued to manifest a high degree of diplomatic solidarity.

The second Northern milieu goal that demonstrated the importance of achieving less conflictual North-South relationships concerned the issue of human values. The mid-1970s witnessed the expression of widely shared concerns over the "value gap" between the United States on the one hand and the Third World on the other. Some of those concerned place their emphasis on differing economic values (e.g., efficiency versus equity); others tend to stress differences in values concerning forms of governmental representation (e.g., democratic versus nondemocratic governments); still others place major emphasis on differing definitions and standards applied by North and South to human rights. Whatever the difference in emphasis, it seemed obvious that continued North-South conflict would seriously constrain Northern (especially United States) efforts to promote the global emergence of values congruent with its own cultural values and norms.

The growing recognition within the North that the levels of North-South conflict reached in the early to mid-1970s were creating problems at many different levels for their own domestic societies and foreign policy goals had led to a growing reconsideration of the relationship between developed and developing countries. While many Northern perspectives on the relationship had emerged, there were five prominent enough to merit special consideration.

Several preliminary points should be made about these five perspectives. First, they are seldom mutually exclusive. They represent five differing frameworks from which North-South relations are now often considered in the North; each framework encompasses a differing mix of concerns. But the same observer may well feel that any improvement in North-South relations will require efforts that address several sets of concerns jointly.

Second, there is a good deal of overlap between several of the perspectives. As their presentation will suggest, it is sometimes difficult to determine exactly where one perspective ends and another begins. Nevertheless, the distinctions are drawn on the assumption that treating them in a discrete fashion reveals much more about current Northern thinking than it conceals.

Third, while representatives of each perspective can be found in all Northern states, it seems clear that some perspectives are more salient in certain countries than they are in others. Where such differences seem to be significant, they will be noted.

A. The Rejectionist Perspective

The rejectionist perspective is one that, politely or otherwise, suggests to the developing countries that they can go to hell in a handbasket, taking their demands for system reform with them. The perspective has generally been more straightforwardly articulated in the United States than elsewhere in the North, perhaps because citizens of great powers are least willing to come to terms with the changing nature of the international system, least able to identify such change, and least threatened by it in any short-term, strategic sense.

Echoing much of the indignation Ambassador Moynihan showered upon his UN colleagues during the same period, Irving Kristol in July 1975 characterized the present North-South conflict as "the new cold war" and wrote the following passage, which succinctly summarizes one major viewpoint inherent in the rejectionist perspective:

There is always a good case, in both principle and prudence, for the more affluent being charitable toward the poor—even to those whose poverty is largely their own fault. Nor is there any reason to expect, much less insist on, gratitude: Such benevolence is supposed to be its own reward. But when the poor start "mau-mauing" their actual or potential benefactors, when they begin vilifying them, insulting them, demanding as a right what is not their right to demand—then one's sense of self-respect may properly take precedence over one's self-imposed humanitarian obligations. If the United States is to gain the respect of world opinion, it first has to demonstrate that it respects itself—its own institutions, its own way of life, the political and social philosophy that is the basis of its institutions and its way of life. Such a sense of self-respect and self-affirmation seems to be a missing element in our foreign policy. It is no wonder, therefore, that we are making such a mess of the "new cold war."[9]

A second element of the perspective is reflected by those Northerners who felt or continue to feel that the Southern unity that greatly contributed to causing developed countries so many difficulties in the early-to-mid 1970s was a temporary phenomenon, one that would soon disappear as the radically differentiated members of the developing-country coalition recovered from the euphoria induced by the 1973–1974 OPEC oil embargo and price actions. Analysts of this persuasion share the view that the developing countries' differing economic structures create sharply divergent needs; that their differing political systems, religious beliefs, and ethnic conflicts defy the capacity for continued diplomatic cooperation; and that within Latin America, Africa, the Middle East, and Asia, bids for regional hegemony and other forms of security threats will soon remove "the South" as a united actor in the international system.

Until the late spring of 1975, United States diplomacy seems to have been based upon this premise. When the United States failed to break the link between the OPEC countries and the rest of the South by that time, United States policy "turned from confrontation to dialogue," in the rhetoric of the period. Even this rhetorical change frightened such rejectionists as Kristol, who found "very worrisome" the "apparent willingness of many State Department officials to reformulate American foreign economic policy in the hope of achieving a more amicable 'dialog' with the so-called Third World."[10] The worry was unwarranted. When the CIEC Conference formally terminated in June of 1977, it was clear for all to see that "reformulation" was yet to become the hallmark of United States (or Northern) economic policy toward the developing countries. The stalemate system still prevailed.

Finally, it is from the United States academic community that what is likely to remain the classic intellectual rationale for the Northern rejectionist perspective appeared, in the form of Robert W. Tucker's *The Inequality of Nations*. While the author disdained involvement in policy prescription, his analysis of the North-South struggle is replete with the implication that Northern attempts at "constructive accommodation" are a fool's work. This is so, he suggests, because Southern governing elites are solely interested in greater status and power according to the rules of the "old" international system. Northerners with qualms about global equity questions are, in Tucker's view, simply making world politics less predictable, more vulnerable to miscalculation and disorder, all for a cause that will benefit not the vast majority of developing-country populations but merely their governing elites. Thus Tucker can conclude that the 1980s will witness the evolution of a new hierarchy, not a new system of global politics.

There are two distinct rationales for the rejectionist perspective. One is that the present international economic system is highly defensible in both normative and efficiency terms, that the Southern attack on this system aims at total replacement rather than measured reforms, and that Northern efforts to "accommodate" will therefore prove self-defeating in the long run. The second rationale, more concerned with international politics than economics, is simply that global politics will be more "manageable" from a Northern point of view without the obstinate presence of a Southern bloc that insists on politicizing such issues as are raised at the Law of the Sea Conference and such institutions as the ILO and UNESCO. But the policy prescriptions that flow from it—to reject all Southern demands and undermine Southern unity—are appropriate only if the bloc is easily broken at small cost. Measured in these terms, the policy failed by mid-1975, and many initial supporters of the rejectionist perspective began to examine others.

B. The "Bring Them into the System" Perspective

Many Northerners, especially those in government-policy-making positions, finally settled on the second major perspective. Some supported it from the outset of the troubled years of the 1970s, while others moved in this direction only after it became clear that the potential costs of the rejectionist perspective were higher than initially calculated.

Those supporting the "bring them into the system" perspective share the following general views: (1) the present system can and should be maintained with a modicum of change to overcome its most obvious weaknesses, (2) a united South poses serious problems for system maintenance, and (3) the most auspicious way to strengthen the system while reducing Southern bloc pressures is to find a much more prominent role for key developing countries within the system. A Trilateral Commission report published in the mid-1970s captured the intellectual essence of this perspective in the following paragraph:

History has often shown that the *greatest dangers to international stability often arise from those nations whose real power is inadequately reflected* in both real involvement in the relevant sets of international arrangements and symbols of status therein. Such nations *can challenge the legitimacy of the system with actions as well as rhetoric*. Much of the current call for a new international economic order flows directly from such concerns. Indeed, only through integration into the management of international arrangements are such countries likely to acquire the systemic interests necessary for the constructive formulation of their own foreign economic policies. (Emphasis added.)[11]

Four points should be made concerning this perspective. First, it most often takes a very narrow view of "the system." Many of those who share it, as the Trilateral Commission report reveals, concentrate almost solely on the international economic aspects of the system. Yet countries knocking on the door of the system in the past have seldom limited their desires for change to the economic (and economic institutional) realm.

Second, as the quoted paragraph suggests, the perspective tends to focus almost exclusively on those Southern countries that have the capacity to destabilize present international economic relationships. Thus the Commission report specifically mentions four developing countries: Iran, Brazil, Mexico, and Saudi Arabia. It suggests that "it might be desirable" to invite the first three to join the OECD and to invite Saudi Arabia "which now has the second largest monetary reserves in the world . . . to meetings of the Group of Ten, which will doubtlessly continue to act as an informal steering group on some international monetary issues."[12] Thus, the approach becomes, in practice if not in original intent, very much oriented toward the sole objective of system maintenance, and the mechanism for achieving that goal is to pay very special attention to integrating the most powerful developing countries more tightly into the present system. The two favored routes to achieve this integration are more chairs at present international and regional organizations for leading LDC candidates and a greater emphasis on Northern bilateral relationships with these same LDCs.

Third, since the perspective does for the most part have a short-term, economic-system-maintenance emphasis, the range of empirical and normative issues that capture its attention is rather limited. The Trilateral Commission report—probably the most articulate and broad-gauged statement yet to appear in this category—does note that new issues, such as income distribution, have arisen as well as new states. In general, however, the focus of this perspective remains heavily oriented toward the exploration of reforms that will ensure the continued operation of the existing international economic system with its values and norms intact.

Finally, it should be noted that it is very difficult to make any judgments concerning the degree to which those groups and individuals who view North-South relations from this perspective also harbor the rejectionist perspective's desire to fragment Southern diplomatic unity. A close examination suggests that while some do view such fragmentation as a welcome outcome that policies developed from this perspective might produce, others are not consciously desirous of achieving this result. They are concerned that "artificial" Southern unity often "politicizes" discussions and negotiations that they believe can and should be guided by more rational, functionally oriented criteria; if a fragmentation of the Group of 77 produced such a change, they would welcome it. But for most of those Northerners who have adopted the "bring them into the system" point of view, a decline in Southern unity seems to be viewed much more as a (perhaps necessary and valuable) side payment than as the policy goal per se.

C. The Global Agenda Perspective

The third major Northern perspective on North-South relations is exhibited by those government officials, scholars, and observers of global politics who see the need for increasingly effective forms of multilateral diplomacy in a world characterized by declining United States hegemony, the growing dispersion of influence and power (especially when measured as control over outcomes) among a broadening number of state and nonstate actors in world politics, and above all the increasing number of global problems that can be contained and resolved only by means of collective action at the international level. Among the problems presently ranked high upon the so-called global agenda are such issues as nuclear proliferation, international rules (a regime) covering the use of the seas and the seabeds, other "international commons" regimes, population stabilization, environmental issues, and a global food system.

Perhaps the classic example of a global agenda item and the difficulties of dealing effectively with it at the present moment concerns the issues that have come together in the complex and time-consuming negotiations to produce a comprehensive law of the sea treaty. The third UN-sponsored Law of the Sea Conference has been struggling for over 4 years to come to grips with such issues as the extension of territorial waters; the boundaries of economic zones that would, for many purposes, be placed under the sole control of coastal states; fishing rights; deep-seabed mining rights; environmental standards and the policing thereof; rules concerning passage through straits; and many others.

During the process of multinational negotiation, three trends have emerged which have troubling implications for other global agenda problems. The first has been the steady erosion of general "global-interest" and "international-interest" themes in favor of specific "special-interest" and "national-interest" proposals. Perhaps the outstanding example of this trend is evidenced by the ever-expanding territorial claims by coastal states and the ever-outward extension of national boundaries. If this trend is finally legitimized in a new law of the sea treaty, the initial theme of a "common heritage of mankind"—which was grounded in the concept of narrow territorial waters and narrow national economic zones, with the vast majority of the riches of the seas and seabed mineral deposits to be harvested and used for development purposes in the world's poorer countries—will have been all but lost in the national- and special-interest scramble for those same sources of wealth.

The second trend concerns the continuing conflict between developed and developing countries. The degree of developing-country distrust of United States foreign policy initiatives has become so strong that an initial United States proposal on ocean issues which contained many elements supportive of the "common heritage of mankind" concept was automatically rejected by the developing countries, which—in LOS III as elsewhere—have continuously caucused and (with but a few exceptions) acted as a remarkably solid unit. Many developing countries with coastal waters rich in fisheries and continental margins rich in minerals have been able to effectively use automatic developing-country distrust of United States policy initiatives in order to enhance their own national interest at the expense of the "common heritage of mankind" approach.[13]

The final trend, implicit in the first two, concerns the extraordinary difficulties of reaching optimal solutions or, indeed, any solutions to this particular global agenda item. Can close to 150 countries successfully conduct multilateral diplomacy? Or does the particular problem in this arena lie with the sheer volume of distinct issues raised by the law of the sea discussions? Finally, does the role of domestic interest groups—which have formed both national and transnational alliances to support, modify, and/or defeat national positions on such negotiations—suggest ever-growing problems with the present mode of multilateral negotiations and force a fundamental reconsideration of the linkages between domestic interest groups, national governments, and the process of multilateral diplomacy?

These are among the major concerns of those who see the world moving into a period in which collective action via multilateral diplomacy will form an increasingly dominant mode of international relations. From this perspective, they are deeply concerned with the potentially destructive effects of continued North-South conflict on global agenda issues. If the conflict continues at its present level of intensity, optimal outcomes from international negotiations will be impossible to realize in sphere after sphere. Not only will talk of a "global community" be dangerously misleading insofar as it suggests a minimum of shared values and norms of international behavior, but it will be next to impossible to make progress toward the formulation of those one or two commonly accepted superordinate goals among states which might form the foundation of a slow but steady move toward a community of nations.

Several points concerning the global agenda perspective on North-South relations deserve mention. First and quite obviously, North-South relations are only one part of a perspective fundamentally concerned with finding that balance between order and justice which will provide for some modicum of world order in the 1980s and beyond. As Stanley Hoffmann noted in urging the Carter administration to make "world order its chief priority: (1) There is no more important matter; (2) there is no alternative; (3) it is a good moment."[14]

Those who share Hoffmann's interpretation of the changing international system, in many ways similar to that described in the preceding chapter, generally share his view that "a great power is often reduced to preventing others from imposing their wills (for they need its contributions), while it cannot impose its own. Recent North-South discussions, as well as bargaining on law of the sea, have confirmed this."[15] While North-South relations are but one element of the problem of world order, the South's veto power over so many needed initiatives on the global agenda makes improvement in North-South relationships a sine qua non of progress toward world order.

A second observation concerns the breadth of the spectrum of views that are included in the global agenda perspective. One might actually conceptualize the spectrum as being delimited by an expansive version of the "bring them into the system" viewpoint at the narrow end and the view that "unlike past crises our current predicament is total"[16] at the broad end. At the narrow end of the spectrum, this perspective may be totally absorbed with current international economic issues. But it analyzes them from what is perceived to be a global point of view involving both institutional and substantive reforms.

From the broad end of the global agenda spectrum, the "bring them into the system" viewpoint seems extraordinarily shortsighted, no matter how defined, in light of the current challenges to the international system in all its component parts: economic, political/institutional, technological, etc. Those observers located at the narrow end of the spectrum argue against issue linkages and politicization and for international organizations that will handle functionally specific tasks. Those at the broadest end of the global agenda spectrum argue that "substantive issue linkage is increasingly expressed in institutional terms and will (eventually) be reflected in the restructuring of the United Nations system."[17] They are predicting quite simply that a *directly political mode* of international decision making is gradually replacing the Bretton Woods *inter-*

national technocratic ("depoliticized") *process* and that the trend *cannot be reversed.* And they therefore turn their attention not to incremental changes in any single arena of the present international system but rather to the extraordinarily complex issue of "the collective elaboration of welfare choices" at the level of global politics. In their view, global agenda problems will have little probability of solution until North and South can agree on new rules and norms for collectively elaborating and making such welfare choices.

This striking difference in the views on how much system change is needed before progress can be made on global agenda items in great part reflects differing views on many of the issues examined in Chapter 2. Has the international system experienced so much change that many of the old responses—ad hoc, incremental adaptations to each new global problem, for example—are now the exact opposite of what is needed? And the differences may also reflect a residual conflict of opinion on the very specific issue of the future of Southern solidarity. Obviously, the range of Northern policy options to achieve a moderate international order in the 1980s will be quite different if the South disappears as a serious diplomatic unit in international relations than if it retains its present levels of coherence. For it is that coherence that permits successful Southern efforts at issue linkage and the politicizing of many issues that might otherwise be treated as discrete, functional problems. The probabilities for continued Southern diplomatic unity are explored in some detail in the following chapter.

Finally, it should be noted that the global agenda perspective highlights a potentially crucial problem for the 1980s but does not suggest any obvious Northern policy options. For even if all observers were to concur that far greater degrees of North-South cooperation were a sine qua non for world order in the coming decades, the "rejectionists" and the "accommodationists" would be no closer to agreement on what set of Northern strategies and policies would produce the necessary degree of Southern cooperation. An examination of existing empirical evidence in later chapters offers some assistance in moving beyond the a priori positions so often assumed by combatants without regard for whatever empirical evidence there is to be gleaned from recent experience.

D.   The Global Equity Perspective

The Northern global equity perspective is in many ways the
analogue of the Southern international inequity perspective. While
the views on why the present system is inequitable to the developing countries may differ considerably, what is shared is the feeling
that the degrees of inequality that now exist between Northern and
Southern states and peoples must begin to be narrowed. Northerners of this persuasion are likely to view such inequalities as
politically dangerous and, perhaps more important, morally
intolerable.

The number of government leaders and analysts of international
relations accepting major overlapping aspects of this perspective is
growing. They are all inclined to view the issue of equity and the
manner in which it is managed internationally as in large degree
determining the course of North-South relations for many decades
to come. It is argued by many that global politics is becoming more
egalitarian than libertarian, that most states in today's world appear
to have far more interest in raising living standards than in the
more abstract concept of liberty. The fear has also been expressed
that America's emphasis on liberty rather than equality as a fundamental societal value may lead the United States into a position
of philosophical and diplomatic isolation unless this nation becomes
more responsive to "a value which has not been central to the
American experience" and begins to take into account the philosophical dimensions and political realities of the growing international emphasis on equity issues.[18]

These prudential concerns with the issue of international equity
are echoed by governments and private groups throughout the
OECD countries with varying degrees of concern. It is also quite
apparent, as the accompanying matrix (Figure 3-1) suggests, that
the equity issue encompasses many different, and often quite divergent, concerns.

First among them is a concern about equity in interstate relations.
Most Northern supporters of various elements in the Southern
demand for a New International Economic Order are persuaded,
in varying degrees, that the present international economic system
does not work in an equitable fashion. That is to say, it is not

Figure 3-1

	EQUALITY OF OPPORTUNITY	EQUALITY OF RESULT
Interstate relations		
Interpersonal relations		

structured in a way that gives most developing countries an equal opportunity to benefit from the operations of the system. It is a concern that fits clearly within the upper left quadrant of Figure 3-1.

The belief that the present international system operates in a manner that primarily benefits the developed countries, often to the detriment of the developing countries, is clearly spreading. As already noted, this view has been taken as an article of faith within the South for decades; a quickening growth of converts is now taking place within the North. Empirical evidence for this assertion can be found in the host of recently published analyses of North-South issues by individuals and groups from many OECD countries. Perhaps the most publicized among them are the Aspen Institute's *The Planetary Bargain*, the Dag Hammarskjöld Foundation's *What Now? Another Development*, and the "Tinbergen Group" report to the Club of Rome entitled *Reshaping the International Order*.[19]

In these and many similar studies produced by Northerners, the conclusion that the present system is inequitable and should be rapidly modified to assist the developing countries results from a highly variable mix of economic analysis and normative judgment. Some writers lean almost entirely on positive analysis of the present international economic system in making their case; a classic example of this genre is to be found in Albert Fishlow's recent essay, "A New International Economic Order: What Kind?"[20] Fishlow suggests that a few significant reforms of the present economic system could remove most of its serious imperfections and assure greater opportunity for developing-country growth while benefiting

Northern economies at the same time. His chief concerns are to improve LDC access to Northern product, capital, and technology markets.

Many Northerners hold the view that these and similar reforms of the present system, by producing opportunities for rapid developing-country growth, can adequately address the global equity issue. Major elements of this "developmentalist" perspective on the equity problem are to be found in the Tinbergen report and a study prepared for the UN by Wassily Leontief in the mid-1970s. Both studies go beyond the relatively modest (if politically difficult) reforms suggested by Fishlow, but both view the equity problem as essentially one of "closing the gap" between Northern and Southern aggregate per capita incomes through reforms that will increase developing-country rates of growth relative to those of the OECD countries.

Within this perspective one notes a constant shifting between positive and normative analysis. Some writers, however, rest their case for reform simply on normative propositions for system change, relying particularly upon the size of the gap between Northern and Southern per capita incomes and upon the plight of the absolute poverty population in the developing countries.

If scientific analysis and normative judgment are often combined by those who adopt this perspective, one also notes in their argumentation a liberal dose of prudential statecraft. For example, it is in the Aspen Institute report that all the global agenda issues noted in the preceding perspective are recalled, the assertion made that their resolution requires greater North-South cooperation, the judgment rendered that North-South conflict will continue until the equity issue is frontally addressed, and the conclusion drawn that a "planetary bargain" to increase global equity must be reached between North and South. While studies of a similar nature produced in European countries often resonate with feelings of guilt, quite possibly linked to former periods of European colonialism, American publications and policy prescriptions on this subject are constructed principally on prudential statecraft with differing amounts of "egalitarian" seasoning.

A second and analytically quite distinct equity consideration focuses not on interstate but on interpersonal equity comparisons.

This Northern focus on individuals often leads observers to significantly different empirical, normative, and policy conclusions than those that emerge from the examination of interstate equity issues. There is generally a clear recognition that changes in the international economic system such as those espoused in the NIEO proposals may have little, if any, effect on the distribution of income, wealth, and life chances within individual developing countries. These observers share the concern expressed by one prominent Southerner that unless governing elites within developing countries are themselves committed to internal equity goals, "foreign donors are completely helpless" to assist in their achievement.[21]

This concern triggers a series of observations about the global equity perspective which growing numbers of Northerners in and out of governments bring to the issue of North-South relations. The first involves the protean character of the term "global equity" and the number of different concerns it tends to encompass.

As Figure 3-1 suggests, the current discussions of equity and "fairness revolutions" often tend to cloud at least two crucial distinctions: the first between states and individuals and the second between "equality of opportunity" and "equality of result." Each of the four potential combinations illuminated by the matrix has its own group of adherents. Each of the four goals suggests its own set of policies; often the policies called for will differ radically.

Some Northern observers, supported by most Southern governments and elite groups, wish to concentrate only on interstate equity issues, fearing that moving into the arena of domestic equity will prove counterproductive to an increased capacity for North-South intergovernmental cooperation. These observers tend to concentrate on NIEO-type issues at the international systemic level.

Other Northerners, supported by those Southerners concerned with new development strategies aimed at serving basic human needs, refuse to focus entirely on interstate equity issues. They fear that such a focus might result in redistributing some wealth and economic opportunity from North to South, but that such a transfer would simply result in the political and economic strengthening of Southern elite groups at the expense of most intra-LDC equity measures.[22]

They have a further concern. It is that unless the intrasocietal equity issue is raised to an equal degree of prominence with the interstate issue, it is highly unlikely that Northern support for international policies that seriously attempt to address the equity issue will be generated and, if generated, will prove to be of more than an ephemeral nature.

Thus the closer one examines the global equity perspective, the more one is aware that the perspective may contain goals and coalitions of support that are very difficult to reconcile in practice. Can equal emphasis on two major concerns—global and intrasocietal equity—hold together reluctant coalitions of support in both North and South? The reluctance will grow when it becomes more apparent that most Northern support is for equality of opportunity and most Southern support is for equality of result. And if coalitions can hold together, for how long and with what prospects for institutionalizing support with new (or refurbished) bilateral, regional, or international programs and organizations?[23]

This problem is raised at what is in two major senses a very inauspicious historical moment. In the first place, it is raised when present degrees of North-South conflict and distrust would almost appear a priori to rule out an effort requiring a significant degree of initial goodwill and mutual confidence. And in the second place, it is raised at a moment when many are questioning whether Northern societies themselves can handle domestic issues of equity and income distribution. This problem will be explored in some detail in Chapter 5. For now it is enough to note that if Northern societies are facing an unknown number of years of stagflation or slow growth, which may well exacerbate present domestic confrontations over income shares, and if "the governability of democracy" problem turns out to be more than a superficial phenomenon, then it may prove to be very difficult for Northern governments to respond to the global equity issue in a manner that is viewed as constructive by holders of that particular perspective (and its Southern analogue, the global inequity perspective).

In view of the potential difficulties posed by going beyond traditional interstate issues and raising questions about domestic equity within foreign countries, cannot policy makers agree to overlook this issue? Probably not. The new constraints on the statesmen, posed by the changing parameters of international politics noted in Chapter 2, are unlikely to allow the problem to be solved in this manner. In the first place, executive branch leadership in the North can no longer count on legislative support for foreign policy initiatives. Indeed, sometimes it cannot achieve support despite the most detailed campaigns to do so. Legislative views will have to be taken into account. And as Northern legislators are becoming increasingly disenchanted with all foreign economic assistance programs not tailored to have a strong domestic equity impact, executive branches of Northern governments will most probably not be able to ignore those legislative views.

In the second place, the nonlegislative, nongovernmental elite networks and institutions that have together played a major role in spreading the global equity view in the North seem unwilling to drop the domestic equity issue. Indeed, the regeneration of the human rights issue within the North as a matter of international concern, while obviously given a prominence it never would have received otherwise by President Carter, began with some of the same groups that provided the intellectual superstructure for the global equity perspective. It is the Dag Hammarskjold Foundation's *What Now? Another Development* that most precisely linked the issues of human rights and of global equity. The report first urged a program of global reform for increased equity based heavily on North-South financial transfers and then concluded that "countries which do not respect human rights should not benefit from [these] financial transfers."

For better or worse, depending upon one's analysis of the problems of global order in the 1980s, the decade will most likely be one in which the issue of human rights in both their economic and political/civil forms becomes a legitimate subject for international observation and discussion if not for certain forms of diplomatic intervention. Of course this process of internationalizing human rights issues has a lengthy history, but not a particularly serious one except as part of the anticolonial struggle. What seems likely for the 1980s is that the issue of human rights in its broadest sense will become a *serious* item on the global agenda because too many groups and transnational coalitions desirous of this outcome exist to be ignored. Southern groups (with some Northern support) will press forward with the interstate equity issue. Northern groups (with some Southern support) will insist on linking the international equity issue to the domestic equity counterpart. The result, as the final perspective to be examined suggests, forces both North and South to face the further, very obvious, link between equity issues and human rights (through the intervening factor of basic human needs).

E. The Basic-Human-Needs Perspective

The final major Northern perspective on North-South relations that merits serious consideration is that of basic human needs. Holders of this perspective are concerned, above all else, with the development of new international (and national) institutions and norms of behavior that would assure, within as short a period of time as is deemed feasible (often the year 2000 is offered as a reasonable time frame), the provision of a minimum standard of living for all the world's people. The approach most generally advocated is to set minimum targets in terms of per capita standards for food, nutrition, health services, and basic education. The more ambitious the program advocated, the longer the needs list becomes; some proposals will be found to include elements such as housing, clothing, clean water, and sanitary facilities. Nevertheless, a review of the literature reveals that the core ingredients are consistently food/nutrition, health care, and basic education. Again the Dag Hammarskjold Foundation and the Aspen Institute have vigorously supported the concept and contributed some initial analytical underpinnings. More recently a study prepared for the 1976 World Employment Conference by the ILO's International Labor Office offered a good deal of empirical data on the problem and suggested many policy options that might be considered in developing a strategy to provide for a global minimum standard of living. It was the World Employment Conference that ultimately declared its support for making the fulfillment of basic human needs the *core* of the UN's Third Development Decade strategy. The winning coalition for this conference decision consisted of Northern government, labor, and employer support on the one hand and labor and employer support from many developing countries on the other. Again, Southern government representatives feared that

Northerners might be preparing to support the basic-human-needs approach as a substitute for the international systemic changes the South was demanding via the NIEO; therefore significant numbers of them refused to endorse the approach as it appeared in initial conference draft resolutions. Finally, the World Bank has been the leading international institution in exploring the conceptual and operational problems of developing a basic human-needs approach that would, in current jargon, "put a floor under global poverty."

The basic propositions generally set forward in support of a basic human needs approach run as follows:

1.   Admitting the difficult problems of measurement, there seems to be growing agreement that close to 1 billion people in the developing world are now receiving so little food, nutrition, basic health care, and education that they are fundamentally deprived of what might best be called equality of opportunity to enhance their own life chances. The result is to severely handicap close to a quarter of the globe's population. Four-fifths of them are estimated to inhabit the so-called Fourth World countries of South Asia and sub-Saharan Africa; the other 200 million are found in the more advanced developing countries (and sometimes grouped in large numbers, as they are in the northeast of Brazil).

2.   The estimated costs of providing these basic human needs to this target population vary enormously. The lack of firm data and the crude methodologies used thus far make any cost estimates highly suspect at this point. One estimate suggests that an expenditure of $12.5 billion per year over a 10-year period could, if properly invested, eliminate what basic human needs supporters refer to as absolute poverty throughout the world and meet the basic-human-needs standards discussed above (i.e., food/nutrition, health care, and basic education).[24] A second estimate, the product of an entirely different methodology, suggests a total investment of $250 billion rather than $125 billion.[25] Finally, some of the most recent costing efforts have highlighted the problem of distinguishing between initial investment costs and annual maintenance costs; the latter had been generally ignored in the earlier estimates. This newest work suggests that those annual maintenance costs might equal annual investment costs, highlighting the degree of long-

term commitment that would be required to reach the desired objective.

3. As noted, much of the absolute poverty population that is the target of this perspective is located in the world's poorest countries. Where high concentrations of target populations are found in the poorest countries, it will undoubtedly be necessary for a basic-human-needs strategy to rely initially on a large degree of Northern financial assistance.

4. In most other developing countries, the problem could be managed by domestically financed programs that restructured development priorities if the domestic political commitment to do so existed. But governing elites and political systems in the majority of these countries—as in most countries—are not inclined to attach high priority to basic-human-needs programs for lengthy periods of time. Indeed, programs with similar intent are of fairly recent vintage within the United States itself and certainly have not yet achieved total success despite significant progress over the past 15 years.[26] Therefore most supporters of this perspective would try to assure that a basic-human-needs approach was not designed to deal with the absolute poverty problem in the poorest countries alone. They look for programs and policies that, with appropriate country-to-country variations, could be applied to the absolute poverty problem in all developing countries.

5. Supporters of this perspective are well aware that any basic-human-needs approach to the equity issue within developing countries raises two intimately related issues of extreme delicacy in the present global political setting. The first is the "domestic elite" problem. No program to eliminate absolute poverty can be constructed and implemented without the necessary degree of commitment of a country's governing elite groups. No amount of foreign resources can overcome domestic resistance or indifference to the achievement of this goal. Thus the first problem: How can that necessary degree of Southern domestic elite support be achieved?

The other side of the coin is the troubling international "intervention" problem. If a basic-human-needs approach to one major strand of the global equity issue is to be internationally sanctioned and supported (whether on a bilateral or a multilateral basis), what oversight or monitoring mechanisms will be necessary and with what implications for national sovereignty? If significant amounts of Northern funding are to support such a program—particularly in its early years—some monitoring will be demanded by Northern legislative bodies, which will seek assurance that the funds are being spent in accordance with agreed policy guidelines. But what kind of monitoring—if any—will Southern governments accept? And if no mutually satisfactory agreement can be reached at the international level, what, if any, will be the impact of a stalemate in this arena upon all the other perspectives examined above, and upon the state of North-South relations in the 1980s? For example, if attempts to address this domestic aspect of the global equity perspective remain deadlocked, can much progress be expected on the interstate aspect, the aspect that contains many salient issues in the eyes of Southern governing groups?

If linkage between the two strands of the equity issue leads to stalemates on both, what becomes of the probabilities for North-South cooperation on those global agenda issues analyzed within that perspective? Perhaps linkages between perspectives are weaker than this line of questioning suggests. Certainly many schools of thought—for example, the *dependéncia* school—would seriously doubt that inaction on the basic-human-needs problem might lead to any serious straining of relations between Northern and Southern governing elites.[27] However, it is quite possible that such a viewpoint overlooks the degree to which Northern elite groups have, in differing ways, been influenced by the equity issue. As one acute observer who remained untouched, indeed mystified, by the growing Northern concern with the global equity issue or any of its component parts noted in the late 1970s:

In a society that remains as rudimentary and lacking in both cohesion and consensus as international society, a growing unwillingness to defend important interests—if necessary, by threat or use of force—is surely in some measure an indication that the legitimacy of these interests has itself been called into question. In the case of the response to OPEC actions by Western elites, this consideration was apparent from the start. A refusal to contemplate force reflected, among other things, the conviction that the interests to be preserved through force were themselves suspect insofar as they formed part of a larger order that has served to sustain radical disparities in income and wealth.[28]

How influential will what Professor Tucker has called this "new political sensibility" prove to be in Northern policymaking circles? This may be the single most important element in the evaluation of North-South relations over the next several years and a fundamental factor in the shaping of North-South relations in the 1980s.

IV

The preceding introductory discussion of the basic-human-needs perspective serves to highlight two problems that must be analyzed in much greater detail before any policy prescriptions are offered regarding North-South relations for the 1980s and beyond.

The first problem is one of understanding the major social and intellectual forces within the North and South in the coming decade which will dictate the probabilities of success of any single strategy or strategy mix in North-South relations. What are the most discernible trends likely to influence these probabilities? Are the oft-cited "cultural contradictions of capitalism" likely to limit the growth of Northern responsiveness to the global equity issue? Will the problems of the "governability of democracy" in the North set sharp limits to a consistent "bring them into the system" approach?

Within the South, will apparent trends toward varying forms of authoritarian government create stronger governing elites that are less willing to allow any forms of foreign (bilateral or multilateral) intervention? Or will the pressures of population growth and unemployment on Southern political systems—authoritarian or democratic—improve the prospects for North-South cooperation on global agenda issues, including basic human needs? The attempt to comprehend the major domestic changes in the North and the South which must be understood before any exercise in policy prescription can be profitably undertaken follows in Part III.

The second major problem is more directly linked to the process of policy prescriptions itself. What are the relationships between domestic growth rates within developing countries and international economic reforms? Much of the disagreement over various

NIEO and related international reform issues stems from this analytical issue. While some observers view the international economic system as the major constraint on rapid LDC growth, others seek to explain domestic growth performance almost exclusively in terms of the adequacies or inadequacies of domestic economic growth policies and the political choices which those domestic policies reflect.

What is the relationship between economic growth and domestic equity? Is there a trade-off between rapid growth and internal equity? If there is, the issue must be recognized in any policy prescription concerning equity issues. If there is not, then this false dilemma (growth versus equity) should no longer influence prescription.

Finally, what is the relationship between international economic reforms, domestic growth patterns, and domestic equity? Can certain international reforms lead to both rapid LDC growth and the fulfillment of basic human needs, making a separate strategy aimed at the latter problem superfluous? Or are most international reforms leading to direct or indirect North-South income transfers more likely to exacerbate Southern domestic equity problems?

In Part IV these issues will be examined as various potential ingredients of North-South strategies are considered. One of the major reasons that economic policy prescription in this area is so difficult is that there remains a great deal of disagreement on these fundamental theoretical and empirical issues. In essence, this means that even if the policy maker knows the end result he wishes to achieve, he does not know with any degree of certainty what policies will produce the preferred outcome. Multiply this by some 150 countries, all seeking somewhat differing end results, and the dimensions of the economic labyrinth of North-South relations are revealed. Add the political and status/identity issues of North-South relations and the policy problems are multiplied still further.

As the analysis in Parts III and IV will note, the changing international system has done far more than spread power (control over outcomes) and undermine issue-specific hierarchy. It has produced a fluid situation in which these two *processes* are unending. Because they proceed at a differing pace in differing arenas of international politics, and because of the linkage strategies employed by states to maximize their bargaining power in each arena (with results extremely difficult to predict), the political game for "influence" is being played by more states in more areas than at any previous time in history. In this context Southern *political* demands, whose historical origins have already been noted, are often so determinative in the formation of economic demands that the latter can be properly analyzed only as an expression of political desires. If examined as economic schemes alone, they will often be rejected as totally lacking in theoretical justification. If examined as symptoms of political goals, they may well lead to counteroffers that shift discussions to issues of analytical and substantive merit, where "accommodation" may prove far superior to "rejection."

In sum, the present North-South relationship is polarized and stalemated because of an historical relationship that has left so much psychological scar tissue, because of the changing structure and processes of global politics, because these changes have encouraged a period of probing for weaknesses and for advantage on the part of both combatants, and because neither Northern nor Southern states have yet come to the realization that a continuation of such behavior is not congruent with the nature of the new system or with the challenging global agenda problems that system must learn to manage.

Of course there remains the substantial possibility that not enough states will recognize the incongruity between traditional state behavior and the needs of the changing global political system in order to successfully achieve appropriate alterations in North-South statecraft. In this case, those who suggest that only the hierarchy of states and not the system itself will change will be uncomfortably close to the truth in the short term. However, that resolution would leave such a degree of instability in the system that it could not last long without inviting seriously destabilizing disorder. If the analysis in Chapter 2 is essentially correct, no new hierarchy that is not congruent with the necessities of a novel global situation can long endure.[29]

NOTES

[1]Stanley Hoffmann, "No Choice, No Illusions," *Foreign Policy*, no. 25, Winter 1976-77, p. 110.

[2]The 10 to 1 aggregate per capita income gap reflects currency conversions based on official exchange rates. Most economists are in agreement that actual purchasing-power conversions would narrow the gap by perhaps as much as 40–50 percent.

[3]Richard J. Barnet and Ronald E. Muller, *Global Reach: The Power of the Multinational Corporations* (New York: Simon & Schuster, 1974), Part II and the studies cited therein.

[4]Mahbub ul Haq, "The Third World and the International Economic Order," Overseas Development Council Development Paper No. 22 (Washington, D.C.: Overseas Development Council, September 1976), p. 24.

[5]On Southern self-reliance and "delinking" see Carlos Díaz-Alejandro, "Delinking North and South: Unshackled or Unhinged?" in Fishlow et al., *Rich and Poor Nations in the World Economy* (New York: McGraw-Hill for the Council on Foreign Relations/1980s Project, 1978), pp. 87–162.

[6]See pp. 76–80 below and chap. 8 for a comprehensive analysis and discussion of the goals, ingredients, and dilemmas of a basic-human-needs strategy.

[7]Colin Legum, "Communal Conflict and International Intervention in Africa," in Legum, Mytelka, and Zartman, *Africa in the 1980s: A Continent in Crisis* (New York: McGraw-Hill for the Council on Foreign Relations/1980s Project, 1979), pp. 21–66.

[8]Jere R. Behrman, *International Commodity Agreements: An Evaluation of the UNCTAD Integrated Commodity Program* (Washington, D.C.: The Overseas Development Council, 1977), p. xi.

[9]Irving Kristol, *Wall Street Journal*, July 17, 1975.

[10]Ibid.

[11]C. Fred Bergsten et al., *The Reform of International Institutions* (New York: The Trilateral Commission, 1976), p. 9. Emphasis added.

[12]Ibid., p. 25.

[13]LOS III presents very interesting evidence of the capacity of the developing countries to play "linkage politics" when it is perceived to be in their interest to do so. This is demonstrated in their linking of NIEO issues to the negotiations over deep-seabed mining and their linking of issues across the three committees within the LOS conference itself.
The conference also demonstrates how close Southern unity has come to cracking on several occasions and on several issues, particularly that of the right of land-locked and shelf-locked states to some of the benefits of coastal states' economic zones. Both for those who scoff at the prospects for "Southern unity" and those who see it as an enduring feature of world politics, LOS III thus far offers a fascinating, if indeterminate, test case. See Edward Miles, *International Organization*, vol. 31, no. 3, Summer 1977.

[14]Hoffmann, op. cit., p. 98.

[15]Ibid., p. 113.

[16]John G. Ruggie and Ernst B. Haas, "Environmental and Resource Interdependencies: Reorganizing for the Evolution of International Regimes," Appendix vol. 1, p. 219, *Commission on the Organization of the Government for the Conduct of Foreign Policy* (Washington, D.C.: U.S. Government Printing Office, 1975).

[17]Branislav Gosovic and John Ruggie, "On the Creation of a New International Economic Order," *International Organization*, Spring 1976, p. 345.

[18]The quotation is from Zbigniew Brzezinski, "America in a Hostile World," *Foreign Policy*, no. 23, Summer 1976, p. 95.

[19]Aspen Institute, *The Planetary Bargain*, an international workshop report, Aspen, Colorado, July 7–August 1, 1975; The Dag Hammarskjöld Foundation, "What Now? Another Development," in *Development Dialog* (Stockholm), no. 1/2, 1975; Jan Tinbergen (coordinator), *Reshaping the International Order* (New York: Dutton, 1976).

[20]Albert Fishlow, "A New International Economic Order: What Kind?" in Fishlow et al., op. cit., pp. 9–83.

[21]Mahbub ul Haq, *The Poverty Curtain* (New York: Columbia University Press, 1976), p. 75.

[22]For an incisive expression of this point of view, see Richard R. Fagen, "Equity in the South in the Context of North-South Relations," in Fishlow et al., op. cit.

[23]The issues raised in this paragraph are analyzed in some detail in chaps. 7–9.

[24]Haq, *The Poverty Curtain*, pp. 209, 229.

[25]Hollis Chenery et al., *Redistribution with Growth*, published for the World Bank and the Institute of Development Studies, University of Sussex (Oxford: Oxford University Press, 1977), chap. 11.

[26]See Henry Owen and Charles L. Schultze (eds.), *Setting National Priorities: The Next Ten Years* (Washington, D.C.: The Brookings Institution, 1976), chap. 8.

[27]An analysis of this issue from the "dependency school" point of view is presented in Richard Fagen, op. cit.

[28]Robert W. Tucker, *The Inequality of Nations* (New York: Basic Books, 1977), pp. 116–117.

[29]Logically, of course, another outcome is possible. It would involve the reversal of several of the major trends creating an altered international system, e.g., the diminishing use of force in the North-South arena, welfare state demands on democratic governments of the North, and requisite degrees of Southern solidarity to play linkage politics in international organizations. If my judgment that no major changes in these trends will take place in the 1980s is incorrect, then the "systemic needs" reified in this paragraph could vanish.

Part III

SOUTH AND NORTH IN THE COMING DECADE: SOME CRUCIAL QUESTIONS OF EVOLUTION

Chapter 4
The South in the 1980s

This chapter, like that which follows on the North in the coming decade, does not attempt a general *tour d'horizon*. Both chapters are limited to an examination of those interstate and intrastate aspects of developing- and developed-country evolution which are likely to play important roles in the unfolding of North-South relationships over the period of interest to us. As noted in the previous chapter, this exercise would seem to be a necessary antecedent to the informed analysis of specific policy questions and prescriptions which remains the ultimate purpose of this book.

The necessity for such an exercise could be stated with more certainty if there were greater consensus on the likely major variables and their probable evolution. As one scans the relevant literature and analyzes the existing empirical evidence, however, it becomes strikingly clear that whether one is examining South or North, there is no existing consensus. This condition explains the eclectic nature of the issues chosen for analysis in Part III and the indeterminacy of much of that analysis. Unlike the previous chapter, which focused on schools of thought, Part III focuses on one observer's opinion concerning the most probable evolution of those

factors—political, economic, and sociopsychological—likely to draw
the boundaries of the policy space for North-South relations in the
coming decade.

I

Will the South continue to exhibit enough diplomatic cohesiveness within in the coming 10–15 years to be considered a major
actor in global politics by the end of the 1980s? Will the developing
countries be able to negotiate common agreements on issues of
major international importance and stand behind them in international forums with enough unity to continue to produce North-
South bloc confrontations and diplomatic processes comparable to
those witnessed during the years since 1973?

As one examines all the available evidence, it becomes increasingly difficult to support the proposition that present degrees of
Southern unity will last through the 1980s. This seems to be the
case whether we are measuring the number of countries constituting the group or the degree of cohesiveness within the group.
Thus by 1990 "the South" may be a term without the same degree
of empirical content that characterized the 1970s, and the empirical
content it still encompasses may be too limited for the South to
constitute a major actor in many arenas of global politics.

This probability may seem unwarranted in view of the evidence
briefly presented in earlier chapters. There it has been noted that
by the early-to-mid-1970s, close to 120 developing countries had
coalesced in one of two major Southern institutions: the Non-
Aligned Countries and the Group of 77. It was also noted that the
degree of Southern institutionalization had increased dramatically
since the late 1960s, that the interests of the Non-Aligned Countries
and the Group of 77 had become almost identical, and that the
degrees of cooperation and mutual support between them had
created an institutional unity and a communications network that
had finally given the developing countries a cohesiveness in a changing international system which greatly encouraged their continued
cooperation.

A moment's reflection on the long and arduous task of building
this structure of Southern diplomatic unity serves as a necessary
reminder that any prediction of faltering Southern cohesion in the

1980s remains a probability at most. No such structure of organization and communication which is built on shared normative convictions and has finally succeeded in controlling international agendas as it has in recent years will atrophy rapidly; some observers would undoubtedly argue that it will show no such symptoms in the 1980s.

While the history of Southern cohesion has roots reaching back to the nineteenth century, our purposes can easily be served by reviewing activities that began with the Afro-Asian Bandung conference of 1955. Interpretations of what was attempted and what was achieved at that conference are as numerous as the books written on the subject. For general purposes it is enough to note that this first major Asian-African conference produced in its aftermath a fairly cogent formulation of a political ideology that until that time had lacked any incisive statement. It was an ideology built upon (1) nonalignment with either East or West, (2) an international self-assertion of former colonial countries, and (3) a militant anticolonialism.

For another decade the countries involved were in dispute over the relative merits of "active" nonalignment (a course of international action favored by India's Nehru to avoid war between the United States and the Soviet Union) and militant anticolonialism as preached by Indonesia's Sukarno. The first Non-Aligned conference, held in Belgrade in 1961, was tilted in the former direction by Nehru with the strong support of Yugoslavia's Marshal Tito.

In Nehru's view, India needed a peaceful global setting in order to concentrate on economic development. The prospects for peace might be helped if India could somehow serve as an impartial mediator in the cold war. A mediator must be nonaligned, and a strong mediator is one who has the support of a large group of nonaligned countries. Thus Nehru's yearnings at several points in the late 1940s and 1950s for the revival of the One Asia idea and of "Afro-Asian solidarity."

While Nehru, Tito, and others emphasized the need for global peace and the role of nonalignment in achieving that peace, several Asian countries and most African states were far more interested in the anticolonialist theme that had dominated much of the discussion at Bandung. Their interests finally emerged at the top of the Non-Aligned agenda by 1964 at Cairo and predominated for the remainder of the decade. In retrospect the death of Nehru, the waning of the cold war, the Sino-Indian and Sino-Soviet conflicts, and the enormous growth in the number of independent African states all gave a sense of inevitability to the emergence of anticolonialism as the leading issue on the Non-Aligned agenda for the decade of the 1960s.

While the Non-Aligned Countries slowly developed a program of action and a strengthened institutional capacity, the same halting steps were reflected at the UN, where a caucus procedure for Afro-Asian permanent representation evolved. But this process also developed slowly and was interrupted when the new influx of African nations into the UN shortly led to the emergence of an all-African caucus, reflecting a different set of interests and priorities.

Southern solidarity was given a major impetus when the developing-country call for a United Nations Conference on Trade and Development was finally and reluctantly accepted by the North and first met in 1964. It was during this first UNCTAD conference that the Group of 77 emerged, representing the developing countries at that conference, and quickly became the most dynamic of the developing-country institutions. Major constituent elements in the development of the bloc represented by the 77 have been the various regional groupings that constitute its overwhelming membership (the Latin American group, until recently coordinated by the Special Coordinating Committee for Latin America; the African group, coordinated through the Economic Commission for Africa and the Organization of African Unity; and the Asian group, the least homogeneous grouping and one almost without an organizational focus). With the UNCTAD secretariat generally acting as a de facto secretariat for the Group of 77 during the interim years of planning for each of the four UNCTAD meetings held thus far, the Group of 77 quickly established a modus operandi, a program of action, and a range of shared values and norms of Southern behavior in international meetings which rapidly spread through the growing network of regional and international conferences of the late 1960s and 1970s. Some of these meetings were part of ongoing international organizational activity, for example, annual UN General Assembly, ILO, and IMF meetings. Others were special: the 1972 Stockholm conference on environmental issues, the 1974 World Food Conference, LOS III, the two Special Sessions (1974, 1975) of the UNGA, and the CIEC (1975–77). The interesting point to note is that the Southern pattern of institutional behavior developed by the G-77 in the UNCTAD forum was used in each of these settings to create the greatest degree of developing-country unity possible prior to each conference and was used to caucus on every point of potential intragroup conflict in an effort to hold that unity in order to derive what was perceived to be maximum developing-country advantage.

As noted in Chapter 2, by 1973 the Non-Aligned Countries had so turned their attention away from their old political agenda and toward the economic issues on the G-77 agenda that the two groups began to interact in a far more supportive way than they ever had previously. If most of the ingredients of the NIEO were standard fare in the UNCTAD setting, they received a major conceptual upgrading at the Algiers Non-Aligned summit; and Algeria, then serving as chairman of the Non-Aligned Countries, was the country that called upon the UN Secretary-General to hold what became the Sixth Special Session of the UNGA in April of 1974. At the session the NIEO received official UNGA blessing, and from that point forward Southern cohesion in pressing on all diplomatic fronts for the policies contained in that document forced the North time and again into meetings it did not wish to attend, agendas it did not wish to consider, and (marginal) compromises it had no initial intention of making. In the process it has linked issues and venues (e.g., NIEO and LOS III) with more skill than the North, has controlled agenda formation in most international organizations, has forced fundamental reconsideration of the North-South "problem" throughout the North, and has demonstrated a marked capacity to restrain potential intrabloc fissures on many occasions.

Underlying this institutional capacity for Southern cohesion among many developing countries are two motivations that have thus far held all forces for fragmentation in check. The first is the widely shared feeling concerning the inequity of the present international system, especially in its economic manifestations. This issue was analyzed when we considered the Southern inequity perspectives on North-South relations. Many observers feel that, whatever the degree of developing-country disagreement over specific policy issues and reform proposals, cohesion at the global multilateral level will endure as long as the "structural inequities" the South seeks to alter remain unchanged. The more closely one examines the many examples these observers list, however, the more conscious one becomes of the potential for fragmentation. This issue will be considered shortly.

The second underlying foundation of developing-country cohesion, more relevant to the countries of Africa and Asia than to Latin America, concerns the "conflicted relationship" between the North and those developing countries that have achieved independence since the end of World War II.[1] Colonial intrusions had enormously destructive effects upon many Southern institutions and attitudes, cultures and societies. The post-colonial Southern search for identity—at both the personal and the societal level—has often led to conflicts between South and North. The difficulties of establishing new paradigms for both individual and state behavior have produced continuous domestic turmoil in many new states. This turmoil has been increased by the processes of social mobilization that accompany the spread of modernization in all Asian and African societies.

In these countries most traditional forms of authority had been shattered by the colonial experience; the rational-legal forms sometimes introduced by the colonial powers seldom proved strong enough to last beyond the termination of colonial rule. Authority in the new states was thus necessarily based rather heavily on charisma, but charisma required results. And results often seemed to come more easily in the foreign policy arena than in the domestic arena, where the problems of economic development in increasingly particularistic societies marked by religious, communal, and interest-group strife often seemed unmanageable. In those fragmented, normless new states, anti-"Western" policies and/or rhetoric provided some of the cement for "nation building," whether in the form of the Non-Aligned Country movement, the anticolonialist movement, or, when the cold war faded and there were few colonies left, the NIEO movement. Each of these "movements" can be partially interpreted as a natural ingredient of the process of state building in an era when foreign policy was recruited to the task of constructing nation-states and, in the process, strengthening precariously placed governing elites. Viewed from this perspective, it is not accidental that the Non-Aligned movement turned to economic issues when it did. There was little left in the old themes of the cold war and colonialism to hold the movement together, but the issue of economic inequality seemed able to serve the same integrating function among the heterogeneous Non-Aligned membership as the old themes had throughout the late 1950s and the 1960s. The new emphasis on economic issues which began to emerge at the third Non-Aligned summit at Lusaka in 1970 once again emphasized, in a new issue area, the bonds among the developing countries vis-à-vis the North. The issue of international inequity was strong enough to overcome the divergent levels of development and economic needs of the countries gathered there, and has been ever since. How much longer can that issue cement an alliance of over 115 countries?

II

The reasons for doubting that currently shared goals for structural reform of the international economic system, currently shared normative goals concerned with equity issues, and currently overlapping governing elite needs will sustain the mid-1970s degree of Southern cohesion well into the 1980s is based on three linked observations: (1) the extraordinarily rapid differentiation that is taking place—and will undoubtedly continue to take place—within the economic structures of Southern states, (2) the challenge this process of differentiation will present to existing Southern capacity for diplomatic solidarity in the presentation of demands for systemic changes in the international economic area, and (3) the noneconomic consequences of this process of rapid differentiation for Southern bloc diplomacy.

The rapid economic differentiation among developing countries is apparent not only in projections for the coming decade, but also in the results of the past quarter century of economic growth. The past two decades have been marked by three outstanding characteristics: rapid average growth rates, wide diversities in country-by-country growth performance, and a rapidly growing disparity between richer and poorer developing countries.

Per capita GNP of the developing countries as a whole grew at an average rate of about 3.4 percent per year between 1950 and 1975 (see Table 4-1). This growth rate, exceeding all expectations, also surpassed any previous historical performance in either the developed or the developing world. But these aggregate figures conceal the marked diversity in developing-country performance during this quarter century. Nine countries, representing close to 1 billion people, grew at average per capita rates of better than 4 percent per year. Another group of nine countries grew at a slightly slower rate, averaging increases between 3 and 4 percent in annual per capita incomes.

In contrast, many countries on the Asian subcontinent and in black Africa grew at only half this rate. Within these two regions, countries representing over 1 billion people increased per capita incomes less than 2 percent per year. Put more dramatically, one can say that for some 40 percent of the people of the developing

Table 4-1   GNP Per Capita and Its Growth Rate, by Regions, 1950–1975

| | | GNP PER CAPITA | | |
Region	POPULATION 1975 (MILLIONS)	(1974 DOLLARS) 1950	1975	GROWTH RATE 1950-1975 (PERCENTAGE PER YEAR)
South Asia	830	85	132	1.7
Africa	384	170	308	2.4
Latin America	304	495	944	2.6
East Asia	312	130	341	3.9
China, People's Rep.	820	113	320	4.2
Middle East	81	460	1,660	5.2
Developing countries*	2,732	160	375	3.4
Developed countries†	654	2,378	5,238	3.2

*If China is excluded, the line for developing countries reads 1,912, 187, 400, 3.0.
†All OECD members except Greece, Portugal, Spain, and Turkey.
Source: Preliminary and unpublished World Bank data.

world the increase in per capita income has approximated $1 or $2 per year for the past 25 years; at the same time, average per capita income for another 33 percent of the developing-country population has trebled.

A part of this growing disparity is captured by the figures in Table 4-1. At the regional level in 1950, average per capita incomes of the richest regions (Latin America and the Middle East) were five or six times those of the poorest (South Asia). By 1975, the multiple for the Middle East over South Asia had risen to thirteen and that of Latin America to seven. Furthermore, when the developing countries are examined according to income levels based on 1975 per capita income, it is clear that today's highest-income developing countries grew fastest while the lower-income countries grew at a considerably slower pace (see Table 4-2).

If we concentrate on a shorter time period, 1965–1975, and projections for the period through 1985, the trends noted above are reinforced. Average per capita incomes in the poorest states, with

Table 4-2   GNP Per Capita and Its Growth Rate,
by Income Groups, 1950–1975

| | | GNP PER CAPITA* | |
| | POPULATION 1975 (MILLIONS) | (DOLLARS) 1975 | GROWTH RATE 1950-1975 (PERCENTAGE PER YEAR) |
Income Group			
Lower-income countries	1,146	265	1.1
Middle-income countries†	1,118	266–520	3.7
Upper-middle-income countries	370	521–1,075	3.4
Higher-income countries	100	1,076+	5.2
Developing countries‡	2,732		3.4

*In 1974 dollars.
†If China is excluded, middle-income countries' population = 298 million, growth rate = 2.4%.
‡If China is excluded, developing countries' population = 1,912 million, growth rate = 3.0%.
Source: Preliminary and unpublished World Bank data.

a total population of 1.2 billion, grew at a rate of 1.5%, or about $2 per year between 1965 and 1975. The remaining countries of the South grew at a per capita rate of about 4% per year. As Table 4-3 suggests, the gap between the poorest, most slowly growing countries and other developing countries has widened and should continue to widen.

Projections through 1985 indicate no increase in growth rates of the poorest countries; 2 percent per capita is viewed as a very optimistic target. Within the group of "middle-income" countries, further differentiation will be very noticeable as growth rates in most oil-exporting developing countries increase while the pace of growth in some of the non-oil-exporting LDCs is at least temporarily slowed. Those middle-range developing countries whose growth prospects will depend to a considerable degree upon the working of the international financial system to cover oil-price-induced current account deficits include Brazil, the Philippines, Chile, Argentina, Peru, and Zaire. Together with Egypt these countries

Table 4-3   Income Disparities between Nations* (in Constant 1975 U.S.$.)

		POPULATION (MILLIONS)	INCOME PER CAPITA[†]		
			1965	1975	1985[‡]
1.	Poorest nations (below $200 per capita)	1,200	130	150	180
2.	Middle-income developing countries (above $200 per capita)	900	630	950	1,350
3.	Developed nations	700	4,200	5,500	8,100

*Data for centrally planned economies are not published and therefore are excluded from the table.

[†]Because the per capita income data in the table are based on official exchange rates rather than on purchasing-power comparisons, which are unavailable, they represent only broad orders of magnitude.

[‡]Long-term projections of economic growth are, of course, highly speculative. They are presented here not as predictions but only to call attention to problems that may develop if action is not initiated in time to prevent them.

Source: Robert S. McNamara, Address to the Board of Governors of the World Bank, Manila, 1976, p. 3.

presently account for nearly half of the developing countries' external debt; the ability to continue to finance that debt while making the necessary structural adjustments in their economies appropriate to new energy prices will be a crucial ingredient in their capacity to continue normal rates of economic growth.

The oil-price problem, the workings of the international financial system, and the growth rates of the OECD countries could all play havoc with these projected trends. This issue will be considered later in this chapter. The figures given here and the analysis based on them represent what might be thought of as the most "surprise-free" or "benign" scenario for LDC economic development over the coming decade.

This brief review of the past 25 years and short projection to 1985 underscores one of the basic hurdles to continued Southern cohesion in the 1980s: the rapidly growing differentiation in economic structures and developmental needs of the countries that constitute the Group of 77. The magnitude of this hurdle is revealed when one examines late-1970s Southern economic demands against the background of rapid change in LDC economic structures and needs.

The major demands the developing countries have thus far been able to present in near unison in NIEO documents and elsewhere are grouped into five different areas: international trade, economic aid, foreign investment (direct and indirect), technology transfer, and the international monetary system.

In the trade field the major demands have been for (1) various forms of international commodity agreements that would raise and stabilize the price of LDC-exported raw materials, (2) a "common fund" that would provide a financial umbrella for these commodity agreements, (3) nonreciprocal reductions in developed-country barriers to developing-country exports of processed raw materials, semimanufactures, and manufactured goods, (4) expanded generalized trade preferences for the developing countries to better enable them to compete with industrial-country production in the markets of the North, and (5) better-financed domestic adjustment assistance programs in the North which, by easing transitional pains accompanying the restructuring of Northern economies, will facilitate imports of Southern manufactured (and some agricultural) goods. In sum, at the aggregate level the South has thus far sought increased relative prices for its raw material exports to the North as well as an increase in the volume of raw material and manufactured exports.

In the field of aid Southern demands have thus far included the following: (1) that the developed countries meet the aid targets most of them agreed to in the International Development Strategy for the Second UN Development Decade (a minimum of 0.7 percent of GNP in the form of official development assistance and 1.0 percent of GNP including private capital flows to the South), (2) that the North increase its financial commitments to all those emergency funds created in response to the food and oil price increases of 1973–75, and (3) that the North be prepared to renegotiate the terms of debt repayment for those Southern countries experiencing serious balance-of-payments problems, including the possibility of significant debt cancellation.

In the area of foreign investment one again finds several distinct Southern goals. One is greater access to international capital markets for Southern countries. A second is the elimination of traditional international legal restraints on the expropriation of foreign direct investments, including the putative requirement of "full, prompt, and effective" compensation. A third Southern goal has been to engage Northern governmental assistance in policing the activities of Northern multinational corporations for the general purpose of increasing the level of economic benefits going to host countries. Such increased benefits might take various forms, for example, greater North-South capital and technology flows, lower charges on technology transfer, less protection for existing (and overwhelmingly Northern) patent rights, and increased developing-country exports to the North of products of foreign corporations.

In the field of technology transfer, Southern demands and objectives include Northern financing earmarked for the creation, expansion, and modernization of Southern scientific and technological institutions; Northern governmental support in "persuading" multinational corporations to adapt their technology to host-country development needs; and international support for changes in patent laws and other measures that will lower the cost of technology transfers to the South.

Finally, with regard to the international monetary system, the developing countries in the aggregate continue to demand (1) a greater voice in the reform and management of that system, (2) more "automaticity" in LDC access to those sources of reserves now available through various IMF "windows" and less IMF surveillance over the use of their funds, and (3) the establishment of an international reserve creation process that automatically places increasing amounts of international reserves in the hands of developing countries.

The above reforms have formed the core of the NIEO demands and have thus far generally evoked a very considerable degree of Southern cohesion in their support. How long can this pattern of diplomatic behavior be expected to continue? Some observers see no reason to expect diminishing cohesion. Their analysis, at its best, runs along the following lines:

Global multilateral politics, acted out largely through the instrument of the 77, generally concerns the status of developing countries in the international economic system and the long-term structural changes they seek. There is substantial disagreement over concrete aspects of their longer-term objectives. *But on the overall structural questions—changed terms of trade, protection of purchasing power, access to markets, monetary reform, increased automaticity of resource transfers, and so on— there appears to be little to disagree about.* . . . In sum, cohesion at the global multilateral level, while involving tension and compromise, is not incompatible with considerable divergence elsewhere.[2]

There are two major problems with this line of argumentation. The first concerns the issue of status in the international system, and the second concerns the static notion of the structural changes that all developing countries will continue to seek in the international economic system.

There is very little evidence that the developing countries will long continue to seek status as a unit rather than as individual states. The constant tension between the Group of 77 and the Group of 19 developing countries that "represented" the G-77 at the CIEC flowed from the concern of most G-77 members that the G-19, which heavily overrepresented the "upper tier" developing countries (and included seven OPEC states) would not appropriately represent the interests of the G-77 in the aggregate.

The growing tensions in the late 1970s between the OPEC states on the one hand and other developing countries—especially those of sub-Saharan Africa—on the other already marked the rising disenchantment with OPEC-country policies on the part of the rest of the developing world. The OPEC countries were simply not financing Southern self-reliance—the dream of the G-77 as late as the Dakar conference of 1975. While channeling considerably more money (as a percentage of GNP) to the developing countries than are the OECD countries, the OPEC countries are doing so through their own new institutions, clearly in accord with their own perceptions of self-interest, and in a manner that is slowly leading to increasingly outspoken criticism from other developing countries. Most Arab OPEC aid goes strictly to Moslem countries, particularly to those states involved in the conflict with Israel. And most Venezuelan aid is viewed, even by its recipients, as calculated to gain increasing influence over states in the Caribbean region. Finally, regional conflicts throughout Latin America, Africa, the Middle East, and Asia suggest that the growing differentiation among states within the South will steadily undermine the willingness of Third World "leviathans" to place their rapidly increasing strength at the service of an aggregate Southern struggle for status in the international system.

The second problem with this line of argument is that the rapidly differentiating structures of Southern economies will soon create— in fact, are already creating—major dissension within the Southern coalition over "the long-term structural changes they seek." For example, beneath the level of rhetoric there is no agreement among Southern states on "changed terms of trade." Just prior to oil-price increases, 40 percent of LDC export earnings were coming from the sale of manufactured goods. Furthermore, those sales were growing at well over 15 percent per year. Those Southern countries whose natural resource base and development strategies called for the export of manufactures and were growing rapidly by following such strategies have absolutely no desire to see global terms of trade alter in favor of raw materials they import in ever-increasing volume. The entire UNCTAD exercise in assembling a list of commodities to be covered by commodity agreements and a common fund revealed that the greater the degree of knowledge about the distributional effects of changing terms of trade, the less the degree of Southern unity over the issue. Changes in the terms of trade produce "winners" and "losers"; and no combination could possibly gain the united approval of all Southern states. Their economies, their stages of development, and their strategies of development are simply too diverse. Only the development of an internal redistribution mechanism to equalize gains and losses among Southern countries could have produced harmony. But as the history of unsuccessful developing-countries regional integration efforts suggests, developing countries have not yet been able to resolve the internal redistribution issue even among small groups of fairly homogeneous states (e.g., three in East Africa, five in Central America). The capacity to do so at the G-77 level of over 115 states taxes the imagination; it may also explain why so many developing countries initially looked to the OPEC states to finance individual commodity schemes.

Analysis of most other demands on the present Southern list for international economic reforms would reveal the same problem of conflicting interests as does the terms-of-trade issue. With the possible exceptions of automaticity of resource transfers and greater access to Northern markets, differences of interest are greater than commonalities. The highly liquid OPEC states do not share typical Southern views on monetary reform. The rapidly industrializing countries, such as Brazil and Mexico, do not share the official Southern view on debt relief; the former countries place continued access to international capital markets well above Southern solidarity on the issue of generalized debt relief and have therefore opposed the majority G-77 position publicly as well as privately.

The burden of the analysis is obvious. The more the economically advanced members of the South are able to achieve their developmental goals within the present global economic system, the less interest they will have in changing it in the ways desired by other G-77 members. Because of the rapidly growing disparity between the rich and poor countries within the South, it will be increasingly difficult for them to agree on the issue of structural reform as the years pass and the intra-Southern gap widens. And to the degree that the North finds and chooses to adopt a variety of options that respond to "status" issues on a state-by-state basis, continued Southern cohesion in support of a broad range of structural economic reforms should prove even more difficult to retain.[3]

Finally, the noneconomic consequences resulting from this rapidly growing structural differentiation in economies of the developing countries are also likely to create major problems for G-77 cohesion in the coming decade. "Noneconomic consequences" of these growing economic structural differences within the South may not be the most felicitous phrasing of the point at issue. What we are concerned with here is essentially the manner in which these growing gaps are likely to lead to Southern state behavior in noneconomic arenas which will present further hurdles to the maintenance of Southern cohesion.

One can already observe modes of emerging Southern state behavior that will test cohesion. In the Middle East, Saudi Arabia finances the Arab cause against Israel. Concentrating on Egypt, it keeps Sadat afloat while he turns away from the Soviet Union to the West for arms purchases and diplomatic support. Then, fearing Soviet influence in the Horn of Africa, Saudia Arabia finances Eritrean and Somalian tests of strength with the new Marxist government of Ethiopia. And as its concerns about Soviet influence in the Red Sea area grow, it reconsiders Arab relations with black Africa. The result: a Saudi pledge of $1 billion in new development assistance to Africa at the first Afro-Arab summit meeting in March of 1977. The gesture prevents the conference from breaking up in acrimony, though black Africa continues to resent the severe impact on African economic development of Arab-induced oil-price increases.

In Northern Africa, Libya finances both efforts to overthrow the government of neighboring Sudan and Ethiopian attempts to defeat the Eritrean secessionist movement. Algeria finances the Polisario guerrilla front in an effort to prevent Morocco and Mauritania from acquiring those portions of the Spanish Sahara ceded to them by Spain in late 1975. In effect, the struggle is one for hegemony in the Maghreb.

In Latin America, a more subtle game of "influence" is being played. Through a series of development assistance programs and joint investment projects developed in the early-to-mid-1970s,

Brazil quietly establishes a set of relationships with Uruguay and Paraguay that increases Brazilian capacity to control events in those two countries, to the dismay of Argentina. Meanwhile Venezuela concentrates its financial assistance in the countries of Central America and the Caribbean, while those countries openly express concerns about the "hardness" of the terms of such assistance and the degree of control Venezuela attaches to its foreign assistance programs.

Further examples would be superfluous, since they simply illuminate an age-old pattern of state behavior that most observers would predict—behavior made all the more predictable given the growing diffusion of global power noted in Chapter 2. The rapidly growing gap in power potential among countries in the South is inviting the upper-tier developing countries to define their own national interest more broadly and therefore to attempt to influence their regional environments. The lower the intensity of the East-West conflict, the generally greater the opportunity for intra-Southern regional conflicts (overt or covert) over influence and/or hegemony. And while such conflicts should not spell the end of Southern cohesion, it is difficult to construct scenarios in which they do not lower the degree of diplomatic unity vis-à-vis the North and increase the range of options for the North in responding to Southern demands. Whether or not this development is conducive to more constructive North-South relations—and it certainly could be—will depend upon Northern motivations and thus on the content of Northern responses.

III

The analysis in the previous section suggests that in the coming decade, existing degrees of Southern diplomatic solidarity will be amply tested by the very large and rapidly growing economic gaps among a group of states already extremely heterogeneous in terms of race, culture, religion, and regime type. Three other considerations that may affect the impact of the strains introduced into the Southern coalition by this growing differentiation deserve brief mention. They are (1) the future behavior of the OPEC countries, (2) the future "responsiveness" of the North to Southern demands, and (3) the growth path of the international economy through the early 1980s.

Ever since their price and embargo actions of 1973–1974, the economic and political behavior of the OPEC states has been a crucial variable in the Southern unity scenario. There is little reason to believe that this element of the North-South puzzle will change.

The North was finally brought to the bargaining table by the South when the United States failed to drive a wedge between OPEC and the rest of the developing countries in the spring of 1975. Only the energy issue was deemed important enough by the North to produce the switch from confrontation to "dialogue"; only after the United States plan to isolate OPEC and deal with the energy question alone failed did it agree to "discuss" other NIEO issues at CIEC in order to open an exchange on energy.

Thus, throughout the early-to-mid-1970s there was a fairly widespread perception in Northern policy-making circles that the South only had one arrow in its quiver, and the arrow belonged to OPEC. Some Northerners suggested attempts to "co-opt" OPEC; others proposed strategies to isolate it. In either case, the fundamental Northern bureaucratic perception of the South was the same: without OPEC, the South as an aggregate would represent a serious international problem in few, if any, foreseeable contexts. Southern countries of significance for various reasons—economic, strategic, etc.—could then be dealt with individually.

Views in the North are changing, as the previous chapter has suggested. But into the early 1980s the degree of Northern governmental attention to the North-South set of problems will most probably be highly and positively correlated with the perception that the diplomatic link between OPEC and the rest of the South remains strong.

It seems obvious that the developing countries are fully aware of this Northern perception of the Southern problem. Otherwise it is difficult (though not impossible, as suggested in Chapter 2) to explain the lack of overt Southern criticism of OPEC pricing policies that probably cost the South close to $40 billion, or 60 percent of its current account deficits, in the years 1974–1975 alone.[4] During these same years OPEC aid flows to the developing countries at most covered one-tenth of that financial burden and, as noted, were highly concentrated in the Middle East.

It is unlikely that the OPEC countries will quickly dilute their diplomatic ties with other developing countries. There remains a degree of shared interest in systemic reform, even if the degree shrinks yearly; there remains a bargaining leverage with the North which OPEC might not be able to exercise without Southern solidarity; there remains Israel. The issue of Israel apart, the slow drift of most OPEC countries (particularly the wealthiest ones) out of a Southern bloc and into a less conflictual, integrated set of political, economic, and security relations with the North seems the most probable outcome of OPEC's present balancing act.[5] The crucial questions in terms of this study are how long this process will take, what kinds of changes might be introduced into the international system as the transition takes place, and how far beyond the energy issue Northern governmental perceptions of the North-South problem will have expanded by the time the transition is completed.

A second test for Southern cohesion in the 1980s is posed by the types and degrees of Northern responsiveness to present Southern demands. Evidence from the Sixth and Seventh Special Sessions of the UNGA have already displayed significant lines of cleavage within the South on modes of negotiation and on what is to be viewed as "acceptable" accommodation. The "radicals" had their way at the 1974 Special Session; the "moderates" dominated the events of 1975. And it was the latter group within the G-77 which reached agreement with the North on what became the unanimous resolution ending the Seventh Special Session and beginning the dialogue at the Paris conference several months later.[6]

An analysis of the G-77 membership suggests that two types of countries constitute the so-called moderate group. One is the middle-range developing country, for which a few significant reforms in the international economic system could help considerably in its further economic development. It is the type of country that is developing rapidly in the present system and wants to assure continued progress.[7]

The other is the country that is not doing as well, but at least at the present time and under present domestic leadership would rather accept what compromises the North is willing to offer than push the present confrontation any further. By 1975 many developing countries clearly felt that they could not afford further conflict. With growth rates falling, exports stagnating, and debt ratios building as current account deficits rose rapidly, these countries were ready to begin serious negotiations with the North rather than continue pressing maximalist rhetorical demands at the cost of what they hoped would be serious bargaining.

As one looks toward the 1980s, this fault line within the G-77 seems unlikely to disappear. There will always be those countries that, out of both strength and weakness, will desire to mix confrontation with compromise, take what they can get, and try for further reforms at a later time. And there will undoubtedly always be those that, for reasons of domestic political necessity or for reasons of conviction that nothing short of "root and branch" alterations will right the perceived inequities of the present system, will press for continued and maximum confrontation from venue to venue, from meeting to meeting. In this context bargaining strategies of the North could well have an influential effect upon the balance of forces within the G-77 itself at any particular moment in time, just as it did at the Seventh Special Session by opting for dialogue. As the brief analysis of the Northern rejectionist perspective in Chapter 3 suggests and as later examination of actual policy options will elaborate, many Northerners would view any attempt on the part of the North to enter this tactical game as a grave error; quite simply, they fear that the tactic could not be controlled, and that concession would follow concession with little analytical thought given to the merits of the temporary bargains being struck or to the momentum being given to a *process* that would prove unalterable. The empirical evidence from the CIEC experience does not support this line of reasoning, but those who favor it seldom examine empirical evidence.

Finally, the performance of the international economy over the coming several years may also influence the degree of Southern solidarity that will be prevalent in the 1980s. Present projections by the IMF, the OECD, and the IBRD all suggest that both global and developing-country growth rates will be somewhat lower over the coming half decade than they were in the 1960s and early 1970s.

However, a period of continued growth rates averaging close to 5 percent for the developing countries is unlikely to have much impact on the issue we are examining. What could lead to a period of intensified North-South conflict would be the combination of a more serious downturn in growth rates, rising current account deficits in the developing countries, and an unwillingness by public and private international financial institutions to lend enough to cover those deficits.

Present projections of growth rates, terms of trade, debt-servicing ratios, and available IMF reserves suggest that there should not be a *generalized* Southern need for debt relief over the coming decade. Nevertheless, projections also suggest that at least as many as five or more major Southern countries could experience serious debt-repayment difficulties. More generally, any optimism about the debt problem in the developing countries is based on projections that could prove as error-prone as similar projections have in recent years. As one expert summarized the situation as of 1977:

While the consensus has it that recovery in the OECD countries will proceed at a moderate, but satisfactory pace, the possibility of sluggish growth or even recession later in the decade cannot be ruled out. Should this more pessimistic scenario occur, many [non-oil-exporting LDC's] would be hard-pressed indeed to meet debt service commitments without unacceptable internal costs.

It is not difficult, then, to imagine a conjunction of debt service peaks and repayments of the [IMF] oil facility credits with stagnating exports and a drying up of private bank credits. While this outcome is not likely, it cannot be excluded. [8]

Should the more pessimistic of these two scenarios prevail, the likelihood of even greater degrees of Southern solidarity and North-South conflict would be enhanced, both because of the broader nature of the problem and because some of the upper-tier countries generally doing well "within the system," such as Brazil, would in all likelihood be among those countries adversely influenced by the "stagnant growth" scenario. Under this set of conditions it is quite possible that OPEC would find it politically advisable to make a greater contribution to ease the growing Southern debt problem;

but it is equally plausible to suggest that the OPEC countries would attempt to cover their Southern financial contributions by increasing their revenues from the OECD countries through oil-price increases.

In retrospect, the challenges facing that Southern diplomatic solidarity which has recently controlled international agendas, forced the North to the bargaining table, and produced marginal gains for Southern development objectives will be significant in the 1980s. The most serious challenge will include growing structural disparities and a consequent heterogeneity of needs and goals within the South, leading not only to contests for regional influence but also to fundamental differences over one of the central issues that has thus far cemented these 115–120 countries: the degree and content of structural change needed to allow the developing countries "equitable benefits" from the international economic system. Closely related to this challenge will be that of the ambiguous role of the OPEC states and the seeming inevitability of stronger OPEC-OECD ties of all types by the latter half of the 1980s; the Northern response to Southern demands, which may please some developing countries and disappoint others; and the performance of the international economy in the coming 5 years.

If they all eventuate in the ways discussed above, the challenges may substantially lessen Southern diplomatic cohesion in the coming decade. But even if this probability is significant—and the judgment itself leaves room for debate—there is little reason to suspect that the Southern institutional structure and communications network so carefully nurtured for two decades will not continue to play an active role in the international politics of the 1980s. Expectations may change, and with them new sources of Southern bloc behavior may appear. But one suspects that the psychological and status rewards that accompany Southern bloc diplomacy are too great to be surrendered even if the challenges to solidarity limit the capacity of an evolving Group of 77 to achieve substantial international economic reforms. If there were no Group of 77, the emerging international political system would invite its creation.

Regardless of the degrees of Southern diplomatic solidarity that characterize the 1980s, the above discussion serves to illuminate two major issues the international political system must be prepared to manage during the 1980s if the moderate international order schematized in Chapter 1 is to be realized. The first is the problem of the so-called upper-tier developing countries; the second is the problem of the growing numbers of the globe's population living at absolute poverty levels. Since this latter problem is particularly acute on the Indian subcontinent and in sub-Saharan Africa, we can think of it in terms of certain developing countries; when viewed from the basic-human-needs perspective the focus is, as noted, generally on people, not countries.

The problem presented by the upper-tier Southern countries— the highly liquid financial powers among the OPEC states; the emerging industrial and export-oriented powers, e.g., Brazil and Mexico; and the few Southern countries being propelled into re- gional military predominance and rapid industrial growth by highly unified leadership, e.g., Iran—can be stated quite simply. If they have not already done so, these states are developing power po- tential to significantly support or complicate the emergence of a moderate international system in the coming decade. Domestic, regional, and international factors will all partially determine the evolution of the foreign policies of these states, making firm pre- dictions of likely outcomes impossible. But in considering North- South issues in the coming decade, the discrete problem posed by the emergence of these states deserves careful consideration. Given the general structure and process elements of the international system outlined in Chapter 2, what reform of present international structures, institutions, and norms of statecraft would optimize the probability that these countries will act in ways congruent with the goals of the moderate system defined in Chapter 1?

The second problem is that of growing levels of absolute poverty. As noted, approximately 1 billion people in the South are now living in what are described as absolute poverty conditions; their numbers are growing in absolute terms; perhaps two-thirds of them are concentrated on the Indian subcontinent; and, as the economic growth projections from Table 4-3 suggest, the size of the problem will increase over the coming decade if not for a much longer period. What problems does this aspect of the South in the 1980s represent for a moderate international order in the 1980s?

These issues will be examined in much greater detail in the four final chapters, devoted to policy analysis. It is sufficient at this point to reiterate that both the "power" and the "poverty" problems which Southern evolution in the 1980s entails must be the object of serious attention in policy analysis and prescription. For no matter what normative perspective is brought to this analysis, an understanding of these two problems will significantly condition one's thinking about North-South relations in the future.

IV

A quite different aspect of Southern evolution in the 1980s, which seems important enough from the standpoint of North-South relations to merit analysis here, involves the high probability that authoritarian regimes will continue to predominate within the South; indeed, it seems more probable than not that their already large numbers will increase. In one subset of these regimes—those found in Africa—an increasing degree of political instability also seems likely to characterize the coming decade's political scene.

As of the mid-1970s, more than half of the sub-Saharan African states were under military rule. It was estimated that three out of every four black Africans lived in countries ruled by the military or by one-party governments. In South and Southeast Asia only four countries were classified—with some leniency—as competitive democracies: Sri Lanka, India, Malaysia, and Singapore. The rest—over 15—were controlled by military regimes, "emergency" regimes (e.g., the Philippines, Bangladesh), or revolutionary, one-party regimes. In Latin America the number of functioning democracies could be counted on the fingers of one hand. Only two remained in all of South America as the rise of military regimes during the previous 10 years cut deeply into the numbers of long-standing democracies (e.g., Chile). Cyclical increases in democratic regimes were expected in the near term, but few experts looked for a secular trend in the democratic direction.

The growth of authoritarian regimes in each region was attributable to a different and only occasionally overlapping set of factors. In Africa, for example, military regimes began to replace the so-called mobilizational, single-party civilian regimes that had emerged during the struggle for independence. These civilian regimes themselves had often been authoritarian in nature. This was not the original intent of many African leaders in the fight for independence, but the many aspects of the culture and societies in which such struggles took place rendered an authoritarian outcome almost inevitable.

Soon after independence the actions of the opposition, or the perceptions of them by the leaders of the governing party; the governing party's conception of nation-building as excluding peripheral, sectional, tribal demands (particularly in states with artificial boundaries imposed by the colonizers); the difficult economic problems; and the problems caused by new expectations of the people led those leaders to prevent, limit, or exclude free political and electoral competition. In many of the states created by decolonization, independence and statehood became symbolically identified with the leader and his party, who often claimed a charismatic authority. . . . The weakness of traditional authority [undermined by the colonial experience] and the lack of understanding of the complexities of legal national authority made the emergence of at least a semblance of charismatic leadership possible. . . . Faced with the problems of national integration, the not-always loyal opposition, and the fear of foreign influence, the *dominant party*, in the context of a political culture that had not institutionalized liberal democratic values, soon became a *single party*.[9]

When these authoritarian parties were unable to control or mediate the demands of the extraordinarily heterogeneous ethnic groups they governed, most were replaced during the 1960s by military regimes. This African contextual ingredient has led Colin Legum to compare today's Africa with 17th- through 19th-century Europe in terms of political instability.

Moreover, Africa has a greater degree of ethnic, cultural and linguistic pluralism than probably any other continent; so the process of nation-making is more complex and potentially more disruptive than elsewhere. All these factors suggest that Africa is at a most difficult and explosive stage of development. All African regimes are essentially temporary, or transitional, since, with very few exceptions, they do not operate within an established framework of viable and widely based institutions, even where they have been legitimized.[10]

As Legum notes, authoritarian rule—in Africa, generally military rule—results in great part from the lack of legitimacy accorded to any regime in a state where ethnic conflict (or potential conflict) is as great as it is in Africa. And his analysis of the four dimensions of the "tribal" problem in Africa—clan, tribe, subnational group, and national group—offers considerable support for his conclusion that

the 1980s will see a continuing, perhaps even a worsening, of communal problems, except in those countries (predictably few) which will succeed in the next decade in overcoming the severe difficulties involved in creating viable institutions and new value systems capable of winning over the loyalty and cooperation of individual citizens, (ethnic) communities, and group interests in making the new system work without undue institutionalized violence.[11]

The spread of military governments and authoritarian regimes throughout Latin America in the past decade shares one similarity with the emergence of military governments in Africa: both trends suggest the lack of institutions and norms that are imbued with legitimacy in the political arena. As Thomas Hobbes once put it, "when nothing else [i.e., some form of legitmacy] is turned up, clubs are trumps."

In Latin America clubs have become trumps in country after country in an entirely different socioeconomic and ethnic environment than they have in Africa. There are few serious ethnic (or communal) problems; per capita income four times greater than that in most of Africa suggests much more advanced and diversified economies and much different class structures; and 150 years of independence have given the Latin American states far more time to develop the institutions and norms suggestive of legitimacy in the political arena.

Yet events of the 1960s and 1970s confirm that the legitimacy issue has still not been resolved in most Latin American states, that mounting civil conflict in country after country both encouraged the military to enter the political arena and created support for such intervention among major civilian groups, and that the 1980s are most likely to witness a continuing swing between civilian and military governments in the region but most probably a trend toward the latter.

In Latin America these authoritarian military regimes are ones in which a coalition predominated by but not exclusively controlled by army officers and bureaucrats establishes control of government and excludes or includes other groups without commitment to specific ideology, acts pragmatically within the limits of their bureaucratic mentality, and neither creates nor allows a mass single party to play a dominant role are the most frequent subtype. They may operate without the existence of any parties, but more frequent is the creation (as in Brazil) of an official government-sponsored single party which, rather than aiming at a controlled mobilization of the population, tends to reduce its participation in political life even in a manipulated form.[12]

These regimes have often emerged when a politically active "popular sector" (e.g., urban workers, lower-middle-class groups, and occasionally peasant movements) developed the political power to make demands that concerned the old oligarchical and new industrial elite elements of Latin American societies. Often the election of "populist" leaders (e.g., Peron in Argentina and Goulart in Brazil) in response to these pressures led to inflationary economic policies, stagnating growth rates, and a potential for class conflict military establishments viewed as threatening to the stability of the state and to the "norms" of legitimate political contest—as they chose to define them. At this point the military as an institution often chose to intervene in the political process to act as a "stabilizing" force. Whereas in earlier decades this pattern of military intervention was usually limited to short transition periods, since the mid-1960s the military in Latin America has increasingly demonstrated the desire to replace civilian political regimes on a longer-term basis and to further the process of national integration and economic development in more "rational" and rapid ways than it believed the democratic political process could provide.

Some analysts tend to emphasize the nonclass aspects of such military takeovers in Latin America. They focus on the emergence of novel concerns and capabilities within a new professional military organization, a desire on the part of the "new professional" for greater national integration and more national industrial growth, and thus the disillusionment with the democratic political process, the willingness to take and hold state power, and the alliance with technocrats and bureaucrats to achieve the new professionals' goals.

Others tend to view this general pattern of military intervention from a more class-oriented sociopolitical perspective.

In a highly modernized context (e.g., Brazil, Argentina) the attempt to exclude and eventually deactivate the popular sector in the absence of the possibility of offering psychological and economic payoffs inevitably required strong and systematic coercive measures. *Bureaucratic authoritarianism*—eliminating political parties and elections and the political personnel sensitive to the demands of the popular sector, domesticating the labor unions by co-optation if not by coercion, and attempting to bureaucratically encapsulate most social sectors to maximize control—was the answer.[13]

In this view most military-bureaucratic authoritarian regimes in Latin America are explicable in terms of a conservative reaction to the strains of advancing industrialization and to the entry of the "masses" into active national political participation. The public bureaucracy and the propertied sectors invited the military to replace an emerging democratic system with their own form of authoritarian regime.

These "models" are generalizations developed from many country-specific cases; in each Latin American country in which the military has recently intervened to assume political power the general models will miss situation-specific variables that may have considerable explanatory power. For our purposes, however, the general explanations are of considerable importance in their illumination of potential trends rather than in their capacity to "explain" fully any specific case. What they suggest is that for the semi-industrialized countries of South America, the 1980s may well be a period marked by a continuing substantial number of military-authoritarian experiments in government and thus a period also marked by a significant potential for political instability. For as all analysts of authoritarian regimes have noted, the problems of ambiguous legitimacy and political institutionalization continue to plague military regimes of the type now so prevalent in South America. As Juan Linz noted recently,

In the Western world, in the absence of an ideological single party, important elites use either the competitive liberal democracies or the dynamic single-party mobilizational regimes as *ideals assuring participation of citizens.* The international linkages with stable democratic advanced industrial societies, while contributing through the linkages of the technocratic elites to the emergence and/or success of those regimes, at the same time also constantly undermine their legitimacy through the cultural influences that conflict with their values. While contributing to the basis for their success, they in the same process contribute to the basis for future crisis; while justifying their existence on technical and economic grounds, they every day contribute to undermining their legitimacy by offering to their citizens an alternative political model and by encouraging them not to give their full allegiance to the authoritarian regime, not to give up hope for a democratic political development.[14]

Thus political projections for Latin America in the 1980s, as for Africa, suggest a high percentage of military/authoritarian regimes, with a good deal of room for continued political instability. The latter projection should be moderated in the Latin American area, however, by two factors. First, the *nation-state* is not challenged by the *communal* or *ethnic* state; where virtually no nation-states in the Western sense yet exist in Africa, they have been a part of the Latin American environment for approximately a century and a half. Second, there is a great deal of evidence that the political culture of Latin America is quite congruent with a particular strand of authoritarianism which most academics refer to as "organic-statist" or "corporativist." The literature on the topic is enormous and the analytical issues involved of equal proportion; what is important for our purposes is simply the possibility that a political culture to which the "corporate state" ideal can appeal with some substantial success is one in which certain forms of authoritarian regimes may not seem as alien or as objectionable to those governed by them as most Northerners may think.[15]

There is no need to examine the problems of authoritarianism, the role of the military in politics, and the potential for political instability in the Asian setting in any detail. From country to country Asia will exhibit the entire range of problems for the 1980s suggested by the preceding examinations of Africa and Latin America. While levels of economic development are generally more advanced than in Africa and the political culture different in many ways, the countries of Asia share some of Africa's responses to the strains of industrialization (as in the Philippines). The region is marked by a high percentage of military/authoritarian regimes, and none of those few countries one would classify as "democratic" exhibit much of a commitment to that regime type. Finally, given the rapid rates of social mobilization, economic structural change, a growing "educated unemployed" problem in the region (at its most severe in Indonesia), and the strains urbanization and industrialization are putting on the region's traditional rural "clientelistic" political processes, many of the standard indicators of political change suggest the potential for substantial instability in the 1980s, particularly in Southeast Asia.

The importance of understanding the political milieu within major regions of the South in the 1980s for the purposes of policy prescription is difficult to demonstrate with a great deal of assurance. If there were any clearly understood causal relationships between authoritarian government on the one hand and such processes or outcomes as rates of economic growth, measures of domestic equity, positioning on North-South issues in general, domestic political stability, and foreign policy goals on the other hand, the purposes of the preceding analysis would be more easily justified. But no such relationships have been convincingly demonstrated, and every generalization has so many exceptions that few are worth stating. Some authoritarian/military regimes have presided over the implementation of highly successful growth strategies; others have failed in the same attempt. Some such regimes are deeply concerned with domestic equity issues; others at best pay lip service to the problem. Some are leading moderates within the Group of 77; others form elements of the Group's radical brain trust. Some have exhibited a great deal of domestic stability; others seem destined for extremely short life spans.

Despite the present lack of understanding of causal relationships between regime types and economic performance, a brief analysis of some of the most salient economic and demographic problems and choices that will face Southern countries in the coming decade may add marginally to our understanding of North-South issues as they will appear over the decade of the 1980s.

In the aggregate, a major problem facing Southern countries in the coming decade will be unemployment and underemployment. The best available estimates suggest that in the mid-1970s well over 5 percent of the developing countries' labor force was totally unemployed and more than 35 percent was underemployed. Taken together, unemployment and underemployment ranged from approximately 45 percent in sub-Saharan Africa to 29 percent in Latin America. Given present demographic profiles and population growth rates in these countries, ranging from approximately 2.5 to 3.5 percent per year, it is obvious that only rapid economic growth rates can prevent employment statistics from worsening during the 1980s.

Even if rapid economic growth rates can be resumed after the global slowdown of the mid-1970s, the magnitude of existing demographic problems suggests the difficulty of lowering unemployment in many countries. Mexico represents what is perhaps an extreme illustration of this problem, as the following facts suggest. While the country's gross national product has grown on the average at better than 6 percent per year in real terms for the past 40 years, it is currently estimated that close to one-fifth of the total Mexican labor force between the ages of 15 and 65 is working (most of it illegally) in the United States. It is also estimated that a Mexican economic growth rate of 6.3 percent per year would be unable to provide jobs for much more than two-thirds of the annual entrants into the Mexican labor force for the next several decades. Some estimates made in the mid-1970s suggest that Mexico would have to grow at approximately 8.5 percent per year to avoid adding to its present relative unemployment and underemployment problems.

Predictably Southern governments will attempt to deal with these problems in a variety of ways. Three of the major determinants in the approach they choose will probably be the socioeconomic level of development of the country involved, the resources available to the government, and the perceived stability of the governing elites.

The lower the level of socioeconomic development in a country, the (politically) less acute will be the problem of unemployment and underemployment. In these (mostly African) cases populations will be close to three-quarters or more rural in makeup, and "extended-family" and other sociocultural systems will give minimum levels of support to the jobless. In countries at higher levels of socioeconomic development, with far larger urban populations, fewer traditional cultural defenses against unemployment, and more of a "participant" political culture and system, the problem is likely to represent a slowly growing threat to governing-elite legitimacy. Thus the same unemployment figures are likely to represent a more serious problem in most Latin American and Southeast Asian countries than they are in Africa.

A second major determinant in governmental response will involve the resources available to manage this clearly projectable problem. Can the government easily increase domestic savings and investment, thus increasing growth rates and decreasing unemployment? Mexico's recent oil discoveries will allow some responsiveness of this type. Can it increase direct or indirect foreign investment? Clearly the answer will depend upon a government's international credit rating, the international economic climate, the government's policies toward foreign direct investment, and the opportunities (market size, raw materials, cheap labor, and others) it has to offer the foreign direct investor.

For those governments that cannot easily increase domestic or foreign investment, a reexamination of present development strategies may follow. Governments in such countries will at least attempt to estimate the extent to which more employment might be provided with the same amount of capital investment (i.e., through the use of less capital-intensive production methods). Whether or not significant changes are attempted in development strategies will again depend on a host of political and economic factors that will vary from country to country. For example, will the easing of one potential political problem (unemployment) create a more serious one (opposition from various economic-elite groups)? Will changes in development policies provide enough new employment to warrant the risks involved in introducing the change?

Additionally, direct efforts to lower population growth may be introduced or reemphasized at higher levels of funding. Approximately three-quarters of the developing countries already support and finance direct programs of birth control; for them the question would be one of emphasis.

Finally, the unemployment problem may not become a major concern for governments that feel themselves to be unchallenged domestically. In the late 1970s many countries with severe unemployment problems but stable governments appeared to have chosen to ignore that problem in the short term, concentrating their resources (as in Algeria) on highly capital-intensive forms of development they believed would provide much lower unemployment at much higher wage levels within another generation.

This brief analysis suggests how speculative projections would be with regard to emerging development strategies, to unemployment problems, to economic growth in individual countries (or regions), and to a host of highly related issues. Many African countries, with the lowest growth rates and the greatest unemployment, may witness the least governmental concern for this issue because attention will be focused on ethnic and other political issues perceived to be of greater importance. A leading Arab socialist state may also pay little attention to unemployment in the 1980s, relying on growing commercial and technological contacts with the North to attempt highly capital-intensive industrial development within two decades. A leading Latin American state may combine workforce emigration, domestic savings from oil sales, and marginal changes toward more labor-intensive growth strategies in the attempt to manage its potentially severe economic/demographic problems in the coming decade.

Perhaps the only conclusion that can be ventured with much assurance is that, in good part because of the demographic and unemployment/underemployment problems, development strategies in the 1980s are likely to be a mix of the old and the new (see Chapter 8), and that the mix will be determined from country to country by all the factors noted above. Foremost among them will be governing-elite strength and purposes, the political culture of each particular society, the health of the international economy, and its degrees of openness to developing-country economies (as measured by degrees of trade liberalization, access to international capital markets, and other relevant indicators). Barring a major period of Northern stagflation, many Southern countries will continue their present policy emphasis on export-led growth. Others will give increased prominence to policy changes to increase the labor content of their production. Still others at lower levels of development will continue to request bilateral foreign assistance and "soft loans" from the World Bank to build basic infrastructures for a broad range of development policies.

V

The analysis in section IV above is of a general nature and is not meant to establish any fundamental causal relationships that will help us illuminate the problems of the 1980s. In the policy chapters that are to follow, however, this brief examination of probable political trends in the developing countries may be of more than marginal significance in distinguishing the plausible objective from the impossible goal and the more as opposed to the less appropriate set of policies to reach plausible goals. Beyond this most general and perhaps most important contribution, the analysis does suggest three more specific parameters to the North-South problem that should be kept in mind.

First, Southern states are likely to be represented by a very large proportion of authoritarian/bureaucratic regimes. There will be many subtypes represented: some of a one-party civilian nature; probably more with a straightforward military core; and many, as in Latin America, that are of the military-bureaucratic-technocratic mix. Finally, within the corporativist subtype, some regimes will display many symbols of democracy but the structure and processes of a particular form of authoritarianism.

We should at the same time remember Robert Dahl's comment that the safest bet about a country's regime a generation from now is that it will be somewhat but not radically different from what it is today. In the African setting we should expect a variety of authoritarian—perhaps even totalitarian—efforts to create stable regimes. In those societies in which authoritarian rule has succeeded premodern authoritarian forms with almost no discontinuity other than a period of colonial rule, pressures for democratic systems may often be very limited. Elite discontent with authoritarianism will contribute to continued instability, but it is doubtful that the instability will lead to anything more than the appearance of new authoritarian regimes. And we should also note that the circumstances accompanying the breakdown of democracy make its reestablishment very difficult, as most Latin American cases demonstrate. All of which leads to the conclusion that "competitive democracy seems to be the result of quite unique constellations of factors and circumstances leading to its inauguration and stability. Many developments in modern societies and in the not-so-modern, particularly in terms of economic well-being, should make stable democracies possible, but those same conditions do not assure a successful process of inauguration of such regimes."[16]

This particular parameter of North-South relations is worth noting for several reasons. It will remind us that any Northern equation of human rights with "representative government" in the 1980s could have disastrous consequences for other efforts to achieve a less conflictual set of North-South relations. It will remind us of the potentially substantial degree of instability in many Southern regimes which seems to accompany almost all authoritarian sub-types. Issue by issue, such instability may represent a problem or an opportunity. It may represent an opportunity where it leads to international efforts to ease some common Southern sources of instability, such as demographic and employment problems (see Chapters 7 and 8). It may represent a problem where it leads to domestic repression and notable deprivations of human rights.

Finally, this analysis of Southern political evolution should remind us of the substantial potential for interstate conflict within the South and the concomitant potential for third-party interventions of an overt or covert nature. This is the second specific parameter of North-South relations deserving of attention. Particularly with regard to Africa, the degrees of regime instability and the communal tensions that constitute much of that instability constantly invite actions by bordering states which involve them in at least covert forms of intervention. When such situations escalate, the prospect of one party or the other calling on outside assistance also escalates. It is the African states themselves, more than the non-African intervenors, who generally take the actions that initiate such interventions.

In the domestic African context this potential problem is likely to increase in the 1980s. How will non-African countries respond? Will Africa become the setting for renewed East-West conflicts? If so, with what impact on the North-South problem and its evolution? All these issues will be paramount in the African setting regardless of the course of events in Namibia, Southern Rhodesia, and South Africa which, whatever their direction, will add another layer of problems to the North-South agenda.[17]

The third and final specific issue raised by the examination of Southern political trends concerns the general issue of human rights. In the preceding chapter it was suggested that, for better or worse, the human rights spectrum of issues could not be kept off the North-South agenda for the 1980s. If this proves a valid assumption, what does the foregoing analysis of developing-country political trends suggest about the potential impact of the human rights problem on North-South relations for the coming decade?

Trouble. In the first place, in countries and regions that are prime candidates for continued communal conflict, the 1980s could witness some dramatic wholesale deprivations of those human rights of most concern to Northerners. And in such cases, where the very existence of the nation-state (and, not unimportantly, the issue of what groups will control it) may well be at stake, human rights appeals are quite unlikely to influence the course of events.

Second, there is probably a high positive correlation between authoritarian regime instability (even without the communal factor) and the deprivation of human rights as defined by most Northerners. The greater the insecurity of governing elites in authoritarian regimes, the higher the likelihood of "illegal" incarcerations, torture, restrictions on press freedoms, etc.

Finally, even in the most modernized of the developing countries (e.g., Chile) it is clear that the process of political polarization that can accompany economic development may produce a subtype of military regime that will violate every human right ever categorized in an attempt to purge its country of the anti-Christ. At the nation-state level, clubs become trumps and political liberties are curtailed when legitimacy deserts the structure and the process norms of a political system. At the individual level, the clubs are turned on people (and the more personal human rights) when the legitimacy of the authoritarian replacement for the previous regime evolves its own opposition because it, too, lacks perceived legitimacy. The greater the legitimacy crisis, the more the opposition; the stronger the opposition, the greater the potential for the violation of human rights in defense of an unstable authoritarian regime.

In retrospect, the Janus-like qualities of the South likely to assert themselves in the 1980s illuminate a conjunction of domestic, regional, and international pressures that defy prediction but suggest several general trends. At the North-South diplomatic bloc level, the Southern network of institutionalization and communication, shared norms of behavior, systemic goals, and conflictual feelings toward the North all suggest that the North-South axis of controversy will remain a permanent fixture for the coming decade.

At the intra-Southern level, rapidly growing gaps in levels of economic development, regional and international influence and power potential, systemic goals (and desires for reforms), political and economic models, and, finally, degrees of regime stability all suggest that, *ceteris paribus*, the South will find bloc cohesion increasingly difficult to retain as the decade of the 1980s passes. If the South is viewed by some as an artificial unit today, it will seem far more artificial in the 1980s. But it is very likely to be found operating as a unit at the rhetorical, international norm-setting level nevertheless.

One of the most serious challenges in reaching a moderate international system in the 1980s will be to maximize Northern ability to work with the developing countries both as a unit and as the increasingly differentiated states and groups of states they are rapidly becoming. It will be a challenge because attempts to work with the South as individual states or small units will constantly be fought by many Southerners who fear that unity is their only assurance of a seat at the present international diplomatic table; it will be a challenge because the South, when operating as a unit that generally necessitates negotiating on the basis of the lowest common denominator, will constantly deal Northern rejectionists a pat hand with which to call Southern rhetorical bluffs (sometimes encouraged off the record to do so by individual Southern states that do not wish to break ranks openly but oppose specific Southern bargaining positions). If the Southern bluff is currently conceptualized in terms of the present NIEO demands in the narrow, technical economic sense, there are many valid reasons to call the bluff. But if it is conceptualized as a diplomatic probe by revisionist states with some legitimate complaints in an evolving international system which encourages such statecraft, then calling the bluff would be more myopic than the bluff itself. For calling the bluff would suggest that a "zero-sum" imagery still controlled the actions of both players in the game. Such imagery is rapidly losing its value for North-South politics in a changing global system.

NOTES

[1]The felicitous phrase belongs to Theodore Geiger, and a full treatment of the theme can be found in his excellent book by the same title. See Theodore Geiger, *The Conflicted Relationship* (New York: McGraw-Hill, 1967), especially chaps. 3 and 4.

[2]Branislav Gosovic and John Gerard Ruggie, "On the Creation of a New International Economic Order," *International Organization*, vol. 30, no. 2, Spring 1967, p. 312. Emphasis added.

[3]The above line of argumentation is always pushed too far by many who would like to see an end to Southern unity. They fail to recognize that with enough internal "logrolling" and "side-payments" Southern states have shown a robust capacity to paper over differences of interest in the past, and will likely continue to do so in the future.

What is being hypothesized here is not the *demise* of Southern solidarity but a *gradual weakening* of the phenomenon due to the rapidly growing differentiation of economic desires and needs. Some observers question this hypothesis on the grounds that the South has been able to overcome most such divisive potential in the past. But as we look ahead 10–15 years, two factors are likely to make past performance a weak indicator of future behavior. The first is simply the continued rapid growth in economic differentiation itself. However differentiated Southern economies were in the 1960s and early 1970s, when Southern unity was for the most part sustained, they will be so much more differentiated in the 1980s that the strains on the process of internal compromise will become extremely strong.

The second factor concerns the increasing probability that the 1980s will witness concrete bargaining between North and South which was, for the most part, absent in the past. As all observers of the UNCTAD process and the G-77 modus operandi have noted, the Southern internal logrolling process constantly produced the lowest common denominator of Southern desires and then presented it to the North in the form of a nonnegotiable demand. One reason that this process was accepted by most Southern states was that the North seldom made any concrete offers (or counteroffers) of its own.

If and when the North begins a concrete bargaining process, however, Southern states interested in Northern offers will find it increasingly difficult to afford to abide by "lowest common denominator" Southern bargaining positions. In this sense, the above hypothesis is built in considerable part on the internal dynamic of the G-77 itself. For an extended analysis of that dynamic see Branislav Gosovic, *UNCTAD: Conflict and Compromise* (Leiden, Holland: A. W. Sijthoff, 1972), passim.

[4]See Gordon W. Smith, *The External Debt Prospects of the Non-Oil-Exporting Developing Countries* (Washington, D.C.: Overseas Development Council, 1977), pp. 8–9.

[5]See Roger D. Hansen, "The Political Economy of North-South Relations: How Much Change?" *International Organization*, vol. 29, no. 4, Autumn 1975, pp. 940–943. Obviously the issue of Israel *could* undermine the entire projection.

[6]See Gosovic and Ruggie, op. cit.

[7]Albert Fishlow, "A New International Economic Order: What Kind?" in Fishlow et al., *Rich and Poor Nations in the World Economy* (New York: McGraw-Hill for the Council on Foreign Relations/1980s Project, 1978), pp. 9–83.

[8]Smith, op. cit., p. 51.

[9]Juan J. Linz, "Totalitarian and Authoritarian Regimes," in Nelson Polsby (ed.), *Handbook of Political Sciences*, vol. 3, pp. 322–323.

[10]Colin Legum, "Communal Conflict and International Intervention in Africa," in Legum, Mytelka, and Zartman, *Africa in the 1980s: A Continent in Crisis* (New York: McGraw-Hill for the Council on Foreign Relations/1980s Project, 1979.)

[11]Ibid.

[12]Linz, op. cit., p. 285.

[13]Ibid., p. 298. Emphasis added.

[14]Ibid., p. 300. Emphasis added.

[15]For a brief analysis of the issue, a discussion of some of the leading literature, and a specific application of the corporativist model to one Latin American country, see Roger D. Hansen, *The Politics of Mexican Development* (Baltimore: Johns Hopkins University Press, 1974), pp. xiii–xxix.

[16]Linz, op. cit., pp. 354–355.

[17]But one too complex and speculative to be added to the analysis undertaken in this book. Like the Arab-Israeli conflict, the southern African problem is simply not examined in any detail in this study for reasons of time, space, and conceptual approach.

Chapter 5
The North in the 1980s

I

The caveats introduced at the beginning of the previous chapter are equally applicable here. What follows is in no way a forecast of Northern evolution over the coming decade. Instead, it is an attempt to illuminate some of the more probable trends within the countries of the North which are most likely to influence Northern policy makers as North-South issues are analyzed and policies developed to deal with them in the 1980s.

It was noted in Chapter 4 how radically the prospects for Southern cohesion and North-South relations might change as a result of unpredictable events in the Middle East or southern Africa. Therefore a kind of *ceteris paribus* condition was attached to those two powder kegs for purposes of analysis in that chapter. In this chapter, the East-West relationship is treated in much the same way. It is simply assumed that "other things will remain equal" in the East-West arena. If they do not, then many of the problems of Northern societies and intra-Northern relations would most likely evolve in a different manner.

Additionally, the two chapters are similar in that it is impossible to draw causal relationships between the probable evolution of sociopolitical and economic trends in the North and policy implications for North-South relations in the 1980s. Therefore the analysis in this chapter is not meant to suggest that any particular set of policies will be the most or the least appropriate for the coming decade or that certain goals will be impossible to achieve while others might seem to be quite reasonable targets. All that analysis can do is to help us understand what the policy space for approaches to North-South problems may look like to the Northern policy maker in the coming decade, and in doing so help us to focus, in the following four chapters, upon goals and policy prescriptions that can be demonstrated to fit within that policy space and within the parameters of the international systemic constraints analyzed earlier.

If there are certain obvious similarities in approach between the previous chapter and this one, there is also at least one significant difference. In analyzing the likely evolution of Southern societies, we see many already very clearly marked trends. A combination of theoretical and empirical evidence created fairly certain groundwork for much of Chapter 4's projections of Southern evolution.

In this chapter, many of the issues being examined are much more problematical. Theoretically, we lack the degree of understanding necessary to discuss many of them—such as the capacity of Northern societies to control inflation or to overcome what conservatives are apt to call "the democratic distemper"—with much certainty. Empirically, we often have very little evidence to work with because the problems seem so novel or are as yet so little understood that we cannot even decide what "empirical evidence" is relevant to the issue being examined. Finally, regarding many of the issues to be explored, it is difficult to judge whether problems are steadily worsening, show no particular trend, or are being resolved.

One example should suffice to portray this type of "judgment call." Can the Northern countries avoid a slow slide into an increasing protectionism that could undermine a great deal of Northern cohesiveness in dealing with the South? To many observers and analysts, the answer is no; the forces pushing Northern societies in that direction are too strong to be checked. Others demur, arguing that "the worst is over" and that new modes of cooperation have already replaced the decaying ones that were an integral part of the Bretton Woods world. One noted international economist, writing in 1977, concluded that "the cup should be regarded as half full rather than half empty. Given the severity and breadth of the most recent recession, I am impressed by the extent to which [Northern] nations have so far avoided resort to protection and other distortions of international transactions."[1]

We will have reason to look at the issue of protectionism, the capacity of Northern societies and the changing international economic regime to contain the process, and the likely outcome for Northern cohesion in some detail below. The point here is simply to note the lack of certainty that attaches to almost every issue we will examine in this chapter. Nevertheless, the issues must be examined because all observers agree that they are crucial even if disagreement concerning outcomes remains. Whitman, for example, at the end of the cautiously optimistic essay quoted above, concluded that "there can be no illusions about the gravity of the threat to the survival of a liberal international economic system."[2]

Even if the magnitude of all the issues examined in this chapter is uncertain and their relationship to North-South issues in the 1980s generally indeterminate, the following schematization should help the reader to understand more clearly which problems are already with us and which may simply be embryonic (and perhaps exaggerated or avoidable); which problems must be dealt with domestically and which also entail serious international efforts at regime building and policy coordination.

Figure 5-1   Major Issues Affecting Northern Societies and Northern Forms of International Cooperation

	DOMESTIC	INTERNATIONAL
Existing Problems	1	2
Potential Problems	3	4

As the following discussion will illustrate, the matrix in Figure 5-1 is artificial in its suggested compartmentalization of four differing sets of issues. First, almost all the existing domestic issues (e.g., inflation, unemployment, fragmented and weak political systems) directly affect the set of issues (e.g., the strengthening of old and new international economic regimes, "neo-mercantilism" and the threat presented by the OPEC surplus trade balance, and progress on trade negotiations) we place in the existing international category. Second, many analysts and interpretations of "existing" problems suggest that they are symptomatic of much deeper problems and conflicts within liberal capitalist societies of the North. Thus it is impossible to separate "existing" from "potential" problems; indeed, if analysts see row 1 problems as little but predictable manifestations of deeper row 2 conflicts, then it is misleading to label row 2 "potential." Nevertheless, this process is followed because the problems to be discussed under the latter label—for example, the "crisis of democracy," the "cultural contradictions of capitalism," "social scarcity" and the inevitable politicization of both domestic and international economic issues in Northern societies— are not yet the objects of enough consensus that they can be labeled "underlying causes" of the problems that appear as row 1 issues.

Those analysts and observers who are so convinced can simply substitute "underlying causes" for "potential problems" as they read the chapter. One advantage of the nomenclature chosen is that it leaves the reader free to further examine the available evidence on the problems raised in row 2 and decide, issue by issue, which problems isolated by analysts merit elevation from a potential problem to an underlying cause. Several probably do on the basis of our present empirical and theoretical knowledge, but a convincing presentation of this point in this chapter would simply divert us too much from the major themes of this book.

The following four sections of the chapter will briefly examine the major problems in each of the four quadrants of the above matrix. The analysis is limited to issues most relevant to our very particular objective in this chapter: a better comprehension of Northern constraints in dealing with North-South issues in the 1980s. This is the litmus test that accounts for the eclectic and unconventional nature of the analysis that follows.

II

Existing domestic problems most likely to influence the range of Northern responses to North-South issues in the 1980s include (1) the domestic aspects of coping with present levels of international economic interdependence, (2) the increased demands upon the Northern welfare state to produce rising levels of economic security and living standards for its constituents, (3) the specific problems of inflation, unemployment, and trade balances, and (4) the apparent weakness of most Northern governments at the present point in time. While each of these problems can be analyzed individually, it is their inextricable linkage that causes far greater concern than would the four measured separately.

It has recently been suggested that "a degree of controlled disintegration in the world economy is a legitimate objective for the 1980s and may be the more realistic one for a moderate international economic order. A central normative problem for the international economic order in the years ahead is how to insure that the disintegration indeed occurs in a controlled way and does not rather spiral into damaging restrictionism."[3] One of the major reasons for such a view is that present degrees of international economic integration appear to be overtaxing the collective willingness of Northern states to pay the price (in terms of autonomy, the domestic ordering of priorities, etc.) for the economic benefits of present levels of integration.

For over 10 years literature on economic integration among the industrialized countries of the North has analyzed the manner in which growing levels of economic interdependence have been posing new problems and hard choices for national policy makers. The point to be made here is that these problems give every appearance of growing in the near to medium term. The stagflation of the mid-1970s, for example, demonstrated not only that Northern countries are now more vulnerable than ever to inflationary and recessionary pressures originating abroad, but also that each country's preferred policy instruments for dealing with the instabilities introduced by greater global integration had grown weaker. The limitations interdependence places on traditional fiscal and monetary policies has been demonstrated for a decade; the past 4 years illuminated the problem dramatically once again.

Further studies have carried the analysis of this general problem from the macroeconomic to the microeconomic level. By this time it has been convincingly demonstrated that national economic policies in the arenas of resource allocation and income distribution are often undermined by present degrees of global economic integration. As one analyst put the problem after assessing governmental goals and instruments in these microeconomic areas, "the nation-state tends to become a less and less efficient unit for decision making, at the same time as they [*sic*] adopt more and more ambitious policy goals."[4]

If the "more ambitious policy goals" were a cyclical phenomenon, then the problems facing Northern states in coping with the demands of increasing global economic integration would be of less concern. But more ambitious domestic policy goals appear to be a fundamental and long-term trend in these same countries, a trend that has its roots in the appearance of the post–World War II welfare state commitment to full employment and price stability. By the late 1970s the initial welfare state commitments looked modest indeed. For in the interim the issues of domestic economic security (and, with country-to-country variations, income distribution) had severely complicated the tasks of the welfare state. Domestic economic security was increasingly being interpreted as a right to one's present job, not simply a job; thus the slow rise in guaranteed-lifetime-employment contracts. Therefore macroeconomic policies that might have assured "full employment" (as interpreted statistically by each state) were becoming less adequate; micro policy adjustments (e.g., trade protectionism for certain industries) were called for—and often delivered—to protect particular job "entitlements." This problem was clearly exacerbated by the declining capacity of governmental macroeconomic performance to assure low levels of unemployment.

Since the issues of income distribution and equity will be discussed below, it need only be noted here that evidence begins to mount in support of analysts who argue that the problem of income distribution will become a significant issue in the domestic politics of Northern states in the coming decade. If the 1960s were devoted to overcoming the absolute poverty problem in the North (as with many of Lyndon Johnson's "Great Society" policies), it is now increasingly predicted and demonstrated (e.g., in Great Britain) that the mid-1970s and beyond will witness a struggle over income shares, further taxing the political institutions of Northern states. For the United States, a prominent United States economist recently prophesied that "income shares and distributional aspects of public actions are going to become a major focus of policy debate in the next few years. I am not predicting how that debate will come out—just that it will take place."[5]

The very serious and specific problems of unemployment, inflation, and trade balances continue to plague Northern economies and, more important for this study, suggest a propensity for endurance that if realized could add significant weight to the potential constraints on North-South policy making being examined in box 1 of our matrix. By the end of 1977 Northern economies continued to live with historically high rates of unemployment. During the first half of that year the overall rate of reported unemployment in the industrial countries was 5.3 percent, just 0.2 percent below the 1975 recession-induced peak of 5.5 percent and almost twice the average that prevailed during the 1960s and early 1970s.

Inflation rates for the industrialized countries also remained very high by comparison with earlier levels. They exceeded 6.5 percent during 1976 and the first half of 1977, compared with a 4 percent average during the period 1962–1972. The persistence of significant inflation left Northern governments facing a severe dilemma. Inflation created substantial political opposition to the use of strong expansionary measures to reduce unemployment, and in doing so it often led governments to adopt other policies—containing substantial potential for intra-Northern conflict—to try to ease the unemployment-inflation dilemma. Some countries tried to "export" inflation (or avoid importing it) through the creation of barriers to exports; most also sought to lower unemployment by restricting imports.

The inflation and unemployment dilemmas were part cyclical, part secular. Economists were baffled by the causes—both domestic and international—of continued high inflation rates and were uncertain about the existence—let alone the parameters—of any trade-off between rates of unemployment and inflation. These analytical uncertainties compounded governmental policy dilemmas, dilemmas already burdened by the overwhelming problem of how to "manage" the $40 billion annual OPEC world trade surplus. By 1977 it was becoming clear that the apparent desire of many Northern countries to run current-account surpluses was once again beginning to pose the problem of inconsistent balance-of-payments targets among the OECD countries. The oil-consuming countries must, as a group, run a current-account deficit corresponding to the surplus of the OPEC countries. Furthermore, contraction on the part of the OECD countries would only throw the burden of the OPEC surpluses onto the accounts of the South, exacerbating the Southern debt problem (thus threatening the international financial system) and increasing the Northern unemployment problem (thus threatening many precarious Northern governing coalitions and even raising the issue of regime legitimacy in some countries).

Thus there emerged a clear need for greater Northern agreement on a mutually acceptable set of ground rules for sharing the deficit caused by the OPEC surpluses. But as the next section will illustrate, the decay of the Bretton Woods system and the temporary absence of anything very substantial to take its place left the United States headed toward a huge ($25 billion to $30 billion) trade deficit in 1977 while other OECD countries continued to run large trade surpluses (perhaps as high as $20 billion for Japan and somewhat less for West Germany).[6]

All the above evidence suggested the need for Northern governments to enter a phase in which the "common good" of the OECD countries is given a higher salience than it might be given in ordinary times. But here one faces the final dilemma of existing domestic problems: the inherent weakness of most Northern governments in the mid-to-late 1970s. Throughout much of Europe, governing coalitions were weak and vulnerable. In addition, potential alternative governing coalitions seemed to be as weak and even more contradictory in makeup. In the United States, the executive branch might have been recovering from the crippling effects of the Watergate years, but the greatly enhanced strength of Congress—for better or worse—continued to limit attempts at executive branch leadership. To cite but one illustrative problem, 4 years after the initial OPEC price actions and the call for "Operation Independence" the United States remained without the semblance of an energy policy despite the increasingly clear costs of this deficiency for the United States, the North, and the non-oil-exporting developing countries. The lack of a serious United States energy policy translates into rapidly growing oil imports from the Middle East, further Northern vulnerability to OPEC cartel actions, and most probably oil prices increasing by more than enough to maintain the real value of petroleum exports.[7] Finally, for the first time in over 20 years the Liberal party in Japan felt challenged domestically and the government correspondingly weakened.

Many of the issues discussed under the category of existing domestic problems were illustrated during 1977 by American attempts to convince West Germany and Japan to reflate their economies at a faster rate and particularly by United States attempts to press the Japanese for further trade liberalization. In the latter instance the United States used both a macro and a micro approach. At the former level, it noted a half year $9 billion Japanese trade surplus and a U.S. trade deficit of over $10 billion and warned that these trends could not be sustained. At the micro level, the United States pressed for the lowering of Japanese barriers that would be of very specific interest to the United States, such as barriers to imports of beef, oranges, computers, and color film. Weakened politically and fearing domestic reactions to trade liberalization under circumstances of slow growth and high unemployment by Japanese standards, the Japanese government vapidly promised to "consider" United States requests. Finally, the United States forced the Japanese government to accept an "Orderly Marketing Arrangement" limiting its exports of color television sets to the United States.

This particular evidence is cited because it contains so many elements reminiscent of the months immediately prior to the "Nixon shock" delivered in 1971, which de facto ended the Bretton Woods era. Many observers who examine the issues briefly scanned in this section share the conclusion that it will be very difficult for the OECD countries to avoid a strong and steady drift away from the open global economy of the 1960s Bretton Woods period and into an increasingly neo-mercantilist world. The term "neo-mercantilism" is chosen to stress the fact that the policies followed by such states will most often be designed to protect interest groups at a *net cost* to the society and the state as a whole. In the aggregate, countries following a general neo-mercantilist path would try to achieve one or many of the following objectives: protection of powerful domestic interest groups, minimum balance-of-payments deficits, avoidance of the importation of inflation or unemployment, expansion of global market shares in high-technology industries as a hedge against a very uncertain economic future, and others less general in nature.

Other observers felt that these neo-mercantilist pressures could be held in check by the evolution of a more managed set of international economic relations among Northern countries. They argued, quite correctly, that more controls over trade and financial flows need not necessarily lead to neo-mercantilism; indeed, many of them viewed more "collective management" as the only viable alternative to the spread of unregulated, unilateral protectionist measures. What seemed unclear in the late 1970s was which trend was likely to prove stronger in coming years: that of increasing multilateral management or that of unilateral neo-mercantilism. Also unclear was the degree to which a Northern multilateral process of economic management might de facto accept increasing doses of protectionism in the name of the "management of the system."

III

Do the types of problems that fall into the second box of our matrix (existing international problems) suggest that the probability of a trend away from Northern state cooperation *à la* Bretton Woods and toward neo-mercantilism is a substantial one? While the reader must continue to accept a considerable degree of indeterminacy, a quick review of those existing international problems pertinent to our theme certainly suggests little beyond the untested potential of "multilateral management" to foreclose a transition toward an international economic system closer to the neo-mercantilist than the "integrated international economy" end of this particular spectrum. This conclusion follows from a consideration of (1) the structural changes that led to the demise of the Bretton Woods system, (2) the rapid development of new norms of international economic behavior that present degrees of interdependence necessitate, and (3) the present environment in which this task of rebuilding must be accomplished (especially the international environmental problems of OPEC surpluses and weak Northern governments).

Again it is possible to see the glass as half full rather than half empty. Thus Whitman's observation in mid-1977 that "today, with virtually all aspects of the [international economic] system in transition, under serious challenge, or embryonic, there is a rare opportunity—as well as the need—to build, expand or rebuild components taking account of their inter-connections and of the need for consistency and mutual support among them."[8] Yet even the new Democratic administration in Washington, which ideologically shared the Whitman vision, was the source of spreading Orderly Marketing Arrangements to set limits on imports from both developed and developing countries (e.g., inexpensive lines of shoes from South Korea and Taiwan, color television sets from Japan). One could, perhaps correctly, have viewed the executive branch's actions as encompassing the minimum protectionist measures which a "liberal-trade" administration felt it had to accept in the face of growing congressional protectionist pressure. For it was strong and growing congressional support for tariff and quota actions that was the backdrop for the Special Trade Representative's negotiation of Orderly Marketing Arrangements, arrangements the administration viewed as less protectionist than the outright use of tariffs and quotas. Nevertheless, the example suggested to many observers that neo-mercantilism might well be leading in the race with new modes of collective management of a non-mercantilist nature.

As the year grew toward a close, congressional pressures mounted for tariff and quota protection for the entire United States steel industry, with threats of unilateral congressional action if the administration failed to protect the industry both prior to and during the Tokyo Round of trade negotiations in Geneva. The steel issue raised one fundamental question for our analysis. Would the Tokyo Round—the seventh round of GATT trade negotiations since World War II—continue the steady movement toward trade liberalization?

Or would it introduce such new mechanisms as sectoral agreements and expanded "safeguard arrangements" which actually begin a process of backing away from present levels of global trade liberalization? In late 1977 it appeared that the negotiations could move in either direction, with perhaps a slight edge toward the latter type of evolution.

From the perspective of North-South relations, a crucial issue was Southern access to Northern markets. If many of the more industrialized Southern states follow growth strategies heavily dependent on the rapid increase of industrial exports to the North, Northern evolution as it relates to trade liberalization becomes a crucial matter. Thus, even if the multilateral management mode of responding to the pressures currently being analyzed were to overcome the neo-mercantilist alternative, the fundamental North-South question–how would multilateral management treat Southern industrial export potential?—would remain unanswered. If the multilateral management mode involved rules and norms that in effect lowered Southern industrial export growth rates from 15 percent to 7–8 percent per year, then *for the South* the dichotomy between neo-mercantilism and multilateral management could become an empty distinction.

While interpretations of the decline of the Bretton Woods international economic order vary in degree, most of them share several central points. The first concerns the growing unwillingness of the system's "leader," the United States, to pay the costs of leadership. This problem might have been overcome if the system had been able to shift to one of joint or collective leadership of three or four major economic powers. This, however, proved impossible because neither the EC nor Japan was able or willing to assume leadership tasks. The EC was too consumed with problems internal to the construction of European union—at whatever level—to turn its collective attention to a global systemic support role; Japan was unwilling to do so.

A second major ingredient in the decline of the system concerned the lowered salience of the East-West struggle and the security issues that attended it. Many Northern economic powers initially accepted United States leadership/hegemony in international economic relations out of national security concerns. Certainly West

Germany and Japan did so, the former most explicitly. But growing ambiguities concerning United States strategic doctrine and its implications for their vulnerability, followed by the decline in cold war tensions of the latter 1960s, lessened general willingness of several Northern countries to accept United States leadership and accommodate its needs in the international economic arena.

These changes are in part reflected in what Stanley Hoffmann long ago referred to as the emergence of "muted bipolarity," "polycentrism," and "multipolarity" in the international system.[9] These systemic changes reduced the strength of United States hegemony; increased the frequency of conflicts between the United States, Europe, and Japan over major international economic issues; and finally produced the United States actions of 1971 (breaking the link between the dollar and gold and imposing an import surcharge) that de facto terminated the Bretton Woods system.

If the ability of the Northern states to patch together the old system—and improve its capacities in the process—is now the center of a widespread debate, this is because events since 1971 do demonstrate both successes and failures. Those who see the glass half full emphasize both political and technical responses to the 1971–1973 breakdown.

At the political level, they point to the institutionalization of Northern economic summit conferences, starting with the meeting at Rambouillet in 1975 and followed by meetings in Puerto Rico in 1976, in London in 1977, and in Bonn in 1978. They might add that these summits have now also institutionalized follow-up conferences in which lower-level representatives attempt to assure that the artfully crafted communiqués of each summit are in fact implemented (wherever an "action item" appears, the identification of which is in itself often a matter of arcane and tedious diplomacy). In this process performances of individual countries regarding such issues as inflation, employment, growth, and balance-of-payments goals are discussed and criticized; international issues, such as the Tokyo Round of trade negotiations and North-South discussions, are examined; and an attempt is undertaken to reach consensus positions on both domestic performance and international negotiating positions. Optimists suggest that such economic summits involving five to eight of the leading Northern economies will give added impetus to the policy coordination efforts carried on for years by the OECD.

Those who feel that solid progress toward the establishment of a reinvigorated system is being made in a technical sense argue that the movement away from fixed exchange rates to "managed flexibility" should, over time, ease protectionist pressures and strengthen remaining Bretton Woods arrangements; and that the significant devaluation of the dollar should eventually ease United States protectionist pressures in particular. And in noting that the North has thus far been able to deal with the huge OPEC trade surpluses without any major internal conflicts, they argue that this singular achievement is the most telling evidence of the resilience of the system that is—informally but steadily—replacing and refurbishing the pre-1971 international economic system.

For those who tend to see the glass half empty, the issue is not the obvious accomplishments in Northern policy coordination and cooperation in the building of new institutions and rules of the game which mark the past 5 years. It is whether those accomplishments are significant enough to overcome both the old problems that led to the demise of the Bretton Woods system and the new problems, domestic and international, stemming from OPEC price actions and the North-South confrontation. From a slightly different perspective, the issue is whether or not the capacities of the renewed, refurbished, or "embryonic" international economic system will grow rapidly enough to meet the escalating demands placed on it.

Skeptics dismiss much of the evidence of "progress" rather swiftly. They note that the Northern economic summits have produced little beyond ambiguous rhetoric; they further note that the heads of state involved listen to one another's views concerning their own growth, trade balance, and other targets, and then return home to do exactly as their own perceived domestic political necessities dictate. Linking this observation to the present electoral weakness of most Northern governments, skeptics are not impressed with the short- to medium-term capacity of summitry to engender new norms of intra-Northern economic cooperation.

These skeptics are also concerned that the new reforms of institutions such as the IMF may not withstand the tests soon to confront them. Much of this doubt was captured by Fred Hirsch and Michael Doyle in a 1977 essay. In noting that the constitutional basis for the prevailing economic system is increasingly questioned, they made the following observation:

The failure to establish a coherent and comprehensive substitute for the Bretton Woods order is a prominent manifestation of these tendencies [toward continuous changing of rules]. The proposed new amendments of the IMF articles, which are now in the process of being ratified, involve nothing less than the abandonment of a specified monetary order.[10]

Pointing out that the only international obligation under the substitute system will be to effect "good behavior," they concluded that

it remains to be seen whether any advance can be made on the existing informal guidelines, which are so general as to be deprived of practical significance in influencing particular actions. The commitment to good behavior is far from unimportant. It represents a facet of the wider commitment to continued international collaboration. *Yet mere commitment to collaborate, without substantive specification of the basis for collaboration, represents a qualitative weakening in the basis of international action.*[11]

Will this depleting legacy of the former economic order retain or renew the capacity to withstand the neo-mercantilist pressures analyzed in the previous section of this chapter? In "normal times" perhaps so. But the late 1970s and early 1980s will not be normal times. Northern countries must agree on ground rules regarding the management of the annual $40 billion OPEC trade surplus, which is not likely to diminish in real terms without the adoption of a major oil-conserving energy program by the United States. The same states must agree on the issue raised by Hirsch and Doyle: What is good behavior regarding exchange-rate policies (and, indirectly, balance-of-payments targets)? Finally, they must make some progress in the present Tokyo Round of trade negotiations or risk a serious reversal of a 30-year trend toward trade liberalization. In one sense such a reversal, if controlled, might be appropriate to the 1980s by relieving some of the pressures on national autonomy accompanying growing degrees of economic openness. But could such a reversal be controlled by weak Northern governments and protectionist-oriented legislatures in an environment of historically high rates of unemployment and ambiguous international economic norms? If, for example, the United States runs a trade deficit of close to $30 billion in 1977 while Japan achieves a surplus of similar magnitude, could 1978 avoid a "Carter shock" even if President Carter wished to avoid one? While most analysts agree that a return to the Northern growth rates of the 1960s would greatly increase the potential for new institution building and rule making, very few are sanguine about the return of such growth rates in the short-to-medium-term future.

Whether one perceives the glass of Northern capacity for global economic cooperation as half full or half empty is, in the last analysis, probably a reflection of views held concerning the issues raised in the following sections—issues often analyzed today by non-Marxist scholars using such terms as the crisis of democracy, the cultural contradictions of capitalism, and the impact of social scarcity on the legitimacy and the policy choices of Northern states.

IV

The third box in our matrix focuses on potential domestic problems within Northern societies, problems that many analysts already consider extant, and the underlying causes of the issues considered in the preceding two sections. All observers would agree that within most industrialized countries facets of the problems to be set forth do exist. What is at issue both for our purposes and independent of them is the nature and the magnitude of these problems, the possibility that they have been "misspecified" and their causes misunderstood, and the resultant possibility that many of them may be cyclical rather than secular in nature.

With these dilemmas in mind, an examination of three particular issues illuminates most of the potential problem areas of interest to this study. They are often identified by the labels (1) the crisis of democracy, (2) the cultural contradictions of capitalism, and (3) the social limits to growth. In considering these issues the skeptical reader should keep in mind that, while using differing terminology and asserting different causal linkages, a growing number of observers from across the conservative-radical spectrum and from a growing number of academic disciplines (e.g., economics, political science, history, philosophy) are giving increased attention to this set of issues.

Our major interest is not in the theoretical or empirical urgency of any particular element to be discovered within this set of issues, but rather, in their aggregate potential to constrain Northern policy making in the coming decade. If evidence suggests that rising rates of inflation in Northern societies are in significant part a reflection of internal distributional battles produced by growing social structural conflicts, it matters little for purposes of this study whether we label this trend an overload of demands on democratic regimes or an example of growing contradictions within capitalist systems. What is important is that we recognize the probable impact of such a trend on the policy space of Northern governments in dealing with North-South issues in the 1980s.

The first theme to be considered is essentially concerned with the following question: Can the liberal-capitalist-democratic regimes that have developed within most industrialized societies— some over several centuries, and some in a much more compressed period of time—successfully overcome what some observers argue are growing threats to their capacity to govern? While the literature this question has produced in the mid-to-late 1970s is enormous, it is thus far disappointingly unenlightening. Much of it can easily be dismissed as an overreaction to a series of fortuitous and quite dissimilar events of the late 1960s and early 1970s. But because they do relate to this section as a whole, two aspects of this theme seem worthy of note.

The first concerns the novel "contextual challenges" that are said to face Northern regimes.[12] Suffice it to observe that they include such obvious factors as the changing international distribution of military, economic, and political power; the changing relations among industrialized countries; and the international problems of inflation, monetary stability, and the "management of interdependence." This range of challenges would present any regime, democratic or not, with difficult policy problems, thus potentially raising questions of regime legitimacy. For the purposes of this book, however, the list serves to remind us less of any crisis of democracy than a potential crisis of Northern solidarity. By themselves these problems are less likely to challenge democratic regimes than they are to challenge Northern cohesion, particularly if governmental responses to the problems of economic interdependence and openness do exhibit a neo-mercantilist trend. Only in instances where regime stability is assumed to stem from Northern cohesion would democracy appear to be threatened by these "contextual challenges."

The second aspect, that of intrinsic challenges to democracy which are purported to grow out of its very functioning, would appear to raise a more serious issue. One summary view of the problem concludes that "the operations of the democratic process do indeed appear to have generated a breakdown of traditional means of social control, a delegitimization of political and other forms of authority, and an overload of demands on government, including its capacity to respond."[13]

Again one might agree with the conclusion that certain problems of "democratic governance" are increasing, without accepting the implicit logic of the above view. It is just as plausible to argue that the so-called overload of demands on government is in essence the inevitable outcome of the continuing clash, within Northern democratic societies, between the logic of (democratic) citizenship and the logic of (capitalist) class structure—a clash that makes class differences less and less "legitimate." What the perspective of the previous paragraph sees as a crisis of democracy, this perspective would be much more inclined to see as a crisis of capitalism. It is unclear, however, that any problems accompanying the expanding logic of citizenship have thus far created a "crisis" for either governance or capitalism. Too many unexplored variables—institutional and cultural—exist to allow very much informed prognostication on an issue of such analytical complexity.

In combination, however, these varying emphases and interpretations give potential substance to the crisis of democracy theme—under whatever label. This point becomes more obvious after we examine the second and third issues explored in this section: the cultural contradictions of capitalism and the social limits to growth. For the central elements in the argumentation underlying both of them tend to strengthen the general crisis of democracy theme through a multiple series of linkages. The term crisis still appears somewhat hyperbolic, but the issues raised in the process of analysis do identify a number of potential Northern societal problems very relevant to North-South relations in the coming decade.

More than any other scholar in recent years—certainly more than any other of non-Marxist persuasion—it is Daniel Bell who has explored what he has called the cultural contradictions of capitalism. Much of his analysis parallels that in Joseph Schumpeter's *Capitalism, Socialism and Democracy*. Bell's explorations lead him to some very pessimistic conclusions concerning the governability of Northern states over the coming decade.[14]

Bell is essentially concerned with what he views as the disjunction between the organization and norms demanded by the economic systems of Northern capitalist states and the norms of "self-realization" that have recently become central to the predominant cultural patterns of those states. The two realms had for centuries been joined to produce a "single character structure"; they have now become sundered, raising serious problems for capitalist economies and even larger problems for Western governments. In essence Bell argues that the problems have arisen with the fading of the Protestant ethic as the cultural paradigm of bourgeois society. When this process accelerated during the early decades of the twentieth century, the capitalist system lost its transcendental ethic.[15] "The cultural, if not moral, justification of capitalism has become hedonism, the idea of pleasure as a way of life."[16]

The results of this gradual change in value systems of Northern states, which can be traced to many social structural origins within industrialized societies, has had an inevitable impact on both the economic and the political systems of Northern countries. In the economic realm the change has institutionalized expectations of continuous economic growth and rising standards of living; "these have been converted, in the current change of values, into a sense of entitlements."[17] If we could rely on continuous economic growth to provide the social solvent it has provided for so many previous decades in Western society, perhaps the change in value orientation would be less debilitating. But for several reasons, continuous economic growth at rates congruent with rising expectations may prove to be both impossible and less rewarding than it once was.

One of the reasons it proves to be less rewarding will be examined under the final theme of this section—the theme Fred Hirsch has labeled "social scarcity." But there are other reasons more central to Bell's exposition. First, continuous rapid growth eventually raised the complex problem of "negative externalities," such as pollution and congestion, highlighting the divergence between the private and social value of certain growth patterns and the need for more government intervention in guiding the process of economic growth. Second, as rising standards of living became viewed as entitlements, a growing bias toward inflation weakened the self-regulating aspects of the economy. In this instance, the economy and the political system came together just as they did when unguided economic growth led to serious negative externality problems. They came together because the legitimacy of Northern governments came to be judged by their capacities to ensure continuous economic growth. And most governments, under the pressure of increasing demands to "perform," were far more inclined to impart an inflationary bias to their economies than risk deflation, higher rates of unemployment, and a consequent loss of political support.

Third, a government's willingness to accommodate inflationary pressures rather than employ the standard deflationary tools raises two more problems that simply complicate its role further. Inflation not only hits fixed-income groups specifically and much of the middle class in general, but also can lead to "stop-go" economic policies when external and domestic targets are brought into sharp conflict. By slowing investment, such policies tend to undermine the capital accumulation process upon which the entire capitalist system of growth is based.

But Northern governments have not been challenged by macrolevel decisions alone. Over 50 years ago Schumpeter noted in a discussion of "fiscal sociology" that governments were becoming increasingly involved in microdecisions, most of which were reflected in annual governmental budgetary processes. The pressures on governments concerning this type of decision have also continued to grow rapidly with the weakening of social and cultural checks on demands for ever-rising living standards.

It is this aspect of Bell's analysis, underscoring the concern with the ever-increasing demands on democratic governments, which is integral to the crisis of democracy theme. In many European countries and in Japan to a somewhat lesser extent, it appears that long-standing societal and cultural barriers to direct citizen pressure on political systems have been weakening in recent years. The result, in Bell's terminology, is to turn the political system into a "cockpit" in which both interest groups and communal groups clash over the distribution of the state budget—which is some 40 percent to 50 percent of total GNP in most Northern countries when local-government expenditures are included.

A final concern for Bell and other analysts of these issues is the judgment that Northern societies in general (though perhaps not all of them, for much analysis is rather narrowly focused upon the United States) now lack any set of values and norms which can "legitimately" be applied to decisions made within the "public household," i.e., governmental allocation decisions writ large. When governmental budgets represented a much smaller percentage of GNP, when the process of economic growth was still not producing as many negative externalities, and when governmental legitimacy was not perceived to be so dependent upon successful macroeconomic performance, there were far fewer contestants in the "cockpit of [fiscal] politics." Furthermore, contestants then tended to be individuals or highly differentiated interest groups, not communal groups; and the issues they fought over were more local (a particular irrigation project) than national (national health care systems, national public education, etc.).

Therefore the need for a national set of cultural values and norms that could influence allocation decisions made in the political arena was far less important than it is becoming. Now that revolutions in technology, transportation, and communication have finally created a national community (regardless of regional variants) and now that 20 years of rapid growth have assured that yesterday's luxuries will be perceived as today's necessities, can Northern political systems retain their capacity to govern without the emergence of a new set of values and norms and/or institutional processes of participation to legitimize the allocative decisions that are increasingly and ineluctably transferred from the invisible market sector to the highly visible government sector?

To the extent that the economic function has been subordinated to societal goals over the past quarter century, the political system becomes "the controlling system of society." But who is to control it, and for what ends? Bell recognizes that this change may simply be interpreted as a displacement of traditional social conflicts from one arena to another. But analysis also suggests that such a change will alter the strength of the contestants as well as the nature of the prizes to be won.

At the very heart of this change and at the heart of the issue of new values and norms to govern industrial societies lies the issue of equality:

What is at stake today is the redefinition of equality. A principle which was the weapon for changing a vast social system, the principle of equality of opportunity, is now seen as leading to a new hierarchy, and the current demand is that "just precedence" of society in Locke's phrase requires the reduction of all inequality or the creation of equality of result—in income, status, and power—for all men in society. *This issue is the central value problem of the post-industrial society.*[18]

Many analysts do not agree with the manner in which Bell states this problem or the stress he gives it, but a large number of commentators do agree on two of his fundamental observations. First, they agree on the weakness, if not the absence, of values and norms operative in today's industrial societies which might serve to restrain the growing pressures put on their political systems for many of the reasons Bell has suggested. Whether institutional changes can modify these pressures through newer forms of interest intermediation is as yet uncertain. To this extent, there is a "crisis of values" that may well constrain the shaping of all Northern governmental policies in the 1980s. Governments in industrial democracies facing alienated, skeptical publics and unable to count on deep-seated, value-oriented claims to legitimacy may seldom feel able to sacrifice short-term gains for long-term benefits. They may seldom take the leadership in the search for and supply of global "collective goods," a role that is often perceived to bear too many net costs in the short run. In sum, they may be generally unable to undertake collectively and effectively the types of global system-building and system-maintenance burdens discussed as part of box 2 of our matrix.

Second, there is increasing agreement that the issue of equality and its redefinition does lie near the center of the set of problems being analyzed in this chapter. To the extent that bourgeois society has—as Schumpeter predicted it would—lost its earlier cultural foundations and has come to depend on economic growth and increased living standards to avoid many value issues, it is not surprising that the issue of equality should be raised at the very time when relatively slow economic growth seems to be losing its capacity to serve as liberal capitalism's "social solvent."

The final theme analyzed in this section is one first given full treatment by Fred Hirsch in his 1976 book entitled *Social Limits to Growth*.[19] From a very different ideological perspective and from a different academic discipline, the Hirsch study lends support to major elements of the argument found in examinations of the crisis of democracy and the cultural contradictions of capitalism.

In an essentially economic analysis, but one filled with psychological and sociological insights, Hirsch arrives at the following pessimistic conclusion concerning the future of Northern industrial societies:

The moral lacuna in the capitalist system no longer appears, in the traditional view of enlightened liberals . . . as a kind of esthetic blemish to be put up with for the sake of its superior efficiency compared to the alternatives. *The absence of explicit moral justification and/or of specified moral obligations within the system is now seen as weakening its operating efficiency in the previously neglected problem of securing the necessary collective goods and socially functional individual norms. Yet dependence on these grows rather than lessens as economies become more interdependent and complex.* Appeal to [Alfred] Marshall's "strongest motive" of private self-interest remains in many situations the most effective instrument available for attainment of the immediate objective. *But by weakening the norms of deliberate cooperation and social restraint, reliance on this appeal as the dominant value of society produces an unstable system over time. The effectiveness of the miracle drug [the mixture of private self-interest and economic growth driven by private needs] is eventually weakened by its side effects.*[20]

Hirsch is in full agreement with all who recognize that the social morality that once served as the ethical foundation of economic individualism has long since disintegrated. But the gradual disappearance of this sixteenth- and seventeenth-century moral legacy

did not begin to undermine the legitimacy of liberal capitalism for
decades. All the justification that seemed to be needed was provided
by the social solvent of growth: "through time, all benefit."[21]

What has finally undermined this amoral justification for the
system, in Hirsch's view, are what he labels . . . "the social limits
to growth." It is their existence, he argues, that has once again
raised in its sharpest form the issue of the distribution of welfare
in liberal capitalist societies. "The internal forces released by liberal
capitalism have exerted pressure for conscious justification of the
distribution of economic rewards, a pressure that undermines the
system's drive and equipoise. That is the current crisis of the
system."[22]

The first social limit to growth concerns the workings of what
Hirsch calls the "positional economy." It relates to all aspects of
goods, services, jobs, and other social relationships that are either
scarce in some absolute or socially imposed sense, or are subject
to congestion or crowding through more extensive use. A Rem-
brandt canvas is scarce in an absolute sense; country club mem-
berships are scarce in the socially imposed sense. The latter can
of course be expanded, but expansion leads to the more extensive
use and "crowding" patterns that slowly undermine the value of
that particular positional good. What everybody can eventually
have is not a positional good. Thus, the definition of positional
competition as "competition for a higher place within some explicit
or implicit hierarchy that thereby yields gains for some only by dint
of losses for others. Positional competition, in the language of game
theory, is a zero-sum game; what winners win, losers lose."[23]

Thus, positional competition introduces an irritant into the socioeconomic system which cannot be resolved by growth. In fact,
growth simply increases the degree of positional competition by
increasing the number of players in the game. The growth of the
material economy can lift all members of society to a level from
which they would like to enter the bidding for positional gains; this
situation only increases the aggregate level of social tensions.

The second type of social limit to growth Hirsch has labeled
"reluctant collectivism." His concern is that economic growth driven by an individualistic ethos of capitalism that has lost its cultural
roots eventually undermines its own foundations. The problem lies

in the need for state intervention and correction to manage increasingly complex and interdependent economies. This trend requires a restriction on the individual calculus of gain in certain spheres as well as a set of shared moral standards among both the controllers and the controlled. Generalized standards of behavior become crucial to the functioning of the economy, but they are constantly at odds with the individualistic ethos of today's material economy.

To cite but two of many examples explored in Hirsch's penetrating analysis:

Business firms are to compete to the hilt to the point where successful competition produces its private jackpot, in the reward of monopoly; but are they thereafter to cooperate fully with the antitrust division? Individual taxpayers must not evade their legal obligations but are entitled to do anything to avoid them. The law has to be obeyed; the spirit of the law does not. [24]

What Hirsch is suggesting is that liberal capitalism, once it shed its moral foundations, created the problem of the rational individualist in a situation of social interdependence. We understand from so-called collective goods theory that the individual does best when *everyone else plays by communal rules and he or she does not.* Therefore—if for quite different reasons—Hirsch shares with Bell the view that Northern (liberal capitalist) societies must evolve a new morality if they are to overcome the present challenges facing them. As Hirsch implies, the challenges could be strong for three reasons. First, an assimilated manual working class, with few channels for individuals' self-improvement, will tend to resort to widespread and unrestrained collective bargaining, with each union attempting to "leapfrog" the gains of the other. Second, in the positional competition arena, growth simply increases levels of frustration. And third, the result is that the distributional issue in Northern societies can no longer be avoided. The Gini is out of the bottle, and only the reintroduction of a moral basis for liberal capitalism which proves acceptable to all significant segments of Northern societies can resolve the major elements in the brewing legitimacy crisis, perhaps most prevalent in Great Britain in recent years.

The three salient and overlapping themes explored in this section may seem novel to many readers and many policy makers. Their examination has remained for the most part within the groves of academe. Two reasons suggest that they deserve much broader consideration. First, when the number of analysts drawn to this set of issues represents such a wide spectrum of disciplines and ideological perspectives, there is a strong likelihood that those issues are worthy of serious consideration. One may well argue with the manner in which different aspects of the problems are linked and described, with the general interpretation of the historical trends involved, with the explicit and implicit policy prescription, and with many other facets of the analysis of these issues as currently presented. But no such caveats would suggest a dismissal of the exploration per se.

Perhaps the most interesting aspect of this set of issues is that the examination of them—from the far Right to the far Left—continues despite the fact that a crisis of democracy to some is a crisis of capitalism to others and that the cultural contradictions of capitalism to some are the political contradictions of capitalism to others. The above analysis has been presented to illuminate the issues, but not to identify with any particular interpretation. One could have raised the same questions about the future of Northern political economy issues by focusing on the Schumpeterian analysis of the "inherent tendency toward self destruction" within the capitalist system spelled out over 30 years ago or by focusing much more closely on major international economic events of the 1970s, paying little attention to the *cultural* contradictions notions of Bell.

Those who choose to de-emphasize the issue of Western values and norms, and analyze the impact of more recent international and domestic economic events of emerging problems of Northern political economy, tend to emphasize the degree to which those events have, perhaps permanently, unsettled the sociopolitical equilibrium attained by most Northern states in the years between 1950 and 1970. A crucial ingredient in that equilibrium was an annual growth dividend to organized labor that continuously increased absolute income without introducing any significant change in relative income differentials. "But, when, for a variety of reasons, these dividends of growth diminished from the early 1970s on, the internal contradictions of the entire institutional arrangement centered around the concept of aggregate welfare became increasingly obvious."[25]

Organized labor, heretofore a willing participant in the liberal domestic and international economic order, assumed a different perspective—in varying degrees—in most Northern countries. Changes in the structure of domestic labor markets unfavorable to organized labor and the virtual lack of manpower policies in most Northern countries exacerbated slowly growing labor disillusionment, thus ending the tacit domestic "social contracts" of the Bretton Woods years and beginning, in several Northern countries, a de jure search for new arrangements to combat the spiraling inflation, high unemployment, and slow growth rates of the mid-1970s.

Observers employing this general approach to examine sources of Northern domestic sociopolitical and economic conflict and to project probable trends in Northern domestic problems (e.g., inflation, unemployment, and the desire for high-technology export industries) onto the international economic scene are in their own way as concerned about a set of issues that overlap with the three themes of this section as are the others analyzed above. And the implications of their analysis for the purposes of this book are equally disturbing. For as Katzenstein notes in concluding his own study,

multiple sources of conflicts are bound to change foreign economic policies of advanced industrial states in the years ahead. The tranquility in which the politics of productivity experienced its greatest triumphs in the 1950s and 1960s is rapidly disappearing . . . foreign economic policy raises basic questions about the legitimation of power and the accumulation of plenty and thus shapes the future governance of advanced industrial societies.[26]

The second reason for examining these longer-term issues concerns the time-frame of this book. In this study we are concerned with the potential evolution of Northern societies over the coming 10 to 15 years. Even if some of the problems raised in the preceding discussion currently seem embryonic at best, they can be ignored only at the peril of misleading policy analysis and prescriptions in the final four chapters that follow. It is obvious that the three linked themes of "the crisis of democracy," "the cultural contradictions of capitalism," and "the social limits to growth"—or whatever labels we choose to substitute for them—raise a wide spectrum of issues relevant to North-South policy prescriptions for the coming decade. They also raise them for a broad range of countries. At the present moment a country like Japan would appear to be at the "least affected" end of the spectrum, while a country like Great Britain would appear to be at the "most affected" end. Surely none of the authors cited nor those uncited suggest that the problems analyzed are at the same level of salience for all Northern societies. Nor would they be likely to disagree that for most Northern countries, a return to a period of rapid and sustained economic growth might substantially ease many of the potential problems analyzed in this section.

What the majority of analysts might agree upon most readily is that Northern societies "may be near the limit of explicit social organization possible without a supporting social morality. . . . The central fact of the modern situation is the need to justify." [27] Beyond that point agreement would shatter, for the appropriate ingredients of "a supporting social morality" are presently the subject of a widespread and often bitter debate, which currently fills the pages of elite journals.

That recognition is perhaps the best note on which to complete our analysis of box 3 of our matrix, potential domestic problems for Northern societies in the 1980s. The potential seriousness of the problems raised by, and the depth of the dispute over, the constitution of appropriate values and norms—particularly economic distributional norms—suggest that no attempt at North-South policy prescription can safely ignore this arena of contention, even though much more data and analysis are needed before conclusions are drawn. For until one can more readily account for such phenomena as the variation in worker and labor union behavior between a Great Britain on the one hand and a West Germany on the other, or the variation in governmental capacities to deflate overheated economies, we certainly can come to no convincing conclusion with regard to the continued efficacy of rapid economic growth (assuming, of course, that it could once again be attained) as a social solvent over a broad range of political cultures.

V

The fourth and final box in our matrix, potential international problems, reflects the impact of the Northern domestic issues just analyzed on the international system of the 1980s. And as those potential domestic problems are a magnification of the existing problems examined in section II, so the international problems at issue here are in most cases a magnification of the problems and issues analyzed in section III. It will be remembered that in that section it was concluded that the decay of the Bretton Woods system, the urgent need for new norms of international economic behavior to support present degrees of interdependence, and existing environmental problems such as the OPEC trade surpluses and politically weak Northern governments all suggested the distinct possibility of the emergence of a neo-mercantilism that might reverse many of the liberalizing trends associated with the Bretton Woods era.

None of the analysis in the preceding section suggests a diminution of this neo-mercantilist prospect. Indeed, to the degree that the three major themes of the last section emerge as significant problems for Northern governments over the coming decade, the race between the strengthening of embryonic forms of international policy coordination and existing institutions that continue their pre-1971 operations (e.g., the GATT) on the one hand and the particularistic (and neo-mercantilistic) demands of individual Northern societies on the other hand may well be won by the latter forces in the 1980s. This evolution seems particularly likely if a rather rapid return to post–World War II growth rates, easing unemployment problems and some of the worst protectionist pressures stemming from large excess productive capacity in many major Northern industrial sectors such as steel, does not occur.

This concern can be overstated. Within the North a great many private and public interests and interest groups are deeply committed to the maintenance and extension of the patterns of liberal economic transactions developed under the Bretton Woods system. Within governments and international organizations, the fight to adapt those organizations and their new rules to the needs of changing international economic realities continues. A great deal of imaginative progress has been made in amending the rules of the IMF to cope with a world of huge OPEC surpluses and a regime of floating exchange rates. The creation of the special oil facility in 1974 and of the so-called Witteven Fund in 1977, the rapid growth in IMF member quotas, and a strengthened Compensatory Finance Facility are all indicators of the vitality of this crucial organization in a period of acute international economic stress. While less of a case can be made for the responsiveness of the GATT, the World Bank, or other institutions, each of them has weathered the international economic storms of the mid-1970s and is capable of resuming its vital activities if the necessary support for such activities from key Northern governments is forthcoming.

But that support from Northern governments, of course, remains the critical issue for the future. Will changes in power potential, particularly in the realms of economic power and vulnerability, paralyze Northern cooperative efforts when swift action is absolutely essential? Will these governments be able to work together on the problems of global inflation, unemployment, international monetary stability, and occasional commodity shortage issues?

To do so means, in effect, agreeing on an international "collective welfare function" for a group of societies that, as suggested by the previous section, are caught in a painful search for domestic consensus on the distribution of welfare. The two processes are most often destined to clash when and if each is a matter of prominence. This tendency could not be more clearly illuminated than it presently is in the field of international trade rules. How much of the OPEC trade surplus should each Northern country be willing to finance? Financing means running a trade deficit, and this issue trains all eyes on the trade surpluses and deficits of each Northern country. It also sensitizes individual industries *within* each country, as the shoe, steel, and electronics industries are currently sensitized in the United States. The pressures they apply on the United States government, directly and via Congress, are, as noted earlier, substantial and growing.

Furthermore, Northern states may jointly bow to the pressures by adding a significant touch of global "cartelization" to the Tokyo Round of trade negotiations. If eventual agreements confirm current de facto arrangements that tend to allocate specific shares of markets to national suppliers, we could be witnessing the beginning of the use of GATT for the purposes of trade restriction rather than liberalization. Much would depend upon the fine print, but the threats are clear in the demands of various national interest groups and in recent bilateral arrangements (involving the United States, Japan, and the EC) covering international trade in steel products.

One reason that these microproblems (or individual industry problems) arise is that Northern governments thus far seem totally unable to come to agreement on the macroaspects of a new international set of economic ground rules. In no area is this clearer than the monetary arena, where huge surpluses and huge deficits are all defended as being consonant with the "rules" of the new monetary system. But, as noted in section II above, there really are as yet no internationally recognized rules for that system. "Mere commitment to collaborate, without substantive specification of the basis of collaboration, represents a qualitative weakening in the basis of international action."[28]

One can summarize this set of problems among developed countries as follows. The weaker the domestic government, the less capable it is of limiting expenditures (and inflationary wage-price spirals) at home. The greater the rates of domestic inflation and unemployment, the more likely the turn to economic nationalism (or neo-mercantilism) to limit unemployment, protect specific import-impacted industries, and prevent deterioration in the balance of trade. While strong governments may *choose* not to adopt increasingly liberal international economic policies in the 1980s in order to slow the growth of interdependence and to enhance the capacity for better Northern policy coordination, weak Northern governments hardly appear able to follow the liberal internationalist path of the preceding thirty years.

Thus, the potential international economic problems likely to cause increasing friction among the Northern industrial societies in the coming decade appear quite formidable. Furthermore, if we were to add to this discussion the issue of possible Northern responses to the North-South set of problems, the potential room for friction would grow. But since this problem is covered elsewhere, all that need be added here is that there is likely to be a considerable diversity in Northern governmental views concerning appropriate Northern responses to Southern demands, a diversity that has been evident for the last several years. Until 1977 one found the United States, West Germany, and Japan grouped near the "rejectionist" end of the spectrum, with the Scandinavian countries and the Netherlands grouped much closer to the "accommodationist" end. The French, as usual, appeared accommodationist publicly while acting rejectionist behind closed Northern doors. With the advent of the Carter administration, positioning became less predictable. All that can be said with much certainty is that Southern bargaining strategies that often politicize all international economic issues will further complicate Northern policy coordination and cooperation despite the eloquent equilibrium achieved in North-South paragraphs of Northern summit communiqués.

VI

To conclude this chapter on the North in the 1980s, it seems appropriate to focus somewhat more specifically on the issue of Northern bloc cohesion as an analogue to the analysis of Southern diplomatic unity in the preceding chapter. While most of the preceding discussion has been concerned with Northern capacity to cooperate and coordinate efforts in building a new international economic system on and with the remains of the old one, the issue of diplomatic cohesiveness per se has not been addressed.

The North contains those countries that, in the post-World War II period, have cooperated to develop the institutions, set the rules, and establish the norms of behavior for the international economic system (which never formally included the Eastern countries that chose not to join). The system may have been initiated by the will of a hegemonic power, but even from the earliest years the United States was forced to entice cooperation rather than command it. United States international economic leadership was often aided by the nation's position of military leadership among the same set of Northern countries. And since it was always in a position to link the two systems, those countries most dependent upon the United States for their own national security were generally willing to accommodate its economic policies even when they disagreed with them and were in a position to challenge them (e.g., demand gold for their accumulating dollar reserves, as did France in the 1960s).

The North was never a diplomatic bloc in the sense that the South is at the present time. If an overriding security concern produced "bloc" diplomatic behavior vis-à-vis the Soviet Union in the early postwar years, the period since the late 1950s and early 1960s has seen a weakening of cohesion on security, political, and economic issues. The growing heterogeneity of goals and policy initiatives was in great part a response to the perceived diminution of the security issue and increasingly became a natural response to the growing relative strength of such countries as West Germany, Japan, and France. Sources of that strength were rapid economic growth, technological advance, and a lessening of asymmetrical interdependence vis-à-vis the United States in the slowly altering international system.

Therefore, the aggregate trends in the North are toward decentralization of leadership (thus the plaintive calls for "collective leadership" and "leadership without hegemony"); toward a more equal spread of power capabilities (with a long way to go and some countries threatening to stumble badly); and toward a differentiation of goals (or strategies to achieve similar goals). All these trends underlay the demise of the Bretton Woods system, and they pose problems for the creation of a replacement. Furthermore, the global diffusion of power potential and capabilities analyzed in Chapter 2 suggests that these trends should continue well into the future unless a major alteration in the global strategic balance annihilates the "other things being equal" condition with which this chapter began.

But these Northern tendencies, which add to the difficulties of policy coordination analyzed throughout this chapter, are of a far different nature from those in the South. Northern states are so interdependent that most of their conflict is really over the rules of cooperation. Furthermore, there is no Northern analogue to the rapid and more fundamental process of differentiation over the entire spectrum of Southern systems: economic, political, and social structural.

These differences suggest that Northern cohesion when faced with Southern demands should be far more resilient than Southern cohesion over time. The difficulties facing Northern social, economic, and political systems reviewed in this chapter, if they assume serious magnitude, may lead to growing conflict (e.g., of a neo-mercantilist nature) among Northern states. But it takes an extraordinarily optimistic Southerner to predict that such a Northern evolution would prove beneficial to the South in the aggregate. The reverse is probably closer to the truth. Two paragraphs should suffice to make the point.

First, let us assume that some major refurbishing of the neoclassical aspects of the Bretton Woods system could prove both helpful to the Southern economic growth process and acceptable as the foundation of less conflictual North-South relations.[29] This effort would require major gains in trade liberalization, a strengthening of international financial institutions, and improved developing-country access to private international capital markets. It is obvious that such an approach would require a *collective* Northern commitment. Without it, private interest groups in countries willing to accept such changes could effectively undermine them by arguing that the "burden sharing" norm among Northern countries was not being observed. The problems analyzed in this chapter suggest how effective such private interest articulation is likely to be in Northern domestic settings in the 1980s unless a collective effort at such reforms is undertaken by all major Northern governments.

In all likelihood, the possibilities for the acceptance of any more fundamental international economic reforms would be even more dependent upon collective action on the part of all significant Northern states. Since many of the more fundamental, NIEO-type reforms are perceived as philosophically alien to Northern economic values and norms, they would be even more exposed to attack from Northern private sectors (and parts of the public sector) than would reforms more consonant with neoclassical assumptions.

Thus, there is an asymmetrical aspect to the issue of Northern as opposed to Southern solidarity. Some Northerners, particularly those sharing the rejectionist and the "bring them into the system" perspectives, may look forward with anticipation to what they hope will be a steady weakening of Southern diplomatic cohesion. Conversely, it is difficult to imagine many serious scenarios in which a weakening of Northern cohesion would produce improvements in aggregate Southern bargaining prospects. To the contrary, a loss of Northern cohesion is more likely to reinforce the present stalemate on North-South issues (occasional bilateral deals helpful to the upper-tier Southern countries excepted).

This follows logically if we think of the rebuilding of a new international economic system as providing a collective good and of the need for all major Northern economic powers to share in the costs of providing that collective good. If the North cannot agree on a sharing of those costs, it is difficult to imagine the emergence of a system that operates optimally even from a narrow Northern point of view, let alone a Southern or a global point of view.

Can the North agree even upon its own version of this particular collective good in the coming decade? Beyond that, can it agree upon one that is also perceived as responsive to major Southern needs, thus lowering present levels of North-South conflict and permitting progress toward a moderate international system in the 1980s? The domestic problems facing many Northern societies in the coming decade do not provide the foundations for a very sanguine response. If domestic determinants alone were to control Northern policy making on North-South issues, the 1980s would probably be characterized by a continuation of the meaningless minuet of the middle 1970s. But given the systemic changes described in Chapter 2 and the changing elite perceptions of the North-South problem described in Chapter 3, this outcome is far from inevitable.

NOTES

[1] Marina V. N. Whitman, "Sustaining the International Economic System: Issues for U.S. Policy," *Essays in International Finance*, no. 121, June 1977, p. 4, International Finance Section, Department of Economics, Princeton University, Princeton, N.J.

[2] Ibid., p. 52.

[3] Fred Hirsch and Michael Doyle, "Politicization in the World Economy," in Hirsch, Doyle, and Edward L. Morse, *Alternatives to Monetary Disorder* (New York: McGraw-Hill for the Council on Foreign Relations/1980s Project, 1977), p. 55.

[4] Assar Lindbeck, quoted in Leon N. Lindberg et al., *Stress and Contradiction in Modern Capitalism* (Lexington, Mass: D. C. Heath & Co., 1976), p. 345.

[5]Alice Rivlin, "Income Distribution: Can Economists Help?" Richard T. Ely Lecture (delivered at the Annual Meeting of the American Economic Association, San Francisco, December 1974), p. 1.

[6]Balance-of-trade figures rather than current-account figures are used in this chapter on the assumption that in the Northern arena described in this analysis, trade figures and their politicization will become the focus of attention in the years to come. Trade figures illuminate the microproblems of industry-specific difficulties and are perceived to illuminate employment problems.

[7]While estimates vary, almost all observers now expect substantial real oil-price increases within the next 5–7 years.

[8]Whitman, op. cit., p. 1. Given the empirical evidence, one is led to believe that this sentence was written when Professor Whitman was in a particularly hortatory mood.

[9]Stanley Hoffmann, *Gulliver's Troubles, or the Setting of American Foreign Policy* (New York: McGraw-Hill, 1968), chap. 11.

[10] Hirsch and Doyle, op. cit., p. 44.

[11]Ibid., p. 44. Emphasis added.

[12]Michael Crozier, Samuel P. Huntington, and Joji Watanuki, *The Crisis of Democracy* (New York: New York University Press, 1975).

[13]Ibid., p. 8.

[14]The following discussion is based in large measure on Bell's book, *The Cultural Contradictions of Capitalism* (New York: Basic Books, 1976).It is interesting to note how many of Bell's observations are congruent with those of scholars of the Left, even though different causal linkages are ascribed in explaining the origins of the problems being analyzed.

[15]For one of the most insightful analyses of this process—which occurred during the late nineteenth- to early twentieth-century transition to "mass consumption" society—see Schumpeter, *Capitalism, Socialism and Democracy* (New York: Harper and Row, 1962), chap. 12 (Harper Torchbook edition).

[16]Ibid., pp. 21–22. Other sociologists examining the impact of industrialization on Western social structures (including the family unit) and value orientations illuminate the same general problem from a different perspective.

[17]Ibid., p. 23.

[18]Daniel Bell, *The Coming of Post-Industrial Society* (New York: Basic Books, 1973), p. 425. Emphasis added. Since all recent studies of income distribution within Northern societies confirm that any movement toward economic "equality of result" remains glacial, one must assume that this particular aspect of the equality battle (1) has been lost; (2) is just beginning; or (3) is projected for the near future.

[19]Fred Hirsch, *Social Limits to Growth* (Cambridge: Harvard University Press, 1976).

[20]Ibid., pp. 157–158. Emphasis added.

[21]Ibid., p. 175.

[22]Ibid., p. 177.

[23]Ibid., p. 52.

[24]Ibid., p. 131.

[25]Peter J. Katzenstein, "Conclusion: Domestic Structures and Strategies of Foreign Economic Policy," *International Organization*, vol. 31, no. 4, Autumn 1977, pp. 918–919.

[26]Ibid., p. 920.

[27]Hirsch, op. cit., p. 190.

[28]Hirsch and Doyle, op. cit., p. 44.

[29] This is the approach suggested by Albert Fishlow. See Albert Fishlow, "A New International Economic Order: What Kind?" in Fishlow et al., *Rich and Poor Nations in the World Economy* (New York: McGraw-Hill for the Council on Foreign Relations/1980s Project, 1978), pp. 9–83.

Part IV
THREE MODAL APPROACHES TO NORTH-SOUTH RELATIONS IN THE 1980s

Introduction

In discussing North-South strategies and policies designed to produce a moderate international system in the coming decade, one is faced with a limitless range of options. A great many policies have been proposed which find some support in both North and South. However, the probabilities for most of these prescriptions are so low that they need not concern us here. The chapters of Part IV focus upon three broad strategies and sets of policies that seem to be the most likely to emerge in one form or another in the 1980s, based on the analysis in Parts II and III of this study. They encompass the strategies of "graduation," "global reform," and "basic human needs."

The range of policies that can be included under each of the three basic elements is potentially quite broad. In each instance one end of the spectrum can be considered "minimalist" in the changes it is willing to consider; the opposite, "maximalist" end significantly expands both the number of policy options to be considered and the *degree* of reform implicit in each option. As the three modal approaches are analyzed, no attempt is made to detail policy packages with a great deal of specificity. Rather an attempt is made to indicate the range of policies that might fit together coherently within each grouping and then to analyze what contribution each set might make to North-South relations in the 1980s. Given the time frame of this study and the difficulties of projection along any single parameter of the problem we are considering, specificity seems far less relevant or helpful to further analysis and policy making than does a clearer understanding concerning what can and might be accomplished within these three general approaches. For the most crucial contribution to more constructive North-South relations in the 1980s will be to alter the *process* rather than the specifics of North-South diplomatic interaction. The North-South diplomatic agenda of the 1970s was perceived as one replete with zero-sum issues; what one side "won" the other side was perceived to have "lost." The fundamental need for the 1980s is to focus the agenda on positive-sum issues of importance to all parties in which both sides can perceive gains from the diplomatic process.

A second point worth emphasis is that what gives coherence to each of these three approaches is the observer's perspective on international and domestic political and economic processes as they relate to the North-South conflict. As noted in Part II, perspectives themselves differ radically. Therefore, two observers with exactly the same normative goals for North-South relations in the 1980s may prescribe very different sets of policies for many reasons. They may disagree on how international political constraints, such as East-West relations and the global strategic balance, will affect any set of North-South policies. They may have differing judgments concerning elite group behavior, North and South, which would affect the potential success or failure of certain policies. They may disagree fundamentally on issues of development economics and propose different policies when each is after the identical end product: more rapid economic development in the South. For these reasons and countless others, some analytical and some normative, policy prescription in this area does and will continue to differentiate even those analysts and policy makers who share the same goals.

A third observation concerns the relationship among the three aggregate approaches examined in Part IV. These approaches are not mutually exclusive. Some observers might wish to adopt the first strategy analyzed, the graduation scenario, then slowly combine it with the second. Others might wish to combine the second and the third strategies—global reform and basic human needs—from the outset, linking the two in negotiations to assure that progress was made in both general areas concurrently. Others might prefer to remain within the general contours of one approach alone.

The occasionally overlapping nature of the approaches underlines the general point concerning the nonexclusiveness of these three heuristic policy sets. Perhaps the reader will note this most clearly in comparing the maximalist end of the graduation approach analyzed in Chapter 6 with the minimalist end of the global reform approach presented in Chapter 7. Despite problems of overlap and nonexclusivity, the general approach in Part IV has been chosen in the belief that the major policy emphases and normative orientation of each of the three approaches is distinct enough to merit separate analysis.

Finally, to return to our point of departure, the three have been chosen because they do seem to cover the range of the probable policy combinations for the coming 10 to 15 years in North-South relations. Within this constraint an attempt is made to analyze the central empirical issues and normative dilemmas raised by policy choice.

In limiting the range to the probable, two of the major perspectives on North-South relations discussed in Chapter 3 have been dropped as specific North-South strategy foci: the Southern self-reliance perspective and the Northern rejectionist perspective. Neither is given major and discrete consideration, on the straightforward assumption that the necessary degree of support to make either perspective a serious contender for prominence in Northern or Southern thinking and action in the coming decade simply will not develop.[1] As noted in Chapter 3, it seems highly unlikely that Southern self-reliance will be adopted by many developing-country governing elites when the concept is defined in terms of breaking economic linkages to the Northern-dominated global economy. To the extent that the perspective is defined in a far less ambitious manner (e.g., more inter-LDC trade, aid, technology transfer, etc.), self-reliance would seem to represent an attempt to alter some global economic *trends* rather than to introduce any abrupt reversals. And in this less ambitious sense self-reliance can be built into any of the three major policy foci presented in Part IV.[2] Finally, self-reliance as a Southern *bargaining strategy* will continue to influence North-South diplomacy despite the growing impediments analyzed in Chapter 4.

Similar reasoning accounts for the lack of a major examination of the Northern rejectionist perspective as a policy focus warranting close scrutiny. First, the initial failure of the policies emanating from this perspective led to changing Northern attitudes on how to cope with the conflicts inherent in North-South relations. Several Northern countries—the United States, West Germany, and Japan in particular—continue to harbor large numbers of "closet rejectionists." But most of them have publicly adopted a less confrontationist pose while others are seriously exploring the "bring them into the system" perspective for ways to ease North-South tensions with a minimum of change.

Second, the majority of Northern governments no longer seem willing to be publicly associated with such a policy perspective. And in the changing international system it is extremely doubtful that even two or three of the most powerful Northern states could impose upon the majority a North-South strategy overtly rooted in such a perspective.

Finally, and linked to the preceding point, the perceived growth (in both numbers and importance) of global agenda problems such as nuclear proliferation and population growth underscores Northern concerns about continued high-level tensions with the South. This perception seems destined to spread over the coming decade, undermining support for the rejectionist perspective.[3]

NOTES

[1]Both perspectives will still retain enough support to influence the shaping of North-South policy packages, marginally at the very least, as the analysis in the next three chapters suggests.

[2]The decision not to devote more direct attention to the Southern self-reliance approach was strongly influenced by the effort to explore this issue by Carlos Díaz-Alejandro in his essay, "Delinking North and South: Unshackled or Un-

hinged," in Albert Fishlow et al., *Rich and Poor Nations in the World Economy* (New York: McGraw-Hill for the Council on Foreign Relations/1980s Project, 1978), pp. 85–162.

[3]Again, to avoid injustice to the presentation of the rejectionist perspective, it should be noted that at least some of those sharing it believe that appropriate responses to global agenda problems cannot be developed unless and until the "Southern bloc" is significantly loosened. The point being made here is simply that, "rightly" or "wrongly," concern with global agenda issues is much more likely to *reduce* than to *enhance* support for the rejectionist perspective.

Chapter 6
The Graduation Scenario: Integrating Developing Countries into the World Economy

I

Perhaps the most predictable aspect of North-South relations in the coming decade is that a major ingredient of any aggregate Northern strategy to ease present degrees of North-South tension and overcome the present stalemate system will be the adoption of a range of policies that attempt to integrate the upper-tier developing countries into the present international system. Any doubts that serious Northern efforts would be made to achieve this objective should have been dispelled with the September 1977 announcement that President Carter planned to visit Venezuela, Brazil, Nigeria, India, Iran, and Saudi Arabia during the second foreign trip of his presidency. Before the strategy is analyzed and evaluated, a few definitional ambiguities should be removed.

Within Northern government circles, an upper-tier developing country is thought of as one that has or soon will have some form of potential power. That potential power can take many forms in the present international system. It can be embodied in (1) rapidly growing industrial strength (Brazil, Mexico), (2) emerging financial importance (Saudi Arabia), (3) actual or potential nuclear power with significant regional military potential (India, Brazil), or (4) natural resource abundance (Nigeria). Other elements (e.g., strategic geopolitical placement) sometimes qualify a country; but for the most part the upper-tier label is reserved for the four categories of states noted above.

What they all have in common is a potential (or actual) capacity to interfere with the achievement of Northern-country domestic and foreign policy goals. Most Northern states will tend to focus attention on those Southern countries that can undermine their economic security. The more global the interests of a Northern state, the more its attention will focus on a broader set of objectives and Southern countries in conceptualizing an upper-tier strategy for North-South relations.

The concepts of graduation and integration imply a reciprocal bargain, tacit as it may remain. The upper-tier countries will be given the rewards and privileges of full membership in the Northern club. They will be made members of the OECD; their voting power will be increased in international institutions; they will become the objects of much greater Northern consultation in both bilateral and multilateral forms. In return, these new members will be expected to share increasingly in the values, goals, and behavioral norms of the status quo powers of the North. Iran will guard its northern marches against Soviet encroachment. Saudi Arabia will help to underwrite the "system-maintenance" costs of international monetary arrangements. Brazil will attempt to influence the course of economic development and political evolution in South America in directions congruent with the objectives of the countries of the North.

Finally, a word of clarification about the phrase "the present international system." When economists discuss the graduation scenario, they generally have a quite specific system in mind: the neoclassical Bretton Woods model with the amendments that have been accepted since 1971. It is essentially the liberal system of the GATT and the IMF, a system in which goods and capital move with a great deal of freedom to maximize global welfare. When capital and technology movements are embodied in the form of the multinational corporation, certain restrictions may be added, but only insofar as those restrictions are thought to assist in the process of global welfare maximization.

The phrase "the international system" loses a good deal of its conceptual clarity as it is applied beyond the realm of economics. In security terms ambiguities emerge. In the strategic balance sense, of course, graduation implies Southern affiliation with the West whenever security issues of an East-West nature arise. But the "system norm" is much less clear, for example, when the security issue concerns such items as nuclear proliferation and conventional arms buildups. Here the reciprocity norm implied by graduation is somewhat clouded. The present Northern norm may have become nonproliferation, but that norm was one all Northern countries were able to accept or reject of their own free will (though not without the presence of strong United States pressures) in the past. Does a new club member have the same right of initial choice, or must it adopt what has slowly become acceptable Northern behavior over the course of several decades? Can Brazil graduate and become a nuclear power at the same time?

Does the system dictate domestic norms of behavior with regard to political and human rights? As noted in Chapter 4, most Southern societies are likely to be governed by military/authoritarian regimes for much of the 1980s. If Franco's Spain could not achieve Northern club membership, can the Shah's Iran or Geisel's Brazil or Obasanjo's Nigeria? If human rights policies become a litmus test of club membership, what becomes of the graduation scenario? And if they do not, what becomes of the "milieu goal" of human rights?

It seems obvious that if the international system is quite narrowly defined—for example, to include no more than the economic system and the East-West aspects of the military security system—the rules of reciprocity in the graduation exercise are fairly clear. But as attempts are made to broaden the definition of the system to include other important Northern foreign policy objectives, rules of reciprocity become increasingly difficult to delineate.

Furthermore, little discussion is needed to illuminate the potential normative trade-offs that will constantly accompany the attempt to implement the graduation scenario. All one need do is to reexamine the matrix initially presented in Chapter 1. How would the scenario perform when measured against the nine potential moderate-order goals highlighted by that matrix? At first glance, not very well. It might score positively at the state-centric, welfare level where welfare was defined in neoclassical terms and distributional issues were not raised. It would also score fairly well if the scenario worked at the state-centric security level for Northern states and new Southern members of the club. But the normative trade-offs are apparent from the likely scores in the other boxes. Unless there is far more North-South agreement on the content of security, welfare, and autonomy as these concepts are applied to groups and individuals in domestic society as well as on those three concepts when applied to nongraduate states, the strategy in and by itself may entail a very high normative cost-benefit ratio. This issue will be considered from many differing perspectives in the following sections of this chapter.

Figure 6-1

	SECURITY	WELFARE	AUTONOMY/IDENTITY
Nation-states			
Groups (ethnic, communal, religious)			
Individuals			

II

It has already been noted that each of the three basic ingredients of North-South strategies for the 1980s discussed in this and the following two chapters should be conceptualized as potentially covering a broad spectrum of policies. This is certainly true of the graduation scenario. Before any empirical and normative generalizations are made about the approach, the breadth of the policy spectrum implicit in it should be underlined.

In section I the discussion of definitional issues tended to portray the approach at the narrow end of the spectrum, leaving the reader with the impression that the strategy would focus exclusively on improving relations between the North and those LDCs that are or shortly will be in a position to cause systemic problems, however defined, and to seriously hinder the achievement of Northern-country domestic and foreign policy goals. While this does remain the sine qua non of the strategy, at the broader end of the spectrum it can include many policies that are at least incrementally responsive to other concerns of almost all Southern countries.

The graduation scenario need not limit itself to concern with co-opting Brazil, Mexico, and Saudi Arabia into the system. When conceptualized as *a longer-term policy of integrating all Southern countries* into the global economic system rather than *a shorter-term policy of co-opting the upper-tier LDCs*, it can be thought of as quite consonant with continuing incremental reforms, particularly in the international economic and institutional arenas. A few examples of the types of reforms most often associated with this general focus should help to underscore the broader potential of the strategy.

In the field of trade policy, advocates of the graduation scenario are often supporters of efforts to continue with steady Northern trade liberalization in the tradition of United States policy since the mid-1930s. In the present Tokyo Round of negotiations in Geneva, they would press for formulas that grant more significant multilateral trade-liberalization benefits to the developing countries, often without significant demands for reciprocity on the part of the less developed countries. Some would also seek to broaden the coverage of the present Generalized System of Preferences (GSP) already extended to the developing countries.

In the highly controversial area of commodity trade policy, many supporters of the graduation scenario are less willing to respond affirmatively to LDC requests, but there is an element of flexibility in their approach. They insist that the discussion of and possible negotiation on international commodity schemes be held on a commodity-by-commodity basis, reserving judgment on whether or not to become a party to each scheme until the results of the negotiation are clear. Regarding the establishment of a common fund to finance commodity buffer stocks, this strategy would remain close to the traditional Northern position of individual commodity buffer stock funding, but might allow a pooling of this funding if such a proposal were deemed to meet the criteria of economic feasibility. Finally, the strategy would be one that continued to view the purpose of commodity schemes to be the stabilization of commodity prices around long-term market trends, and not, as the developing countries demand, the raising and/or indexing of commodity prices.

The graduation strategy conceived broadly has considerable room for increased flows of economic assistance for development. Many Northern countries whose strategies now exhibit a close fit with the graduation scenario are on record as agreeing that more Northern Official Development Assistance is needed and warranted. Several Northern countries presently speak of doubling aid flows by 1980–1981, implying increasing amounts when measured as a percentage of total GNP.

Further, the scenario is quite consonant with a strengthening of such institutions as the IMF and the World Bank in ways that can be of incremental assistance to the South. By the late 1970s graduation scenario enthusiasts were considering significant increases in IMF quotas, which would give developing countries access to larger amounts of international reserves. They were also active in the support of increasing the capital base of the World Bank in order to allow the IBRD to continue raising its real rate of lending to the South each year.

Beyond these incremental changes, however, the graduation strategy enthusiasts are generally skeptical of further reforms. They oppose any generalized debt-relief proposals introduced by the developing countries, believing that such an action would undermine further activity of the international capital markets in lending to developing countries in the future. They also doubt that a step of this magnitude is needed. Their view is that "careful" domestic debt management by each developing country can avoid any generalized debt problem and limit the need for debt relief to a very few developing countries. In these latter instances, they suggest the use of traditional lender institutions (e.g., the "Paris Club") and norms of behavior. In sum, this scenario would not include much more than a defense of present international economic policies and mechanisms beyond the incremental changes noted above. It would continue to resist demands for a code of conduct for multinational firms along the lines proposed by most developing countries; it would resist any movement toward global planning of the allocation of international production (as called for in the Southern Lima Declaration of 1975); it would resist codes on technology transfer which interfered with present interpretations of property rights, although it would continue to support developing-country research institutions working to identify and develop "appropriate technology" for LDC development.

In characterizing the graduation strategy, therefore, perhaps the following three points are the most important:

1. Its *major* concern—and policy emphasis—is devoted to the process of integrating the upper-tier developing countries as defined above into the international system. This implies that these countries receive *top priority* in several senses: institutional reforms to increase their status, economic policies to meet their further development needs, increased bilateral contact and consultation, and (most probably, judging from existing evidence) a willingness to limit criticism of them on other grounds (e.g., political and human rights issues and weapons-procurement policies, among others). It is hoped that the graduates will reciprocate by accepting the norms that accompany club membership.

2. The strategy nevertheless contains enough flexibility to accept some limited incremental changes that respond to the needs of nongraduating developing countries. The most obvious areas for such flexibility are foreign aid, trade, and the strengthening of international financial institutions that can in turn assist the development process. If this flexibility is not used for these broader purposes, the graduation scenario in effect becomes simply a Northern strategy of co-optation of a very few of the most powerful developing countries.

3. What clearly distinguishes the graduation scenario from the other two basic elements in North-South policy, to be analyzed in Chapters 7 and 8, is its system-maintenance viewpoint. This fundamental orientation—conscious or subconscious—is reflected in its demonstrated belief that incremental changes in a limited number of fields are enough to ease North-South tensions and to manage the problems the international system of the 1980s is likely to face. The belief is demonstrated in both

the policies graduation enthusiasts propose and those they oppose.

The characterization of this strategy as one built on a system-maintenance orientation carries no pejorative connotation. As the reasons for its support are analyzed below, it will become clear that any such connotation would be inappropriate. The normative and empirical judgments that come together to support this particular aggregate approach to North-South relations are not of a lower (or higher) order of morality or perceptivity than those that produce support for the other major approaches. They simply reflect different normative orderings, empirical judgments, and estimates of what problems will be most prominent in the coming decade.

III

Support for the graduation scenario as a fundamental ingredient in North-South policy prescription for the coming decade derives from economic, political, and security perspectives. It also derives from a combination of positive and normative analysis. This section will examine the bases for this support; the following section will present a critique of the graduation scenario as a basic guideline for policy prescription.

The Economic Perspective

In the economic arena, there are four prominent lines of positive and normative thinking in the North which suggest that the graduation scenario will be a major North-South policy reference point in the coming decade. In summary form, they run as follows:

1. The present international economic system is at best a minor source of the economic problems facing developing countries. Incremental reforms can resolve whatever problems the international economic system creates for the development process.
2. Economic development is an overwhelmingly domestic challenge, and developmental success depends upon domestic political decisions to implement economic policies most appropriate to the resource base of each developing country. Countries that develop strong sociopolitical and human re-

source infrastructures can achieve rapid economic growth. Those that do not are unlikely to benefit more than marginally from the receipt of major foreign assistance and international economic reform, whether in the form of "free" Northern aid flows or greater developing-country access to Northern commodity markets, technology, and international credit mechanisms.

3. When closely analyzed, many of the specific developing-country proposals that have dominated the North-South dialogue over the past decade are not even in the aggregate long-term interests of most Southern countries. Therefore a North-South strategy and set of policies that was more forthcoming on the part of the North could very quickly prove to be counterproductive to Southern economic development and consequently to North-South relations.

4. The present international economic system can be destabilized if several emergent Southern powers do not cooperate with the North in its management by accepting the "duties" of club membership. For the system to operate optimally, countries such as Saudi Arabia, Iran, Brazil, and Mexico must become supporters of the norms of behavior that allow the system to function as it should. Greater status, befitting their growing economic power, should be conferred upon these states in order to assure their integration into the system and their acceptance of its requisite rules of behavior.

The intensity with which these judgments are currently held within Northern policy-making circles assures their continuing influence on North-South policy space in the 1980s. Furthermore, at least some of those Southern countries chosen for graduation will most probably attend the commencement exercises understanding and accepting the reciprocity implicit in the ceremony, further strengthening support for the policy prescriptions that flow from this focus on North-South problems.

Each of the four major economic arguments listed above is defensible at the proper level of generalization. Regarding the first point—that the present international system is at worst a minor source of the economic problems facing developing countries—the following indirect evidence is generally offered. During the 1960s the aggregate growth rate of the developing countries was well over 5 percent per year. This rate was thus higher than the First Development Decade target, one chosen as the maximum feasible in light of historical experience. This rate increased during the late 1960s and early 1970s. Moreover, a number of Southern countries have developed so successfully that they are often compared with Japan in the 1950s. The comparison is meant to suggest that these countries have reached that point in the development process where they are ready to utilize fully the potential role of comparative advantage and international markets in order to grow at even more rapid rates than those of the past decade. (For over 20 years Japan grew at a real rate of better than 10 percent per year.) Thus, for developing countries that are able to build strong sociopolitical institutions and implement appropriate economic policies, the international economic system is at the very least congenial to rapid economic growth.

To the extent that the international economic system does contain impediments to LDC growth, it is assumed that continuing marginal changes can remove these obstacles. For example, the monopoly or oligopoly power of multinational corporations vis-à-vis the developing countries is believed to be diminishing because of the growth in competition among multinational corporations (MNCs) from many Northern countries. The bargaining power of developing countries is thereby strengthened, improving their terms of access to Northern technology, capital, and domestic markets. Thus many of the worst market imperfections that the MNCs once represented are viewed as rapidly diminishing, particularly as knowledge of their operations and their technologies spreads among the developing countries.

Another weakness of the system is lessened as the growth of the Eurodollar market increases developing-country access to an international capital market, a market free from the political pressures that, in the past, have been associated with national capital markets. Further, easier LDC access to larger amounts of foreign exchange through the IMF's Compensatory Finance Facility has markedly increased the capacity of developing countries to finance short-term foreign-exchange shortfalls that the global economy may unexpectedly inflict upon them. Many other incremental improvements of the system from the perspective of developing-country needs could be cited, several dealing with the longer-term strengthening of the IMF and the World Bank in matters affecting their capacity to assist the development process. The conclusion drawn from all this evidence is that major reforms of the existing international economic system are not needed. Old minor problems are being removed, and new ones are being acted upon as they arise.[1] From this reading of the evidence, an accommodating Northern response to more fundamental NIEO economic demands would be of little assistance to the process of economic development at best and positively harmful at worst.

This point of view is not weakened when the issue of Southern domestic income distribution and potential causal linkages to the international economic system are raised. Prominent economists have hypothesized for years that the choice of domestic development policies is the most crucial determinant in the distributional effects of economic growth within developing countries and have argued that choice generally remains in the hands of Southern governing elites.[2] While the evidence remains inconclusive, it is clear that a compelling causal linkage between the international economic system and the domestic inequity issue in many developing countries has yet to be demonstrated.

The second major economic argument supporting the graduation scenario and its implicit policy prescriptions is that success or failure in fomenting economic development is, to an overwhelming degree, determined by domestic rather than international policies. This viewpoint is very widely accepted by Northern policy makers and by the great majority of non-Marxist Northern economists. Those holding this viewpoint would not deny that greater access to foreign exchange at certain critical stages might ease potential development bottlenecks, and they would agree that more aid, export opportunities, and access to international capital markets could therefore assist growth at various stages of the development process. However, they would argue that there is a great deal of substitutability between international and domestic measures to overcome these "development bottlenecks." To cite but one example, LDC-manufactured exports grew at over 15 percent per year in the late 1960s and early 1970s and by 1973 accounted for 40 percent of all developing-country nonoil exports. The conclusion drawn is that the international economic system was highly congenial to appropriate domestic development policies and that the "scarce-foreign-exchange" problem could be overcome through domestic efforts without the assistance of constantly growing international aid transfers. Interpreted more broadly, the evidence is read to suggest that developing countries with capacity to design and implement appropriate development strategies can overcome any obstacles to growth. Without that capacity, no amount of international economic reform can produce development—if what is meant by development is the institutionalization of the growth process itself.

The third economic argument favoring the graduation scenario asserts that the current set of developing-country reform proposals—including many that are given prominence in the NIEO list—is replete with analytical flaws and contradictions and by no means represents effective approaches to assisting development. The "integrated commodity scheme" and a common fund to finance buffer stocks necessary to the operation of that scheme, given absolute priority by the Group of 77, faces enormously difficult technical problems, will almost surely prove unacceptable to the North if it is constituted as a price-raising rather than price-stabilizing mechanism, and is likely to have very perverse distributional effects within the South itself. Many of the largest potential gainers would be found among the richer LDCs; some of the net losers would be found among the poorest of the developing countries.

Likewise, the proposed debt moratorium is viewed as a serious error for the development process. Such a move would weaken the growing capacity of developing countries to borrow funds in private international capital markets at the very time that this added source of development funding is becoming increasingly available to them with the fewest strings attached. Many Southern states agree with this line of argumentation, thus explaining the split among the developing countries on this issue at the Colombo summit meeting of the Non-Aligned Countries in the summer of 1976 and at the joint IBRD/IMF meeting in Manila later that year.

Additionally, it is argued that Southern demands for nonreciprocity and broader generalized preferences in trade negotiations with the North have perverse effects on Southern economic development. The granting of such demands would allow many developing countries the unaffordable luxury of postponing necessary domestic reforms that would make their products competitive in world markets without artificial discrimination in their favor—a policy that could be undermined quite easily by domestic protectionist pressures within the North.[3] While this list, too, could be greatly lengthened, it is sufficient to indicate the deep skepticism with which Northern policy makers and most Northern economists view the NIEO-type proposals as potential contributors to the development process.

In this connection it is interesting to note that one highly respected Northern economist and sometime government official whose deep sympathies with Southern development problems are unquestionable dismisses many of the NIEO proposals in his own reading of Southern wants and needs. Albert Fishlow, in a 1977 essay, suggested that what most developing countries are really interested in are (1) greater assured access to Northern markets (traditional trade liberalization), (2) greater access to Northern capital markets (acceptance of the international capital market structure if they can gain better access to it), and (3) a modified system of technology transfer that would give the South access to Northern technology at lower cost.[4] Thus Fishlow suggests that moderate reforms of the present system, stripped of much NIEO rhetoric and many of its demands, are what the South is really seeking and what the North should be willing to concede, because it is optimal for global welfare as well as supportive of LDC development.

Finally, the fourth major line of economic argumentation concerns the need to "bring selected 'newcomers' into the inner circles of international decision making."[5] As noted, this argument is based on a systemic necessity: If those developing countries that now have the power to disrupt the effective operation of the economic system are not given seats at the table and do not accept the system-supporting responsibilities that are the reciprocal of increased status and voice, real damage can be inflicted on all states, North and South.

As noted in Chapter 5, the international economic system is in a period of precarious passage, even if analysts are in disagreement over its next port of call. Oil price and production policies will be a major determinant of the health of the global economy over the coming decade. Saudi Arabia will soon hold more international monetary reserves than any other country in the world. Without Saudi cooperation, the passage could prove disastrous; ergo the first drumrolls of the graduation processional. Brazil and Mexico have private international debts that exceed those of almost all other Southern countries combined; their present levels of development make them leading Southern exporters of manufactured products; their domestic markets make them major targets of Northern private-sector economic opportunity. Thus the second bars of the processional. Increased membership on the board of directors is a small price to pay if there is a strong conviction that the system thus being maintained is one that fully merits the effort, in terms of both positive and normative analysis. And as all the preceding economic arguments suggest, supporters of the graduation scenario have no doubt that the effort is merited in the present instance.

The Political Perspective

The political support for this approach to North-South policy prescription for the 1980s rests upon three major lines of argument, not all necessarily held by each proponent of this general persuasion:

1. This is the most realistic starting point for North-South policy prescription in the 1980s. Therefore it would be imprudent to deviate too far from the parameters it suggests whether or not one is normatively comfortable with those implicit limitations.
2. For the North to attempt greater degrees of accommodation is simply to invite escalating Southern demands. The result would be to increase present levels of tension, not reduce them.
3. The graduation scenario has a high probability of success. That very success would weaken the Southern bloc as a united international diplomatic actor and in doing so promote greater opportunities to (a) diminish the North-South confrontation and (b) resume less politicized multilateral efforts to deal with problems emerging on the global agenda.

The argument that the graduation scenario is the most realistic starting point in policy prescription for North-South relations in the coming decade is supported by a majority of Northern policy makers, analysts, and observers. Some embrace the argument and its policy implications warmly, others reluctantly. The latter group joins the former in support of the approach because both share certain fundamental assumptions about the dynamics of world politics. While emphasizing different constraints on state behavior in international relations, they agree generally on the following line of analysis. [6]

Other things being equal, states will seek to maximize their security/status/power positions in the international system. Of course this "first cut" at explaining state behavior is an oversimplification, but particularly with regard to North-South relations it still reveals more than any other single statement about the ultimate motivations underlying state behavior in world politics. Even if the pattern of behavior suggested by this characterization is weakening considerably when it is applied to Northern interstate relations, the same cannot be said when it is applied to North-South or intra-Southern state interaction. [7] The implicit model may no longer be adequate to predict with much accuracy the policies of industrialized states whose governments, as noted in Chapter 5, are increasingly perplexed in and consumed by the need to satisfy the welfare desires of their citizens and therefore are increasingly forced into modes of interstate coordination and cooperation in their efforts to satisfy those desires. Among these states, it can be and increasingly is being argued, conflict is over modes of cooperation.

For two reasons, however, the constraints slowly undermining the predictive power of the old model do not appear to be growing with anywhere near the same rapidity in the sphere of North-South relations. The first reason concerns the present stage of evolution of Southern states. Most developing countries have yet to taste the sweet (and bitter) fruits of "power, glory, and idea." Never (in recent centuries) having possessed international power and status— indeed, most having suffered the humiliation of subordination to Western civilization—their governments retain many of the goals of pre–welfare state Western nations. Obviously part of the explanation lies in the fact that at their present levels of economic and sociopolitical development, many of these Southern governments face neither the identical types nor degrees of domestic pressures for welfare performance currently being experienced in the North. Furthermore, they perceive a series of foreign and domestic policy alternatives (e.g., territorial expansion, the spread of regional influence, roles in the North-South conflict, authoritarian experiments in governance and development) that may be successfully substituted for improved domestic welfare performance. For these and many other reasons, Southern state behavior is unlikely to be limited by the same constraints now influencing Northern governments.

The second reason the old model is still viewed by many as quite relevant to North-South relations is that the types and degrees of interdependence that affect intra-Northern state relations do not yet constrain North-South interstate behavior. Without reviewing the entire "threat from the Third World" debate, it can simply be noted that the threat was always overstated. The argument was built upon a series of linkages (e.g., OPEC money supporting other Third World raw material cartels) that have proven to be far too weak to give much substance to the threat. While trends in North-South transactions—trade, finance, direct investment, etc.—are moving toward increased interdependence, the aggregate relationship is still highly asymmetrical. The North is simply not yet perceived as being vulnerable to the economic actions of Southern states. Oil is the exception; growing economic powers such as Brazil and Mexico are the exception. But they also represent the very explicit targets of the graduation set of policy prescriptions. Therefore, barring Southern refusals to attend the graduation exercise, whatever there was that constituted the threat from the South at this level of analysis will vanish, and North-South relations are unlikely to be constrained by the same interdependence relationships that influence intra-Northern state behavior.[8]

This type of logic has led most Northern policy makers and analysts to hold to the old model of interstate relations in thinking about North-South issues. Add one novel constraint, the growing unwillingness on the part of Northern states to use military force in North-South conflicts, and the graduation scenario becomes a most plausible guideline for prudent statecraft. If North-South relations are now characterized by too little interdependence to demand a mutual search for more cooperative modes of interaction, but the use of overt force by the North in North-South conflicts is increasingly viewed as illegitimate, Northern co-optation of those Southern states potentially capable of inflicting damage on the Northern-dominated system almost seems too obvious a policy prescription to necessitate lengthy and careful scrutiny. To attempt less would risk easily avoidable system damage on the part of the Saudi Arabias and the Brazils of the South; to attempt more would invite increased conflict because of the very novelty and consequent misperceptions that a more accommodating effort might produce.

The latter point is the essential ingredient of the second major political argument supporting the graduation scenario. Given the traditional norms of statecraft, major Northern attempts to accommodate Southern demands are viewed as more likely to result in their continued escalation than in diplomatic détente. Whether or not this judgment is accepted, it is certainly the case that the NIEO demands go well beyond the realm of economics; therefore, political analysis and judgment is a crucial ingredient in any attempt to prescribe appropriate North-South policy guidelines. The simplest possible hypothetical example of the potential concern in this area might run as follows:

1. Northern government A finally achieves domestic and intra-Northern support for what is perceived in the North to be a major move toward North-South accommodation. This is accomplished against all the background problems likely to be faced by any Northern government in the 1980s, as outlined in the preceding chapter.
2. The Southern reaction to the Northern accommodation is to escalate demands, international organizational rhetoric, and resulting tensions.
3. Northern legislatures respond with a series of retaliatory amendments to all authorization and appropriation requests affecting foreign assistance, trade policy legislation, or other policy proposals affecting North-South economic relations.
4. Under resulting backlash pressures, Northern executive

branches of government reconsider any further attempts at accommodation.

Simplistic as the scenario may seem to some, to others of all normative persuasions it appears to merit a distressingly high degree of probability (except, perhaps, for step 1). Indeed, with the exception of step 1, it is a pattern of North-South interaction quite congruent with the probing for weakness and division characteristic of the 1970s stalemate system in North-South relations.

A final prominent political argument is that the graduation scenario itself has a high probability of success. At the narrow co-optation level, for reasons of security, status, economic welfare, or political stability, most of the upper-tier Southern states can be expected to offer de facto support for system maintenance if they are given a bigger personal stake in the system's continued operation. At the broader integration level, success may be achieved by hastening the incremental reforms of most importance to the remaining developing countries. Certainly, the incremental reform process might be accelerated if the new members of the club, desiring to retain their *bona fides* with the rest of the South, pressed for reform from their new positions as club members. Finally, the scenario might succeed in lessening the degree of confrontation and politicization presently characterizing North-South discussions of substantive problems.

Those who are inclined to accept these political arguments recognize that there is no guarantee of success in attempts to integrate upper-tier Southern countries, accelerate the process of incremental reforms, or increase the capacity for constructive multilateral diplomacy. They simply view the strategy and resultant policy prescriptions as deserving of priority for the following reasons:

1. The high probability they attach to the capacity to achieve the co-optation of the upper-tier Southern countries
2. The crucial nature of this achievement

If it is successful, then economic system maintenance is assured— at least for some years to come—whatever the response of the rest of the South. Further incremental reforms and depoliticized international institutions might help to produce a constructive change in North-South relations, but they are in fact second-order considerations. If the remainder of the South continues united and "confrontationist," it would also be very much weaker and represents no short-term threat. If the remaining unity dissolves, so much the better for "global issue" negotiations based on straightforward "national self-interest" rather than "artificial blocs."

The Security Perspective

As noted earlier, the graduation scenario is most often invoked by those who are concerned with international economic system maintenance. Nevertheless, the same modes of thought can be and are applied to international security issues. One substantial problem for the scenario is the potential incongruity between policy prescriptions that flow from the previously analyzed economic and political perspectives and those flowing from the security perspective. Will the economic and security perspectives produce complementary policy prescriptions for Saudi Arabia? The answer will depend upon how one interprets Northern (perhaps almost exclusively United States) security interests in the Arab-Israeli conflict. From the economic security perspective the integration of Saudi Arabia is a sine qua non for system maintenance; from a military security perspective the issue becomes much more difficult to assess.[9] At stake is not only the security of Israel but also the perception of the value of United States international commitments. At the very least, this is the issue that will be perceived by many.

The uncertain implications of the graduation scenario for United States–Saudi relations (or United States–Brazilian relations) are only the most obvious of potential conflicts that arise when the security dimension of this general policy prescription is analyzed. Northern (again, particularly United States) security interests are often equated with the safety of sea-lanes. This perspective suggests the need to deal very cautiously and circumspectly with the present evolution of Northern relations with South Africa. At the very least, short-run conflicts between economic and military security perspectives are therefore likely to arise; the former will tend, for example, to focus heavily on the co-optation of Nigeria; the latter will focus on maintaining as amicable a set of diplomatic relations with South Africa as possible in a difficult decade. What happens if (or when) Nigeria decides to nationalize all foreign direct investment from Northern countries maintaining normal diplomatic and economic relations with South Africa?

Clearly co-optation can in theory be highly consistent with a traditional national security perspective. When, to use Samuel Huntington's phrase, Southern "local leviathans" can be integrated into a Northern security system, the outcome is applauded, and for normative as well as prudential reasons. Henry Kissinger is hardly alone in insisting that no normative goals can be achieved unless the East-West strategic balance remains intact; the co-optation of local leviathans into all elements of the Northern system can presumably help to solidify that strategic balance.

If there is a potential case-by-case conflict between the military and the economic security elements of a graduation-type policy guideline, there will most probably be more instances of congruence. Furthermore, it should be noted in concluding this exposition of the graduation scenario that there is a strong normative congruence—easy to overlook by critics of the scenario—among its constituent parts.

It is very easy to portray this general line of reasoning and the policy prescriptions that flow from it as the reflection of self-serving pragmatists whose only concern is the retention of their place in the present international hierarchy. And certainly that characterization is not inappropriate in a great many individual cases. But it must be recognized that it is very logical at a normative level to support this scenario as a basic element of a North-South policy prescription for the 1980s if one believes in the economic and political analysis that underlies it. If the present international economic system, with continuing incremental adaptations, does not present obstacles to rapid economic development, the scenario is highly defensible. If Southern bloc behavior is responsible for a growing set of economic demands that are not very conducive to overcoming Southern developmental problems—viewed from either the aggregate growth or the domestic equity perspective—the scenario is highly defensible. And if Southern and Northern government behavior is likely to approximate the traditional model of interstate behavior with the few crucial novel constraints noted above, the scenario is highly defensible. The fact that it will probably be perceived as patronizing at best and Machiavellian at worst by most Southerners is, from a normative perspective, beside the point.

From a political standpoint, of course, Southern perceptions are not at all beside the point. If this scenario were perceived as patronizing, Machiavellian, and a major obstacle to the achievement of the goals of Southern states by most developing-country elites, the probabilities of success in the crucial graduation exercises would need to be very high in order to proceed with the scenario. But it should also be remembered that the more offensive aspects of this scenario as perceived in the South could at least be partially overcome if there were several additional basic ingredients in an aggregate North-South strategy which removed some of the graduation scenario's rough edges.

IV

A critique of the graduation scenario is best begun by accepting the frame of reference implicit in the approach and examining its fundamental analytical underpinnings. Then the critique must be expanded to question the frame of reference itself. Given its system-maintenance orientation, does it by its very nature overlook issues and problems that, in reviewing the evidence and analysis of the earlier chapters, seem destined to emerge in the coming decade? Finally, recognizing that the scenario is not consciously intended by many of its proponents to foreclose other major elements of a North-South strategy for lessened tensions and increased cooperative endeavors, the compatibility of this general policy perspective with others should be briefly examined.

Potential weaknesses in the economic underpinning of the graduation touchstone to North-South policy prescriptions can be succinctly summarized through a focus on the following three issues:

1. The number and degree of market imperfections present in today's international economic system
2. The potential in at least some Southern proposals for major benefits to the development process
3. The potential gains to the *North* as well as the South which might emerge from a greater Northern willingness to examine more fundamental reforms of the present system

In the case of the first issue, the critique consists of some very technical questions concerning the degree to which the present international economic system is free of major market imperfections. If it is relatively free of them and if those that do exist (for example, the current norm that developing countries are given rather wide latitude to promote infant industries and subsidize entry into export markets) are generally supportive of the development process, then the economic rationale for the graduation option is strengthened. However, to the degree that market imperfections do prevail, especially those that would, a priori, be suspected of impeding Southern economic development, the economic case for this genre of policy prescription is weakened. The greater the market imperfections, the weaker the economic arguments for economic system maintenance with incremental reform via integration of upper-tier Southern countries.

An analysis of the individual market imperfections issues is already the subject of an enormous literature. A summary of the debate and the (sometimes conflicting) findings is all that is needed for present purposes.

The burden of the evidence and the conventional wisdom among most economists is that the present international economic system contains many serious market imperfections and in that sense alone is far from optimal for North or South. It is also agreed that if major market imperfections exist, any a priori case for "free market" orthodoxy is seriously undermined. In academic terms, we are then into the "theory of the second best" world, which can lead countries to introduce major deviations from neoclassical orthodoxy in order to overcome distorted market signals.

The real debate concerning the economic rationale for economic system maintenance is not whether we are operating in an international economic system free from serious market imperfections but whether or not those that do exist are major, whether or not they are in the aggregate biased against the developing countries, and whether more optimal alternatives require incremental reforms or major surgery. Among the more obvious imperfections are the following: very little international labor mobility; for most Southern countries, only slightly more inward capital mobility; many tariff and nontariff impediments to the free flow of commodities; a considerable degree of oligopoly power in many product and technology markets; and, perhaps most debilitating to the developing countries, the bias in the availability of market information. All these imperfections suggest significant limitations in the graduation scenario's modest commitment to continued incremental change.[10]

Is there a bias against the developing countries? The weight of evidence suggests an affirmative response. Again, speaking in aggregate terms, typical developing-country manufactured and semi-manufactured exports face higher tariff and nontariff barriers than do products of developed countries; capital market imperfections (of both a de jure and a de facto nature) have burdened the developing countries more than the developed countries; it would surely be difficult to argue that the restrictions on immigration into high-wage Northern countries from the developing countries have been offset by capital flows from North to South or by liberal Northern trade policies that might, in great part, have eased the problem of the general international immobility of labor; and, as noted above, the bias in market information heavily taxes the South.

Finally, it should be noted that these aggregate-level considerations do not begin to examine imperfections in individual markets for specific commodities and specific technologies. Such an examination would tend to confirm the structuralist notion that the very rules and behavioral norms of the post–World War II economic system introduced a subtle bias against the South in economic exchanges between developed and developing countries in the day-to-day process of trade, foreign investment, and technology transfer. These arguments are often overdeterministic, implying that developing countries have had far fewer options in choice of development policies than has been the case. But as in the case of MNC activity and other forms of technology transfer, they highlight the degree to which the structural foundations of the system allowed, if they did not actively encourage, a pattern of North-South economic transactions that supported Northern capital accumulation more than it did Southern economic development.[11]

If the present system does contain significant biases against economic activities of the developing countries, how can they best be overcome? If the system is not free of such biases, shouldn't the North examine developing-country proposals much more closely?

And if they are found wanting in theoretical merit, shouldn't Northern policy makers attempt to point the policy debate toward some of the more fundamental problems and market imperfections (the two are not always the same) that have often engendered "misdirected" Southern policy proposals? In the trade field, for example, is the North prepared to undertake major reforms in the fields of tariff and nontariff barriers which either remove present anti-Southern imperfections or introduce some countervailing pro-Southern biases? If it is, wouldn't contentious discussion of fourth-best solutions, such as generalized tariff preferences and joint commodity funding schemes (whose aim is to raise commodity prices), be redirected into a more constructive channel? In the case of a global food regime, is the North prepared to tackle domestic-interest-group constraints on the evolution of an optimal global food regime? Or will it continue to follow the incremental trail, giving little more than lip service to more fundamental reforms such as those suggested by the 1974 World Food Conference?

This type of consideration leads to the third and final economic issue. Whether analyzing such problems as food production and distribution, environmental decay, or use of the international commons, it seems obvious that both North and South may often benefit from examining the pros and cons of a more global perspective. An aspect of Fred Hirsch's social scarcity problem (more specifically, the collective goods problem) here appears at the international level rather than the intrastate level. To cite one example, it is clear that failure to achieve a "maximal sustainable yields" solution to the global fisheries problem will be detrimental to both Northern and Southern interests and will certainly be less than optimal in a global welfare sense. Can a perspective that focuses so intently on the day-to-day management of the present international economic system, considering only incremental changes as major problems arise, ever turn significant attention to such "marginal issues" before they become major problems with only second-best solutions to them still possible?

Put simply, how much flexibility to deal with North-South issues of growing legitimate economic concern can be built into a North-South policy touchstone that is so oriented toward system maintenance in the economic realm? Add the fact that the neoclassical

norms and values that imbue the system contain the inherent contradictions examined at the Northern domestic level in the preceding chapter ("cultural contradictions," "social scarcity," etc.) and
the potential limitations of the economic underpinnings of the graduation scenario increase in magnitude.

There is a logical congruence between the economic and political
critiques of the graduation scenario on the part of most analysts.
First, the political critique questions the assumption that well-
designed reforms in the economic (and international institutional)
realm will of necessity lead to greater demands from the developing
countries. Second, it generally exhibits the concerns that dominate
the global agenda perspective analyzed earlier. It suggests that the
degree of international collective action necessary to achieve progress in these areas will be forthcoming only if more accommodating
policies to ease present levels of North-South tension through cooperative efforts on Southern developmental problems are
implemented.

The congruence stems from the judgment that there is a need
for more than co-optation and incremental reforms that would be
responsive to perceived developing-country concerns and would
moderate rather than escalate Southern demands. Empirical evidence often focuses upon the "reemergence of the moderates" as
the dominant force within the Group of 77 since the Seventh Special
Session of the UNGA and on their ability to sustain relatively
fruitless negotiations for 2 years after that Special Session without
losing control of G-77 leadership.

Two other strands of essentially political analysis produce doubts
concerning the capacity of the graduation scenario to achieve moderate goals in the 1980s irrespective of the economic issues involved;
and they would appear to contain diametrically opposed implications for policy. On the one hand, there are those who feel that
Southern cooperation can be achieved at a modest price when
compared with the costs of continuing the stalemate system. These
observers are generally willing to pay a cost in terms of second-
best reforms to aid Southern developmental needs on the assumption that a quid pro quo will develop in terms of cooperation on
efforts to make progress in such areas as nuclear proliferation, the
international commons, and environmental decay. They oppose the

graduation scenario on the assumption that because of its narrow focus on a very few Southern countries, it will not enhance the capacity of multilateral institutions to overcome their present North-South–dominated stalemates.

On the other hand, there is a small but influential school of thought that argues that a graduation scenario draws its inspiration from a domestic societal model that is wholly misleading, runs substantial risks of failure vis-à-vis the upper-echelon Southern states themselves, and will accomplish nothing but further disorder in the broader North-South arena. These views are most cogently expressed by Robert Tucker:

As applied to North-South relations the difficulties attending a strategy of cooptation through accommodation arise in part because international society is not domestic society. It does not follow that the success of such a strategy is precluded in international society, only that it is made more difficult and uncertain. Its difficulty today, moreover, is due not only to the absence of a social framework that provides some stability to the process of accommodation but to the markedly heterogeneous character of the parties involved in this process. This pervasive heterogeneity finds no meaningful parallel to the differences that earlier separated classes within the state. Where class conflict issued in successful accommodation, it was because adversaries ultimately shared the same values. However much one side may have denied these values in practice, in the end this common commitment—even though attended by the threat or actuality of force—provided the balm of compromise. In the international society of today, it would be ludicrous to attempt even the vaguest articulation of those values common to the participants in the struggle over a new distribution of wealth and power. . . . *It is chiefly for these reasons that a strategy of co-optation through accommodation must be viewed with a substantial measure of skepticism. It may be argued that despite the hazards of this strategy there appears no viable alternative. Even if true, those hazards ought to be recognized for what they are.*[12]

The message of this argumentation is that the graduation scenario would succeed only in the narrowest (and normatively least compelling) sense of separating the upper-tier developing countries from the rest of the South. Their adoption of Northern systemic goals and norms would be ambiguous and unassured; their lack of concern for the rest of the South would become increasingly likely;

and "world-order politics" would escape the grasp of all parties. All one need do to confirm this possibility is to examine the revealed foreign policy goals of Iran, Saudi Arabia, and Brazil. They contain major potential for clash with moderate-global-order norms, with system-maintenance norms, and with both international and domestic equity norms.

Given the potential for failure in the co-optation approach, little further need be added in a separate security-oriented critique of the graduation scenario. On the one hand, it may accomplish too little vis-à-vis those countries that are its primary targets. They may gain in power and status without accepting the reciprocal obligations implied in the process. The rest of the South, left to fend for itself, may do so by continuing to stalemate progress on such issues as proliferation, commons regimes, and others in international institutions. Finally, as noted earlier, major military security aspects of the graduation scenario may clash with economic and political aspects from the very outset. In sum, from a national security or a "global-world-order" standpoint the graduation scenario involves a gamble on a series of linked behavioral hypotheses and probabilities that are very uncertain and highly difficult to measure.

V

A serious potential flaw in the graduation scenario concerns the central thrust of this conceptualization of the North-South set of problems and the way to manage them. Given the scenario's system-maintenance orientation, does the very dynamic of policy thinking that informs it *necessarily* overlook issues and problems that seem destined to emerge along the North-South axis in the coming decade?

One way of illustrating this potential was noted in section I by reexamining the matrix containing nine possible goals of a moderate international system in the 1980s. There it was noted that policies developed in accordance with the graduation element were likely to make limited contributions to most of those goals, with the possible exceptions of state-centric economic and national security goals for the North and for those Southern graduates that joined the system. How far beyond these states economic and security gains would spread is uncertain, as the analysis of the economic and political underpinnings of the scenario suggests. On the one hand, one can imagine the following optimistic scenario in which benefits are broadly spread:

1. Co-optation works: the upper-tier Southern countries join in support of the present international economic system and help to stabilize the East-West strategic balance.
2. The international economic system approximates the behavior—and therefore the results—predicted by its supporters. If so, it will offer no constraint to rapid Southern economic growth except where individual developing-country domestic policies undermined the development process.
3. The system will continue to be the object of incremental change that rids it of remaining major imperfections and, under constant normative pressure from the co-opted newcomers, introduces special forms of assistance to the developing countries.
4. The net effect of these achievements will be a gradual diminution of present levels of North-South conflict and a rising capacity to conduct constructive North-South diplomacy.

On the other hand, the following scenario is viewed by many as just as probable:

1. Co-optation may take place, but it will not be of the reciprocal nature envisioned by its advocates. The price charged for co-operation (by a Saudi Arabia, an Iran, a Brazil) may be quite high at the outset and subject to constant escalation as each Southern co-optee becomes more crucial to system maintenance. This, in effect, is the course of events Tucker predicts.
2. The economic system being maintained by the process of co-optation is far more flawed by imperfections biased against the South than its supporters realize (or admit). Therefore system maintenance does little to assist Southern development in the aggregate, even if individual "success stories" continue to appear.
3. The pressures against an incremental reform process that would benefit the South—e.g., pressures for increasing Northern

protectionism, lowered levels of foreign aid, diminishing real rates of lending to the South by the IBRD and the Eurodollar market—outweigh any pressures for accommodating reforms. The brunt of the analysis of Northern societal evolution suggests how probable the rise of the nonaccommodating pressures will be.

4. The aggregate result of these trends will "serve only to increase, rather than to allay, the struggle for wealth and power."[13]

Unfortunately, the probabilities attached to these opposing scenarios are so difficult to "guesstimate" that they will vary widely from analyst to analyst.

Another method of judging whether the graduation scenario contains an inner dynamic that inherently narrows its focus is to measure it against the emerging Northern and Southern perspectives analyzed in Chapter 3. The narrowing tendency is again confirmed.

From either of the two significant Southern perspectives—global inequity or basic human needs—the graduation scenario has nothing to offer beyond the promise of the "old system" strengthened, it is hoped, by the graduation ceremonies. As noted earlier, developing countries in the aggregate have grown at historically high rates under that system. Nevertheless, the global inequity and basic-human-needs perspectives are not concerned with aggregate growth rates. The former is concerned with the perceived inequity of present international economic rules and norms and the North-South income gap, the latter with the problem of absolute poverty. Therefore, in terms of Southern perceptions, a return to 6 percent aggregate growth rates is not as relevant an indicator as it may appear to proponents of the graduation scenario.

The same generalization applies to three of the emerging Northern perspectives: those focusing on the global agenda, global equity, and basic-human-needs issues. The latter two are Northern analogues of the Southern perspectives just reviewed, and the objections of Northerners embracing these perspectives to the limitations of the graduation scenario reflect shared concerns. And as the previous section of this chapter has already suggested, most policy makers and analysts concerned with the need to break out of present North-South deadlocks on a growing number of global management issues view an approach to North-South policy making based substantially on the graduation scenario with a great deal of skepticism.

VI

In concluding the analysis of this initial basic ingredient in an aggregate North-South strategy, it must be recalled that many supporters of a graduation approach would insist that it be conceptualized as only one of several guidelines for North-South policy making in the 1980s. What they are arguing is that it is the sine qua non for improved North-South relations: if the present economic system is not strengthened by the graduation of the upper-tier developing countries, no concrete accomplishments can be expected and further deterioration is projected.

In the minds of most Northern policy makers, there appears to be a general acceptance of this judgment: a grudging acceptance on the part of those who focus upon the inherent limitations of the approach and fear that the sine qua non will inevitably establish itself as the *primus inter pares*, and a benign acceptance on the part of those who are disinclined to worry about global agendas, global equity, basic human needs, or the potential dynamic of a system-maintenance perspective.

A crucial issue for the global politics of North-South relations in the 1980s, therefore, concerns the degree to which the system-maintenance outlook that will inevitably act as one major Northern parameter of North-South policy making can be successfully melded with other core ingredients of a North-South strategy to limit its inherent defects and build upon its potential strengths. A successful melding process will need to resolve at least four major problems presented by the graduation strategy: the perceptual problem, the co-optation problem, the world-order-politics problem, and the equity/distribution problem.

If the co-optation effort is perceived as a Northern attempt to weaken Southern cohesion and diplomatic strength, this perception will surely embitter North-South relations for a number of years. It will also create substantial problems for upper-tier developing countries caught between Northern invitations and Southern suspicions. Thus the manner in which the process of intergration is attempted will be extremely important. Unless it is perceived as part of a broader effort at North-South constructive endeavors, the side effects, though unpredictable, would at best invite increased distrust and the solidification of the present stalemate system. The conflict and distrust between the G-19 and the G-77, discussed in Chapter 4, suggest how sensitive the weaker developing countries are about any move in the direction of upper-tier cooperation with the North.

The co-optation process involves unpredictable consequences for North-South relations arising from the potential behavior of the co-opted countries themselves. Will they accept the reciprocal system-maintenance behavioral norms that would be expected by the North? Or will the heterogeneity of their levels of development needs and goals simply enhance the conflict over power and wealth predicted by many observers? What can be added to a nucleus of North-South policy ingredients to limit the potential magnitude of this problem?

The world-order-politics problem encompasses the concerns of a broad spectrum of analysts and practitioners of statecraft. Their analyses of the problems confronting successful world-order politics go so far beyond the agenda of the graduation scenario and raise such fundamental philosophical and behavioral doubts about the congruity between economic system maintenance and the systemic world-order needs of the 1980s that one must face the possibility that these two major levels of concern and sets of policy prescriptions may not be amenable to successful melding. The creation of new systems or the removal of contradictions in old ones is unlikely to be accomplished while one system—the economic system—is held constant. If norms underlying new systems are in conflict with economic system maintenance, and they will be on many occasions, pressures will build for change.

Finally, the issue of equality must be considered. Whether one is focusing on interstate or interpersonal relations, on equality of opportunity or equality of result, it is apparent that the rising challenge to inequality is both strong and widespread. It pervades the international environment; it jars Northern domestic tranquillity. Several years ago, Zbigniew Brzezinski made the following observation about the global equality issue:

It is to be expected that in the next two or three decades we will witness an intensified crisis in the developing world brought about by the twin impacts of demographic growth and the spread of education. Both will make global inequality even more intolerable at a time when equality is becoming the most powerful moral imperative of our time, thus paralleling the appeal of the concept of liberty during the nineteenth century.[14]

At the United States domestic level, the analysis presented in the preceding chapter suggests that the issue of income distribution will increase in prominence over the coming decade. Several years ago, Robert Lampman noted the typical American ambivalence on the subject:

Each program for redistribution, be it public education, unemployment insurance or public housing, has its own philosophy that informs the design of the American standard distribution of income. The latter is, then, a performance indicator to which no social policy is directly keyed. The hiatus is significant. It means that the income distribution is not used in deciding who should help whom; apparently, it is not considered to be a reliable road map for social intervention. It may also mean something else: namely, that Americans don't really seek any particular degree of income equality, but rather seek a system of sharing that recognizes *human needs*, restrains certain arbitrary or capricious inequalities, and serves social purposes.[15]

Despite this American ambivalence, analyses of social change in America and the rest of the North over the coming decade lend support to the view that the distributional impact of government policies will increasingly become a major subject of debate in the United States; this debate is already on the uptrend in many other Northern societies.

The question for North-South relations and the graduation scenario in the 1980s posed by the international and domestic equity issues is at once very simple and extraordinarily complex. It is simple in that the graduation scenario must be melded with some policy prescriptions that are at least perceived to deal somewhat more directly with the issues of both global inequality and basic human needs than the "trickle-down" dynamic of the neoclassical growth model.[16] It is complex because of the potential for efforts to redress international and domestic inequity to conflict rather than to converge. We have already noted this tendency in two disparate instances: (1) the extremely costly impact of OPEC oil-price increases on other developing countries and (2) the potential that Northern domestic conflict over income shares in the context of relatively high rates of inflation and unemployment will lead to protectionist measures and lower aid appropriations, both trends inimical to a narrowing of the relative North-South income gap. Will the list prove to be infinitely expandable? One can hazard the opinion that if and when economic growth is no longer viewed as the great social solvent, the neoclassical perception of economics as a positive-sum game in which all can win will be quick to lose its allure and the list will expand even if, under certain conditions, the perception remains an accurate one. But if and when that point will be reached is still a matter of conjecture.

It seems certain that the graduation scenario will have to be melded with policy prescriptions responding to each of the four problems noted above if North-South relations in the 1980s are to become supportive of a moderate international system. Each prescription will be difficult to fill, and perhaps none more difficult than the equity issue. The development of norms to overcome the potential conflicts in the various perceptions of equality and equity as those perceptions are emerging toward the end of the 1970s may ultimately present the greatest challenge of all.

NOTES

[1]Recent examples of innovations to ease new problems include the oil facility and the Witteveen Fund, both innovations aimed at increasing the IMF's lending capacity to meet the sudden oil-price- and recession-induced foreign-exchange needs of both developed and developing countries.

[2]For the supporting economic analysis the many Yale University Economic Growth Center papers by Gustav Ranis over the past 5 years should be consulted. For an opposing argument based on sociopolitical analysis, see Richard Fagen, "Equity in the South in the Context of North-South Relations," in Fishlow et al., *Rich and Poor Nations in the World Economy* (New York: McGraw-Hill for the Council on Foreign Relations/1980s Project, 1978), pp. 163–214.

[3]In late 1977 the Amalgamated Clothing and Textile Workers Union filed petitions with the Commissioner of Customs seeking "appropriate countervailing

duties" on textile and apparel imports from South Korea, Taiwan, India, the Philippines, Brazil, Argentina, Uruguay, and Colombia. AFL-CIO President George Meany indicated at a news conference held on the day the petitions were filed that this was organized labor's opening volley in a campaign against "unfair trade practices" that, he suggested, were followed in many developing countries.

[4]Albert Fishlow, "A New International Economic Order: What Kind?" in Fishlow et al., op. cit.

[5]C. Fred Bergsten et al., *The Reform of International Institutions*, Triangle Paper no. 11, p. vi.

[6]For an essay on the differing levels of constraints on state behavior which remains as engaging as it is insightful, see Kenneth Waltz, *Man, the State, and War* (New York: Columbia University Press, 1959).

[7]Even two leading exponents of the view that the statement is losing much of its explanatory power in intra-Northern situations of what they call "complex interdependence" would not appear to object to this judgment. See Robert O. Keohane and Joseph S. Nye, *Power and Interdependence: World Politics in Transition* (Boston: Little, Brown & Co., 1977).

[8]Other forms of "threat"—such as failure to cooperate on global problems— were never a part of this line of analysis.

[9]In the security arena, graduation need not generally imply the same degree of "integration" into the Northern "system" as it does in the economic arena. Often it may involve no more than Northern (generally United States) support for a Southern regional power that serves as a force for stability (and Northern influence) in a given area of the South. What is at issue here are those cases in which Southern states tapped for "economic" graduation (co-optation) have foreign policy goals or concerns that conflict with Northern (United States) security goals. It is in these instances that conflicting security goals may well undermine the positive, economic system–maintenance benefits the North seeks from the graduation scenario.

[10]The reader should remember that what is being questioned here is the adequacy of co-optation plus *incremental change* in the system of the late 1970s. If the verdict is "inadequate," then the *pace of change* should accelerate. But the *nature* of that change is indeterminate. At one end of the spectrum it can be of a "system-perfecting" nature (à la Fishlow); at the other end it can be of a radical alteration nature.

[11]Empirical evidence on this issue suggests the dangers of unqualified conclusions, as do some of the theoretical underpinnings. And the mere fact that a considerable number of Southern countries have been able to overcome many such biases—even turning some of them to their own developmental advantage— suggests how overdeterministic many of the so-called "structuralist" interpretations are. But overstated generalizations on the one hand should not lead to total

rejection of a significant problem on the other. For an exceptionally well-balanced analysis of the "market imperfections" issue see Gerald K. Helleiner, *World Markets and Developing Countries* (Washington, D.C.: Overseas Development Council, 1978).

[12]Robert W. Tucker, *The Inequality of Nations* (New York: Basic Books, 1977), pp. 199–200. Emphasis added. A different type of skepticism concerning the prospects for a successful co-optation strategy, based on judgments concerning regime fragility and rapidly altering foreign policy phases and goals, is found in George Liska's *States in Evolution: Changing Societies and Traditional Systems in World Politics* (Baltimore: Johns Hopkins University Press, 1973).

[13]Tucker, op. cit., p. 198.

[14]Zbigniew Brzezinski, "U.S. Foreign Policy: The Search for Focus," *Foreign Affairs*, vol. 51, no. 4, July 1973, p. 726.

[15]Robert J. Lampman, "Measured Inequality of Income: What Does It Mean and What Can It Tell Us?" *The Annals of the American Academy of Political and Social Science*, September 1973, pp. 90–91.

[16]See Chapter 8 for an explanation and analysis of the terms and issues raised in this sentence.

Chapter 7
The Global
Reform Ingredient

I

The Northern attempt to co-opt Southern upper-tier states will unfold inevitably, whatever we choose to call it and whether or not it bears any early fruit. "Prudential" Northern statecraft of the most traditional type will find it impossible to avoid this superficially perceived low-risk/high-payoff response to the present North-South diplomatic stalemate. Whether in fact the approach leads to the results expected by some of its warmest advocates or to the less sanguine outcome projected by others remains a judgment reached on such little empirical or theoretical evidence that further speculation about the graduation scenario per se is unwarranted.

More fruitful at this point is an examination of other basic elements of North-South policy prescription that may limit the most obvious shortcomings of that scenario. What can be added to overcome what we have called the perceptual, world-order, and equity/distribution problems that are either created or magnified by the co-optation approach?

One major policy guideline can be found in a Northern willingness to suspend skepticism and examine with far greater seriousness than exhibited in the mid-1970s a broad range of international systemic reforms that were by then being suggested in both the South and the North. Within the developing countries these proposals come from governmental bureaucracies; within the North most have emanated from the private sector and the academic community. The goal of such a Northern governmental examination would be to open discussions and negotiations with the South on those system-reform proposals that, with appropriate alterations and refinements, could be successfully supported before Northern legislatures and publics.

Before proceeding to examine several examples of such proposals and to analyze the potential costs and benefits of the general approach, four preliminary observations are in order. First, it should be emphasized that this basic element of North-South policy prescription does not limit the definition of "system" to economic issues alone. Even though most of the reforms themselves have a strong economic orientation, the raison d'être of the approach is to strengthen the capacity of the international system in the aggregate to move toward the highly generalized goals of a moderate global order set forth in Chapter 1. More directly, it is to overcome the present North-South stalemate that so often prevents such movement. Therefore the calculus of costs and benefits is complex, since one is speculating about the impact of certain policies across differing subsystems of global politics. If the implementation of a reform in the international economic arena would seem, by neoclassical economic measurement, to be of marginal benefit globally and of even more questionable benefit to the South in a distributional sense, is the effort worth it? The answer must be calculated in terms of the impact of that reform (and similar ones) on the aggregate North-South *diplomatic relationship*. In making such calculations in the North it would be well to remember two aspects of the Southern scene that are often ignored or given little attention. First, the promise of dialogue alone, without a single advance promise of any substantive worth, was enough to allow moderate Southern leadership to take control of the Southern negotiating position after the Seventh Special Session of the UNGA. And second, many precariously placed Southern governing elites need symbols of Northern accommodation for domestic purposes. From this perspective, reforms of marginal economic consequence may have much greater political impact than Northern policy makers ever consider. Such oversights in what are admittedly difficult calculations are likely to become increasingly costly.

The second preliminary observation concerns the breadth of the spectrum of global systemic reforms that might be—indeed, are being—examined. They can be conceptualized as beginning at the most flexible end of the graduation approach and running all the way to the formal proposals of the NIEO. An additional ingredient—most radical of all in the change it implies in the structure and process of international politics—can be found in the writings of certain United States scholars who, with an eye to a time frame somewhat lengthier than the 1980s, are currently asking how much longer incremental and unconnected policy formulation can be afforded on issues not unconnected in the physical world (e.g., population growth, food production, raw materials, consumption, and pollution).

The third preliminary point is that across this very broad spectrum of reform proposals one uncovers enormous differences in motives (e.g., normative, prudential), in judgments (e.g., normative, empirical), and in strategic and tactical considerations. Many of these differences seem to find their roots in the divergent perceptions of the North-South problem analyzed in Chapter 3. Since each perspective is characterized by a differing order of values and normative concerns and since each looks at different empirical evidence and submits that evidence to different tests, there will never be agreement on the appropriate scope and specific content of a global systemic reform "package." Perhaps the most that can be hoped for is agreement on the legitimacy of the *process* of trying to identify and implement reforms that incorporate elements responsive to divergent (but not always conflicting) motives, judgments, and concerns, North and South.

Policy makers, analysts, and readers of this book would undoubtedly much prefer a more precise conceptualization of the objectives of this particular "global reform" approach. For better or worse, we may all simply have to live with such imprecision as slowly altering forms of North-South statecraft are tested. If the analysis thus far underlines one central problem for North-South relations in the coming years, it is the uncertainties that are destined to attend these relations. This conclusion is nowhere more dramatically supported than in the analysis of the North-South relationship by some of the subject's leading students themselves.

Robert Tucker suggests, as we have noted, that current North-South issues will result in nothing more than some shift in the hierarchy of states; the international system's structural and process elements will otherwise remain unaffected. At the same time he suggests that Northern elite groups—governing elites and others— are so uncertain about the moral and ethical foundations of the present system that their "new political sensibility" is producing a very significant alteration of Northern state behavior in the face of Southern demands. Can he be right on both counts? The answer would seem to be that while such an outcome is not logically impossible, his own analysis opens up a wide range of potential outcomes that go well beyond some new partners for the same diplomatic minuet.

Similar ambivalence is to be found in the writings of Mahbub ul Haq, one of the most prominent Southern analysts of many issues central to this book. On the one hand Haq can make a statement of the following nature:

Let us make quite clear in our future negotiations that what is at stake here is not a few marginal adjustments in the international system: *it is its complete overhaul.* We are not foolish enough to think that this can happen overnight. . . . But we are not willing to settle for some inadequate, piecemeal concessions in the name of a step-by-step approach.[1]

In the same analysis, however, Haq also makes the following observation:

If we are going to opt for negotiations in our search for a new international economic order, it is essential that whatever proposals we formulate balance the interests of both rich and poor nations. It is easy to formulate partisan positions. But we live in an interdependent world. If we are to live without major confrontations, we should think of proposals which, while benefitting the Third World, do not hurt the interests of the world as a whole and which can obtain more willing cooperation from the rich nations. . . . It should be possible to evolve arrangements which balance the interests of both sides.[2]

Again, as in the case of Tucker, the two themes of the Haq analysis are not of logical necessity mutually exclusive. Nevertheless, emphasis on the need for "complete overhaul" surely suggests the desire for a major change in the distribution of benefits from the international system. The path from that objective to an outcome that "balances the interests of both sides" is not self-evident.

Yet another example of the inherent ambiguities of the issues themselves are highlighted in the writings of two prominent United States scholars, Ernst Haas and John Ruggie. In many of their joint and separate writings during the mid-1970s, they focused upon the evolution of international organizations and international "regimes" (e.g., for the management of the oceans, environment, and raw materials). Concerning regimes, they note that

all regimes are predicated upon the definition of a purpose, but in virtually all cases the purpose of the collectivity [all states involved] is subordinated to the disparate purposes of national policy. As environmental and resource interdependencies become more severe, however, one might expect the emergence of regimes in which the disparate purposes of national policies are redefined in terms of the larger collectivity.[3]

They observe that the process of the "collective elaboration of welfare choices" internationally is in a very rudimentary state. They see its beginnings in the cases of food allocation schemes, fisheries management, and public health. And they observe that

to the extent that collective welfare choices are beginning to be made, however, *they result from one or another of two superordinate purposes: the global redistribution of income, goods, and services (from North to South), and the improvement of the quality of life by controlling those characteristics of science and technology which undermine it.*[4]

Then the authors complicate the issue by adding that "obviously, there exists no agreement on either of these."[5] By this time it should be clear that the complexities of North-South relations lie in the issues themselves and not in the minds of the analysts. From a totally different perspective, with very different interests, and trying with great success to bring some conceptual clarity to the analysis of "interdependence" and "global agenda" issues, Haas and Ruggie confront the stubborn complexities of North-South issues within the framework of a slowly altering international system. The results of science and technology on the one hand and political perceptions and choices on the other have pushed global politics to the point where, consciously or unconsciously, government leaders are reluctantly forced on occasion to participate in the "collective elaboration of welfare choices." What purposes guide states when they participate in this form of global diplomacy? Haas and Ruggie rightly note that one of the two purposes that are at least embryonic in this process concerns a transfer—a redistribution of income or opportunity—from North to South. Yet they also realistically observe that whatever agreement exists on this "superordinate purpose" is still extremely fragile.

The Tuckers, the Haqs, the Haases, and the Ruggies of the world may share little else in their views concerning North-South relations but this: an acute appreciation of the ambiguities and uncertainties of that relationship in the present international setting. It is that same appreciation that informs the eclectic discussion of international systemic reforms in this chapter. It is possible that the very exercise of analysis, discussion, and negotiation of some of the reforms briefly sketched below will be as beneficial to North-South relations as the quantitative results of any of the reforms themselves. For those who can live with George Kennan's view that what is often needed to achieve progress toward more constructive relations between states is "gardening" and not "engineering," the approach and the prescription informing this chapter should be understandable.

The final preliminary point concerns the constant tension between the issues of interstate and intrastate equity which is revealed as one examines proposals for global system reforms that are already before the public and the policy makers. A few rhetorical flourishes aside, most Southern proposals of the 1970s concentrated exclusively on the interstate equity issue. In contrast, most of the major proposals that were set forth by Northern groups and governments paid very significant attention to the intrastate equity issue, generally incorporating the basic-human-needs approach to the elimination of the absolute poverty problem.

Given the present degree of mistrust characterizing North-South relations, these differences in emphasis on the equity issue could become thoroughly polarized unless serious attempts are made to strike a balance in which the concerns of *each side* are addressed. Without such a balance, Southern leadership will become increasingly suspicious of articulated Northern concerns about basic human needs and the North will become increasingly skeptical of the intent of Southern governing elites. Chapters 7 and 8 attempt to strike that crucial balance. This chapter focuses primarily on the interstate equity issue, presenting sketches of reform proposals that should appeal to most Southern states. Indeed, many of the proposals are directly responsive to certain NIEO demands. Chapter 8 then focuses on the intrastate equity issue to complete the balance.

II

In this section six examples of global systemic reforms are examined. We begin with some of the most commonly discussed proposals and move toward some of the more novel and complex reforms. Unfortunately there is little correlation between the commonly discussed and the politically feasible. If there were, several of the potential reforms noted below, beginning with the very first one, would have been implemented years ago rather than becoming a more and more controversial target of reform with each passing year.

1. Significant Trade Liberalization

Trade liberalization remains a classic example of positive-sum reform on the North-South agenda. That is to say, it is a reform that would be of demonstrable benefit to both North and South. At the same time, it would be directly responsive to one of the South's long-standing (and most accurate) complaints about the "imperfections" of the present international economic system. Further, it would be very supportive of the South's desire for a greater share of global industrial production. Finally, there are two other elements involved in this reform which should be appealing to even the most skeptical Northern critic of Southern demands and/or motives. The first is that it is clearly a reform that falls into the equality of opportunity rather than the equality of result category. Trade liberalization creates the *opportunity* for developing countries to compete in Northern markets on equal terms with Northern producers, but it offers them no special advantages. Second, the spread of this particular economic norm strengthens global acceptance of the philosophical core of the neoclassical values and behavioral rules that lay at the center of the Bretton Woods system.

A few figures will suggest what the South is already accomplishing as a result of present levels of trade liberalization and what might be accomplished if a major reform—such as a Northern willingness to eliminate all barriers to trade in manufactured goods—were to be implemented.

Recent projections by the World Bank suggest that, under quite feasible assumptions, per capita growth rates of 2 percent a year in the poorest developing countries and rates of 4 percent in the more developed countries could be sustained between 1977 and 1985. This projection assumes no additional trade protectionism in the North and also assumes that LDC-manufactured exports would rise from $33 billion in 1975 to about $94 billion in 1985 [measured in constant (1975) dollars]. These figures suggest how great the dependence of the South is on present levels of international trade liberalization and the magnitude of the opportunities for Southern growth that inhere in successful Northern resistance to the neo-mercantilist pressures analyzed in Chapter 5.

The same World Bank estimates then suggest that, if Northern countries were to dismantle all trade barriers against manufactured goods of the developing countries, those countries could be earning $24 billion per year in addition to the amounts projected above. Finally, the Bank has recently estimated that, under free trade conditions, the developing countries could earn another $21 billion per year in manufactured exports if they could overcome supply constraints on their own productive capacity. "In other words, if fully rational policies were pursued by importers and exporters alike, the developing countries' export earnings from manufactured goods would increase by $45 billion per year above the levels which will result from a continuation of past policies."[6]

Recognizing the political and technical impossibility of moving so quickly to dismantle present trade barriers and increase LDC productive capacity, the World Bank then produced Table 7-1 on the basis of three assumptions: (1) the Tokyo round of trade negotiations would lead to tariff reductions of 50 percent; (2) a partial Northern relaxation of nontariff barriers (NTBs) on the export of LDC manufactures would increase their earnings by $6 billion per year; and (3) the capacity of the LDCs to exploit 50 percent of their unused export potential through greater efficiency and further reduction of supply constraints would develop.

The figures in this table are interesting for several reasons. First, they indicate how much potential for industrial growth the present system already contains for developing countries that have reached the stage where they can avail themselves of the opportunities it presents. The middle and upper range of LDCs should be able to increase their manufactured exports from $30 billion to $87 billion in 10 years with *no* policy changes. Second, the figures reveal that with liberalization falling far short of free trade, the figure would grow to $103 billion in 10 years. And finally, they thereby demonstrate that there are *some* issues in the NIEO reform demands which simply borrow a page from Adam Smith. It is extraordinarily

Table 7-1   LDC Earnings from Export of Manufactures
($ billion, 1975 prices)

	POOREST COUNTRIES	MIDDLE-INCOME COUNTRIES	TOTAL
1965	$ 2.4	$ 7.6	$ 10
1975	3.4	29.6	33
1985 Present Policies	7.3	86.7	94
Possible additions from:			
·Tokyo Round	.3	3.7	4
·Partial relaxation of non-tariff barriers	1.0	5.0	6
·Improved LDC policies	2.5	7.5	10
1985 New policies	11.1	102.9	114

Source: Robert S. McNamara, Address to the Board of Governors of the World Bank, Washington, D.C., September 26, 1977, p. 17.

easy for Northern economists to ridicule some ill-considered Southern proposals; unfortunately, they often do so in print, apparently without considering the possibility that some of the less enlightened NIEO demands simply reflect growing frustration with protracted Northern nonresponsiveness to more enlightened Southern proposals.

The dangers of Northern regression rather than progression in the field of trade liberalization have already been noted in earlier chapters. While many examples of United States restrictions were cited, the problem is endemic to Northern societies. During the latter 1970s the European Common Market countries imposed various kinds of import restrictions on steel, shoes, textiles, and electronic gear as well as food; many of these new restrictions significantly affect developing-country exports. But this line of observation speaks to the inherent difficulties of structuring a comprehensive and internally consistent set of North-South policy guidelines and prescriptions for the 1980s, and not to the obvious magnitude and merits of this particular international systemic reform.

2. A Major Strengthening of International Financial Institutions and Mechanism

A second area in which there would appear to be room for at least a quickening pace of incremental reform if not the consideration of more dramatic changes is the operation of the formal and informal institutions and rules of the international financial system. The process of reform is already well advanced in this arena. During the mid-1970s several changes were adopted that are of substantial benefit to the developing countries. Within the International Monetary Fund, expanding member quotas have increased LDC access to foreign exchange; a major increase in the funds available under the so-called Compensatory Finance Facility and an easing of conditions of access to those funds have also provided developing countries with balance-of-payments assistance when suffering from unpredictable export earnings shortfalls. Finally, the agreement in 1977 to establish the so-called Witteveen Fund of about $10 billion to ease temporary payments imbalance problems will, provided that it is ratified, be of further assistance. Had some of these changes been introduced sooner and in greater magnitudes, thus providing developing countries much more assistance in coping with fluctuations in prices and earnings from their major exports, there is good reason to doubt that the North-South dialogue in the mid-1970s would have focused so single-mindedly and fruitlessly on the issue of commodity-price problems.

Changes in the World Bank, which border on systemic reform if pressed forward continuously, are also evidence in the decision of 1977 to expand substantially the capital base of the IBRD. While no final decision was made on the size of the expansion, agreement in principle was reached to allow the Bank to continue its lending activities in the developing countries at annual real rates of increase for at least the rest of the decade. Should the capital expansion (and further expansions as needed) continue to allow Bank lending to grow in real terms, the middle-range developing countries—those also able to benefit from trade liberalization—will find their NIEO demand for increased access to international capital markets met in a combination of ways. First, the expanded IMF facilities will ease short-term, unpredictable foreign-exchange problems. Second, World Bank lending will continue to assist in providing capital for industrial infrastructure and other investments necessary to increase the productive capacities of these countries. Finally, the aggregate assistance from these international financial institutions should, *ceteris paribus*, continuously improve the credit ratings of many of these countries in private international capital markets, particularly the Eurodollar market.

While each of these individual actions may appear quite incremental in nature, the aggregate *process*—which, in the long run, is the more important issue—may come closer to the "World Development Authority" ideas of Mahbub ul Haq (Chapter 3) than individual actions suggest.

This process could be strengthened even further if a new mechanism could be developed to institutionalize the handling of severe debt burden problems in a way that aided individual developing countries in need of assistance without weakening the growing capacity of developing countries in general to tap private international financial markets. Many proposals that attempt to isolate and aid individual debtor nations without creating an adverse impact on other developing-country borrowers or on the distribution of foreign assistance have recently been put forward.[7] Were the North to advance some of these alternative proposals to Southern generalized debt-relief demands, two major benefits would be derived. First, the Southern perception that the North was unwilling to recognize that LDC debt problems deserved any special attention would be erased. Second, if the proposals proved negotiable, the international economic system as a whole would be strengthened. Again, as in the case of trade liberalization, all the ingredients of this reform option are in the nature of a change that could benefit all parties, North and South. That they have not been perceived in this "mutual gain" framework is again more of a commentary on the state of North-South relations in a changing international system than on the potential reforms themselves.

3.   Foreign Economic Assistance

To complete the list of traditional arenas where Southern reform proposals have been prominent, a word should be addressed to the issue of foreign economic assistance. As noted in Table 3-1, Northern Official Development Assistance has not only failed to reach the 0.7 percent target listed in the UNGA's Second Development Decade strategy; it has steadily deteriorated. At 0.52 percent in 1960, it had fallen to 0.34 by 1970; in 1976 it stood at $14.8 billion, which translated into 0.33 percent of DAC-member GNP. In fact, in real terms ODA has been essentially stationary for the past decade, during which time real income of the OECD countries has risen by 40 percent.

For years it has been argued by some elements within Northern policymaking and academic circles that the 0.7 percent target represented no more than a compromise number pulled out of a hat during a UN hallway caucus, and that there was—and still is—no compelling logical, ethical, or economic argument to support that target. Yet the issues analyzed in previous chapters, the numbers scanned thus far in this chapter, and the examination of a basic-human-needs ingredient in North-South policy prescriptions in the following chapter all begin to provide a rationale for some such target, and the 0.7 percent number is mentioned here simply because it is an integral part of the current dialogue.

The rationale for a serious Northern effort to set and achieve some such target is, admittedly, of the gardening variety, not the engineering variety. It would run somewhat as follows:

(a) The North will, come what may, follow a graduation scenario strategy as one basic element of North-South policy in the 1980s. This strategy may leave the North with many problems and an upper range of LDCs with relatively fewer.

(b) As the examination of growth trends, manufactured exports, access to capital markets, and other indicators suggests, unless the world economy slumps again or moves into a period of marked neomercantilism, the middle-range developing countries could find themselves growing at an historically high per capita rate of 4 percent per year. This very process will produce more "voice" in the system through further graduations, more "symmetrical interdependence," and growing quotas and votes in such institutions as the IMF, the IBRD, and others.

(c) From a state-centric point of view, this process leaves the least developed countries at the unpleasant end of the growing Southern gap analyzed in Chapter 4. The countries of South Asia, sub-Saharan Africa, and the Caribbean area will be likely to grow at half the per capita rate of the rest of the South at best. Here the need for increases in foreign assistance has been clearly documented.

(d) From a non-state-centric perspective, both the rapidly growing developing countries and the least developed, or poorest, countries will contain about 1 billion people living in absolute poverty. Lack of basic nutrition, health care, and education will continue to mock the phrase "equality of opportunity" when it is applied to this stratum of developing-country populations.

(e) If, as expressed in legislative intent, the World Employment Conference, and elsewhere, Northern Official Development Assistance is to focus on the problems of the poorest people of the world, a dual rationale for an ODA target emerges. The first rationale is of a moral/ethical nature. If Northern countries have the potential capacity (at an extraordinarily small marginal cost) to increase the life chances of 1 billion people in the world who are otherwise permanently caught in absolute poverty, is it not integral to the continued nurturing of fundamental values and norms of Western culture and civilization to make the effort? Obviously this rationale is highly correlated with the degree to which ODA funds do achieve the purpose of permanently lifting the globe's absolute poverty population out of its present conditions.

The second rationale is more in the nature of prudential statecraft. For such a small cost, shouldn't the North attempt to establish as an international norm the obligation of the rich to help the poor? Considering that the distribution of those funds would ultimately remain under the control of Northern governments, allowing them to demonstrate to Northern legislatures, taxpayers, and themselves that the funds are being spent in ways that further the development process (to say nothing of other Northern foreign policy objectives), it simply seems like one of the easiest reforms to undertake if Northern governments are willing to spend some political capital on this issue. In undertaking such a reform the North might even retreat from the 0.7 percent target to something like 0.5 percent. The "reform" would lie in the acceptance of a *commitment to meet the target*, whatever its level.

Before considering the three final examples of reforms that are all part of the potential global reform spectrum, it is interesting to note how much might be accomplished of an economic developmental nature simply if significant progress is made in the three areas already examined. The analysis suggests how much might be accomplished for a very considerable range of developing countries through increased trade liberalization, strengthened international financial institutions and rules of the game that implicitly strengthen LDC access to private capital markets, and a commitment to increase ODA to an annual figure in the 0.5–0.7 percent of GNP range.

The potential inherent in these three reforms will come as no surprise to the many developing countries that really desire more productive participation in the system rather than its drastic overhaul. [8] Nor will it come as a surprise to those analysts who continue to view the international economic system as relatively free of imperfections that are biased against the development process. Most of them would probably find reforms of this nature quite acceptable, viewing them as incremental reforms that can quite easily be appended to the graduation scenario.

"Quite easily" in a conceptual sense; politically quite formidable, as Chapter 5 suggests. But if significant elements of this minimum global reform package cannot be sold to Northern governments, legislatures, and publics over the coming half decade, it is doubtful that *any* package of reforms to complement the graduation scenario will prove acceptable.

4. Automatic Resource Transfers

Many developing countries of the Third and Fourth worlds often face "foreign-exchange bottlenecks" to continued rapid economic growth. Simply put, they are often unable to acquire enough foreign exchange (through export earnings; borrowing from the IMF, the IBRD, and the private international capital markets; or restraints on nonessential imports) to purchase the imports needed by a rapidly developing economy. As a part of the global systemic reform ingredient in North-South strategies and policy prescription for the 1980s, alternative methods of increasing the flow of foreign exchange to these countries would be explored which would be automatic (i.e., not dependent upon the political decisions of individual Northern countries or even of the developed countries as a group). This avenue of exploration would again be a direct, positive response to a long-standing Southern request.

Potential sources of revenue for such automatic transfers have been analyzed for years, although no concrete results have thus far been achieved. Taxes on international trade (or on certain commodity groups within this trade), the allocation of the IMF's Special Drawing Rights (SDRs), a percentage of the proceeds of a deep-seabed-mining regime, and the potential tax returns from a global fisheries regime have all received considerable attention as possible sources of "automatic transfers." Each scheme would involve a different type of "cost" and a different method of allocating the proceeds. In some instances, the cost might be measured in terms of Northern abstention from claims to an as yet unappropriated source of wealth (e.g., the profits from deep-seabed mining); in others, the North might be expected to bear the major burden of an international tax because of its weight in the system (e.g., an undifferentiated tax on international trade). In still other cases, such as an ocean fisheries regime, the potential revenues might flow from taxes established in order to optimize global levels of fish harvests. In this instance the purpose of the tax would be to help resolve a "global agenda" problem—overfishing and thereby depleting the ocean's natural resources—and by global agreement the proceeds would be allocated to Southern developmental purposes.

The unwillingness of Northern governments thus far to acquiesce in any such automatic forms of transfer might suggest that little could be gained from further exploration of this general approach. But in addition to the needs of the North to overcome the present stalemate system for its own purposes, change in the very issues of international relations is currently increasing the scope for automaticity and suggests that a new examination of the problem is merited. As the examples of regimes for deep-seabed mining and ocean fisheries suggest, global agenda issues of the 1980s may often involve novel resource allocation decisions. When and as those decisions are being made, opportunities will be presented for the gradual emergence of new international norms on global distributive issues. It is in these new areas that Northern governments will likely possess much more flexibility than they do in areas where the issue is perceived as one of redistribution rather than as an initial distribution or as an efficient response to a new "global management" problem.

Again the individual decisions may seem marginal while the process established may in truth be much more central. It has been estimated that several billion dollars would be generated by an appropriate tax within a global fisheries regime alone. Should several new regimes with similar potential be developed in the coming decade, and should Northern governments agree to allocation principles that had the effect of making the Southern development process the major beneficiary of such resources, another significant step in the direction of the "collective elaboration of welfare

choices" with a bias toward Southern developmental efforts would
have been taken.

5. The Construction of Global Regimes

The coming decade will witness the construction of a growing
number of global or quasi-global regimes to regulate state activity
in discrete areas of endeavor. The need for such regimes is the
result of scientific and technological advance on the one hand and
political perceptions on the other. For the most part, states are
driven to regime building only when they perceive that unregulated
activity in certain areas is no longer in their own self-interest:

Multilateral arrangements are considered only when it is recognized that
a valued objective cannot be attained without them. The evolution of
multilateral regimes for dealing with a scarce resource—whether this be
money, clean air or water, fish, radio frequencies, or radiation safety—
is thus a function of a general recognition that these goods cannot be
obtained through institutionally "cheaper" arrangements [e.g., unilateral
or bilateral methods]. This means that no arrangement [for new rule
creation, or regime creation] is concluded until such a recognition has
occurred. [9]

As most of the examples noted above suggest, the expansion of
scientific knowledge and technological capacity is now creating a
perceived need for many new international rules and rule-making
bodies to optimize the continued attainment of "valued objectives."
The seas are being fished well beyond so-called maximum sustainable yields; various pollutants are being discharged beyond the
capacity of the globe's environment to safely absorb them; sources
of radiation are perceived to be spreading more rapidly than the
regulatory norms that could limit margins for error within acceptable boundaries.

In the previous discussion of automatic resource transfers we
examined the constitution of such new bodies of rules and rule
making as a novel interstate activity in which the North should
examine the potential for resource transfers where such transfers
would not interfere with optimal organization of new regimes. In
this discussion the focus is upon the consideration of regimes that
would *themselves* be of particular benefit to the South if their needs

were appropriately represented as the regimes were being constructed. A regime for food in the coming decade can be used to
illustrate the approach being suggested here.

Can a global food system be developed which addresses (1)
emergency shortage problems, (2) major price fluctuation problems, and (3) the longer-term problem of increasing the capacity
of the developing countries to feed themselves through greatly
expanded domestic production? Since the 1974 Rome World Food
Conference there has been much international discussion devoted
to these subjects, but so far very little action. Most of the lack of
progress can be traced to sharp differences between the United
States and the European Common Market on the operative rules
that would control the working of a grain-reserve system; each party
to the argument has put forward proposals most congruent with
the perceived needs of its own agricultural constituencies.

What thus far continues to be ignored—to the eventual detriment
of whatever global regime for food production and international
distribution should emerge—are the needs of the developing countries and the implications of those needs for the North as well as
the South in the 1980s. The problem starts, as the National Research
Council of the National Academy of Sciences concluded in its 1977
World Food and Nutrition Study, with the obvious need for the
developing countries "to double their own food production by the
end of the century. We are convinced that this can be done given
the political will in the developing and higher-income countries."[10]
This necessity is based on projections that suggest the inability of
most LDC food-importing countries to earn enough foreign exchange to meet domestic food demand through an exponential
growth in their food imports.

From the Northern point of view, a global food regime that had
short-to-medium-term goals of famine prevention through the
stocking of emergency reserves (or cash to buy food to meet local
famine situations), price stabilization through the medium of a
global grain-reserve system, and the *longer-term goal* of major
increases in developing-country food production would be an em-
inently sensible objective for several reasons. Regarding the two
shorter-term goals, econometric studies suggest that global reduction in grain price fluctuations would create welfare gains for North-

ern consumers that exceed by 100 percent the probable cost of such a program. "These benefits do not include any macroeconomic output gains that might also be achieved as the result of reduced difficulties in managing inflation and resulting increases in employment permissible with macroeconomic unemployment-inflation target alternatives; nor do the benefits include any valuation placed on increased price certainty itself."[11]

The longer-term goal also concerns the issue of inflation versus price stability. Projections for the coming 20 years suggest that demand for grains will increase in the developed countries by one-third (the equivalent of total United States output today) and in the South by 100 percent (or 150 percent of present United States output). Quite simply, if developing countries continued their past production trends, their import needs would more than double before the end of the 1980s; and the extra demand on United States production capacity would greatly increase food costs for all the world's consumers, North and South. All studies of trends in per-unit production costs in the United States presently confirm this projection.

For all these reasons there is a significant and growing consensus among both agricultural and developmental specialists supporting the National Research Council's conclusion that the only sensible approach to a food regime over the longer term is to work as swiftly as possible to increase the capacity for food production within the developing countries themselves. The only alternative—constantly growing dependence on United States food exports, whose prices will rise because of rising per-unit production costs—will both undermine the Southern development process and add permanently to the inflation problem within Northern societies.

As the National Research Council's study notes,

There are large reserve assets in the developing countries that can be applied over the long run to increase world food production, and research can help make them more useful. These assets include large areas of land suitable for farming; grossly underutilized water resources; many sources of fertilizer and animal feed . . .; food currently lost during or after production; and large quantities of waste products from grains, oilseeds, fish, and animals that are now thrown away or used for nonfood purposes.[12]

Can Northern diplomatic efforts eventually turn United States–European Community bickering over the shorter-term elements of an embryonic global food regime into a significant global reform ingredient in North-South relations? The challenges are obvious; too often ignored are the potential benefits that would redound to the North as well as the South in the forms of (1) consumer welfare benefits and (2) important limitations on new global inflationary pressures of both a cyclical and a secular nature.

6. A "Holistic" View of the Population Stabilization Issue

The previous examples of the types of global reforms the North might well examine and present for discussion and negotiation with the South have—with the possible exception of the fourth and fifth examples, both involving global regimes—been fairly discrete and traditional in nature. And perhaps that is the only genus of reform that national bureaucracies are yet capable of conceptualizing. This shortcoming is not one of bureaucratic intelligence, but rather one of bureaucratic fragmentation. If the old aphorism "where you stand depends on where you sit" continues to reflect a good deal of bureaucratic truth in the 1980s, the approach to global reform issues of great potential benefit to the North-South stalemate situation, illustrated by this final example, is unlikely to provide a constructive opening. Nevertheless, we briefly examine it in order to illuminate once again the degree to which one's views on the need for novel approaches to the consideration of serious reforms affecting present North-South relations depend upon one's perception of major international issues for the 1980s and the role of North-South conflict and compromise in constructively addressing those issues.

The population stabilization approach discussed here is intimately connected with the basic-human-needs approach to economic development, examined in the following chapter. Therefore all the difficult questions concerning implementation of that strategy will be set aside for purposes of this discussion and examined as part of Chapter 8. It should also be noted that the *rationale* for considering the population stabilization/basic-human-needs set of issues in this chapter is quite different from the one presented in Chapter 8. Here we consider the issue as a final example of the global reform ingredient in North-South policy prescription in the

1980s, as one in a spectrum of reforms that might contribute to more constructive North-South relations by introducing changes that can range far beyond those expected to accompany the graduation scenario.

The discussion of basic human needs in the following chapter concerns the need for a third and final basic ingredient in North-South policy formulation in and of itself, one which is informed much more by normative concerns and equity issues at the *intrastate*, or individual, level. The fact that a basic-human-needs approach to development strategies and their reform may also play a very positive role in achieving global population stabilization sooner than might otherwise be expected is an important *additional* reason for giving the highest priority to the search for an effective approach to abolishing absolute poverty and guaranteeing the lower strata of the developing-country populations minimum standards of nutrition, health care, and education.

In 1976 the world's population passed the 4 billion mark. Population growth rates in the developing countries averaged 2.2 percent, more than twice the average in the developed countries. If current trends in fertility rates continue, with crude birthrates in the developing countries falling by approximately 6 points per decade, a net reproduction rate of 1.0 percent would be reached in the year 2020 and a steady-state population of some 11 billion would be reached approximately 70 years later.

If the trend of falling birthrates in the developing countries could be increased in order to reach a net reproduction rate of 1.0 percent two decades earlier, i.e., in 2000, the stationary-state population would be reduced by 3 billion, from 11 to 8 billion (a figure still representing twice the 1976 global total). This achievement would significantly ease the economic growth problems of the developing countries; limit eventual population pressures on global food production constraints, environmental constraints, and all other forms of actual and potential scarcities; and lower many forms of international conflict that may easily accompany rapid population growth rates (e.g., Mexican and Caribbean illegal immigration into the United States) and a massive increase in global population (e.g., greater concerns over and conflict accompanying the staking of claims to raw materials, for reasons that may be rational or irrational).

The unsettling implications of developing-country population growth rates have been a cause of concern in the North for many years. But within the past 15 years, many developing countries have openly or tacitly acknowledged that these growth rates are now perceived as a problem and have begun to implement a wide range of programs to lower them. The recent dramatic conversions of India and Mexico to this point of view have received extensive publicity, but actually the decade of the 1960s began to witness a rapid growth of antinatalist movements throughout the developing world. At the present time, over 70 percent of the world's population lives in countries that offer family planning in their existing public health services, over 80 percent of the developing world's population is located in countries that sponsor official family planning programs, and over 90 percent of the people in Asia live in countries whose deliberate policy is to reduce fertility.

Given the growing Northern and Southern convergence of policy objectives in this area, what implications, if any, follow for North-South strategies? The first would be to continue all scientific efforts to understand the key determinants—complex as they are—that appear to link fertility reduction to certain specific elements of socioeconomic development. The generally positive correlation between socioeconomic development and falling birthrates has been noted for years. That correlation now appears to be more specifically related to literacy, nutrition, and falling infant mortality. Furthermore, there no longer seems to be any doubt that an improvement in the welfare of the poorest strata of developing-country societies "appears to be essential before fertility can fall to developed country levels."[13]

In an address to the Massachusetts Institute of Technology in 1977, World Bank President Robert McNamara summarized the present state of knowledge and the policy implications in the following manner:

1. A significant decline in fertility may finally have begun in most developing countries.
2. For every decade of delay in achieving a net reproduction rate of 1.0—replacement-level fertility—the ultimate steady-state world population will be approximately 15 percent greater.

3. The key linkages between fertility reduction and socioeconomic development appear to be basic health care, basic education, economic growth that includes rising standards of living for the poorest members of society, urbanization, and the enhanced status of women.
4. There are two major policy implications:
    (a) Those of a broad developmental nature, designed to encourage couples to desire smaller families
    (b) Those designed to provide parents with the means to implement that desire.

The first implication calls for policies to accomplish the following goals:

*   The reduction of infant and child mortality
*   The expansion of basic educational opportunities (for females as well as males)
*   Increased productivity of rural smallholders and nonagricultural workers
*   More equitable distribution of income and services in the process of economic growth
*   Enhanced economic, social, and political status for women

The second implication calls for the following policies:

*   Provision of a broad choice of contraceptive techniques
*   Development of an improved contraceptive delivery system
*   Expansion of research seeking better contraceptive techniques and services. [14]

Most of these policy implications may seem to be limited in relevance to Southern governments alone. But if global population size is perceived as important to the North as well as the South—and certainly a great number of Northerners share this perception—then the question arises: What, if anything, can Northern governments do to assist in the implementation of such policies? Clearly they can assist at the level of the second policy implication by continuing research (and funding of research) on birth control techniques and their dissemination, working directly with Southern governments when asked to do so. They can also support loans and grants to Southern governments for such purposes.

The first policy implication—development strategies aimed at patterns of socioeconomic development that channel more resources in the direction of programs to set minimum living standards for the poorest—raises a set of complex questions about economic development in general and the appropriate role of Northern governments in attempting to influence strategies of development. This issue will be fully explored in the following chapter, but for present purposes the question can be posed from the perspective of a "global population regime." Does it not make eminent sense for Northern governments to assist those Southern governments desiring financial and technical help in attempts at both the broad development strategy level and the more technical birth control level to move as quickly as possible to replacement-rate levels of reproduction? This conclusion would certainly seem logical if population stabilization were viewed as a public good from which all countries benefit.

This, then, is an example of the mode of thinking that more "holistic" approaches to global problems of the future would encourage. The approach often suggests perspectives on North-South relationships and policy conflicts which are otherwise not apparent. Its merits will be judged differently by all those interested in the present problems inherent in North-South relations, as the following section suggests.

III

Three lines of argument support the contention that a more active examination of potential global reforms should form one of the fundamental ingredients of North-South policy prescription in the coming years. The first is normative, the second prudential, and the third technical.

In the arena of norms and values, the search for reforms extending far beyond those that might automatically accompany the graduation approach is congruent with the view that present per capita income differentials between North and (non-OPEC) South are ethically unacceptable. Were the present relative income gap between developed and developing countries narrowing, or if projections suggested that it would begin to narrow in the near future, a more cautious incrementalism might be acceptable. In fact of course, as Table 7-2 suggests, in both absolute *and* relative terms the gap continues to widen; in absolute terms the probabilities are that it will continue to do so for centuries. Those concerned with inequalities at the *interstate* level and more concerned with equality of result than of opportunity simply find this an intolerable future and insist on the search for ways in which to alter present trends.

Those less concerned with the more abstract issue of interstate inequalities but vitally concerned with the equity issue as it affects the absolute poverty population throughout the developing world will tend to stress those global (and accompanying domestic) reforms that will have the greatest probability of eliminating absolute poverty as quickly as possible.

Concerns with this aspect of the normative issue of inequality lead to the consideration of global food regimes and population stabilization regimes that would, it is hoped, begin to have a direct and positive impact on the absolute poverty problem during the coming decade. These concerns also merge to support the basic-human-

Table 7-2 Relative Income Gaps: Developing-Country Per Capita Incomes as a Percentage of Developed-Country Incomes*

	1950	1960	1975
Developing countries:			
Poorest†	6.1	4.0	2.6
Middle-income	20.8	18.3	17.0
Oil-exporting†	n.a.	16.1	22.6
All developing countries	11.9	9.7	9.2

*The income data used to prepare the table reflect currency conversions at official exchange rates rather than comparative purchasing power. Had purchasing-power comparisons been available, they would probably have shown similar income trends but gaps of lesser magnitude.

†Indonesia is included in the "poorest" category.

Source: Robert McNamara, 1977 Address to the Board of Governors of the World Bank, p. 8.

needs element of North-South policy making, but they support many ingredients of the global reform approach as second-best efforts to achieve their ultimate aim: the abolition of absolute poverty.

The prudential arguments favoring the global reform approach are based on two premises about developing-country needs and desires. First, they assume that most developing-country governing elites are truly interested in economic development issues as well as issues of power and status in international politics. And the arguments are surely correct in the aggregate. With many developing countries facing the tensions caused by high birthrates, increasing unemployment and underemployment, and social mobilization, rapid economic growth provides LDC governing elites with the same social solvent it has provided Northern systems of governance in decades past. Therefore relatively few elites desiring to remain in power can afford to be uninterested in increasing growth opportunities, especially those that come at the expense of outsiders (in dollar or "adjustment" terms).

The second assumption underlying the prudential argumentation for the global reform approach is that Northern treatment of Southern ecomomic demands as serious and negotiable issues will produce positive gains for the entire process of multilateral diplomacy by easing the most confrontational aspects of North-South diplomacy. Thus the conviction that a broad examination of potential reforms in the international economic system—with a bias toward the hope that mutually satisfactory responses to a significant number of Southern demands can be found—will provide for that minimum degree of North-South understanding needed to begin constructive work on the array of global agenda items the North will face in the coming decade.

This viewpoint is not without supporting empirical evidence. When the United States switched its position between the Sixth and Seventh Special Sessions of the UNGA and pronounced itself ready to enter a period of negotiation on the issues raised by the Group of 77, the "moderates" were able to resume leadership of the Southern coalition and begin a process of dialogue at CIEC which was continued for close to 2 years with far less rhetoric and public confrontation than had characterized the previous 2 years.

Even in the months following the futile denouement of CIEC, the moderate forces within the Group of 77 continued the process of quiet diplomacy to explore what might be salvaged from the abortive Paris meetings.

Other fragments of evidence suggest the same interpretation of the benefits to be derived from a less rejectionist, more cooperative Northern endeavor simply to explore potential avenues of reform. Often cited is the role played by the Organization of African Unity in moderating resolutions at the Fall 1976 UNESCO conference on issues ranging from Israel to the treatment of the Northern news media in developing countries. The conclusions drawn from such evidence, although admittedly fragmentary and open to differing interpretations, is that Northern unwillingness even to examine the range of economic reform issues that would be scrutinized along with others under this particular policy prescription is as much responsible for the current impasse in North-South relations as is Southern "stridency."

Finally, there is a body of straightforward technical argumentation which supports this basic global reform ingredient in North-South policy prescription for the coming years. It is drawn from those analysts of the economic issues raised before, during, and since the "great NIEO debate" and of the performance of the international economy since the early 1970s who are convinced that many of the issues similar to those put forward as illustrations in this chapter would prove amenable to positive-sum reforms in which both North and South would be the beneficiaries. Obvious examples of such reforms are the construction of international food and fisheries regimes and the process of further trade liberalization. If one adds the potential assistance that trade liberalization and a global food regime could give to the fight against Northern inflationary pressures, the calculated benefits from such reforms must be considerably increased.

It is this technique of scanning the horizon for growing problems that will require international cooperation for effective resolution within the coming decade, and of seeking "positive-sum" outcomes that combine efficiency and equity norms to win both Northern and Southern support, that totally distinguishes this global reform approach from the incremental approach implicit in the graduation scenario. It is an approach concerned with tomorrow's problems, not today's. It is an approach that attempts to link predictable problems whenever the linkage is likely to produce more effective analysis and management of the problems involved (as a food and/or a population stabilization regime). And it is an approach that, if followed with constant attention to "global agenda" issues on the one hand and the need to ease North-South tensions on the other hand, could produce far more policy space than current levels of rhetoric and concern about the "inevitable" clash between efficient solutions and equitable solutions suggest.

IV

The approach to the examination of more-than-incremental global economic reforms suggested in this chapter seems merited on two major counts. First, it serves as a partial response to three problems caused by the graduation scenario: the perceptual problems accompanying a co-optation strategy, the world-order-politics problem, and the equity/distribution problem. And second, if pursued with analytical rigor and political acumen, it is clearly capable of assisting Southern developmental efforts and Northern economic difficulties as well. The farther into the future one projects both Southern and Northern economic dilemmas, the more plausible become the arguments for sustaining the analytical and diplomatic efforts that would be entailed in this examination of global economic reforms.

Nevertheless, it would be an injustice to all parties to the North-South confrontation not to recognize the potential weaknesses inherent in this approach. As with each of the three basic ingredients of policy prescription analyzed in Part IV of this study, an over-enthusiastic embrace of any single element is quite likely to produce costs disproportionate to benefits achieved. Perhaps the best manner in which to illuminate the potential costs of embracing the global reform ingredient with an excess of *brio* is to focus first on the problems of North-South *negotiation* and second on the problems of Northern *implementation*.

The problems likely to arise during the negotiating process stem from the differing perceptions concerning the role and effectiveness of the present international economic system (defined as a set of rules, norms of behavior, and institutions to enforce and/or alter those rules and norms). Most Northern policy makers and economists view the present system as—at minimum—a fairly effective instrument for achieving the optimal use of global resources. Turning specifically to the issue of Southern economic development, they observe that over the past 25 years, Southern states have grown at both aggregate and per capita rates that have never been matched by any other group of states. And thus their concern is as much to keep the system at its present levels of "openness" to Southern developmental efforts as it is to seek major alterations that in the eyes of many appear unnecessary.

These perceptions are not shared by most Southern policy makers, in great part because their major concern—to the extent it is an economic and not a political concern—is not with the day-to-day functioning of the system but rather with the North-South gap problem, which the system is admittedly not "resolving." Northern policy makers who are party to the North-South debate judge the system according to its responsiveness to the problems of *economic development* and give it good marks; Southerners often judge it according to its *gap-closing capacities* and give it failing marks. In view of the questions each group is asking, both are right.

Given these differing perspectives—which are only slightly caricatured—there is an obvious danger inherent in the process of negotiating reforms of the system. It lies in the significant probabilities that the goals of the two parties to the negotiation and to any schemes that emerge from such negotiations will remain in conflict. And that conflict could well guarantee the failure of the reforms themselves. At a minimum the reforms would produce a Northern perception that the South was guilty of a misuse of such reform schemes.

An obvious example of this danger can be discerned in the commodity agreements issue. Government representatives from most developing countries have already declared that one of the major purposes of such agreements is to increase the price of raw materials covered by the agreements with no reference to longer-term, market-trend forces. Northern countries for the most part have insisted that the role of commodity agreements should be limited to stabilizing prices around long-term market trends. The obvious concern arises that such a fundamental conflict would tend to be papered over during the course of a negotiation in which the North was searching for "constructive compromise," but would reappear as soon as a commodity regime had been officially negotiated and constituted. At that point Northern governments would be faced with two unpalatable alternatives: a failure and breakup of the regime or further Northern compromises that would eventually legitimize the price-raising goals of the developing countries. Either outcome would be likely to have serious adverse consequences: the first for North-South diplomatic relations, the second for the working of the international economy.

Two other valid concerns that also stem from the conflicting goals of the two parties are raised with regard to the global reform approach at the negotiating stage. First, where the North will be looking for the longer-term, positive-sum reforms that can benefit all countries, Southern goals will lead Southern negotiators to focus more insistently on shorter-term zero-sum reforms that are most likely to produce immediate gains for the South at the expense of the North. Thus the South will focus on higher (and then "indexed") commodity prices, a general moratorium on international debt repayments, and the assurance of SDRs with an aid-SDR link.

Second, once such negotiations have begun, the South's proven capacity for cohesion may on certain occasions outlast that of the North. Many European members of the OECD seem more willing than the United States, for example, to accept reforms of dubious value to the global system *or* to the Southern development process simply for tactical, diplomatic reasons. And thus the fear on the part of many Northerners that the international economic system, which is not perceived as the imperfection-ridden, Northern-biased culprit in the present North-South drama, would be subjected to the risk of serious weakening by the inherent dynamic of the North-South negotiating process that opened the system to major reforms.

The second area of potential cost to North-South relations lies in the post-negotiation stage of Northern implementation. Here one runs directly into the numerous problems of Northern domestic constraints which will face all reforms that might manage to clear the negotiating hurdle. Given the problems and projections discussed in Chapter 5, it is clear that in a potentially neo-mercantilist Northern environment many negotiated reforms may never successfully run the Northern legislative gauntlet. Well-analyzed precedents for such a prediction abound in the trade-liberalization and foreign assistance areas. And even those reforms that are endorsed by Northern legislatures are likely to have loopholes added to them that when activated may lead to serious Southern disappointments and exacerbated North-South conflict.

Two classical forms these loopholes may take might be noted to illustrate the broad and still growing magnitude of this problem. The South's access to the markets of the OECD countries for its manufactured exports is constantly in jeopardy of being limited through the use of domestic "escape clauses," Orderly Marketing Arrangements, and other forms of voluntary and involuntary restraint. Thus the advantages of trade liberalization and the growing Southern capacity to export manufactured products at highly competitive international prices can be seriously undermined as the result of political pressures within developed countries which Northern governments may be unable or unwilling to resist. While the degree of importance attached to this problem is clearly related to assessments of the present strength of Northern governments to withstand such pressures, preceding analysis does not suggest a very sanguine outlook.

The second example of the implementation problems to be expected concerns the potential impact on global reforms of "linkage politics" and "extraneous" events at the Northern domestic level. Within the United States, for example, Congress has increasingly placed basic-human-needs and human rights performance "strings" on United States foreign aid programs. Congress has also barred the OPEC countries from access to trade preferences granted to developing countries under the GSP program. Many other examples from the United States and other Northern countries could be cited to illuminate these problems of domestic implementation raised by legislative branches of government—often in response to private-sector pressures for "protection" of one sort or another.[15] It is certainly plausible to suggest that many of the global reform approaches noted in this chapter might find themselves subjected to similar "extraneous" congressional riders.

In earlier decades, seemingly stronger executive branch leadership was able to defeat such pressures, particularly when national security arguments could be employed against the more particularistic pleadings of special-interest groups. Now executive leadership is weakened, at least for the short term, and the national security rationale has been replaced by pleas for world-order politics, eloquent statements concerning international equity, and warnings about the complexities of global agenda issues and the consequent need for Southern cooperation. These changed circumstances are not particularly conducive to optimism regarding the prospects for a warm congressional embrace of the Aspen Institute's latest rendition of a "global bargain."

V

The global reform approach suggested in this chapter would be an integral part of a Northern initiative to move North-South relations beyond their present stalemate position, and the critique of that approach has attempted to assess the capacity of this particular ingredient of a broader North-South strategy to respond to the needs of the diplomatic situation within the parameters set by Northern domestic constraints. The degree of Southern support for this basic element in an overall North-South set of policy guidelines would clearly be a function of the nature of the actual reforms to be considered, the speed with which they would be examined and negotiated, and the degree to which the problems potentially associated with Northern implementation actually appeared. Many Southerners would welcome the general approach and would partake of the process as they did for 18 months at the Paris CIEC meeting, since many issues similar to those on the NIEO and CIEC agendas would be reconsidered even if the perspective for such reconsideration were altered. It is also to be expected that, because of the CIEC failure, a new round of dialogue would have to overcome a good deal of initial skepticism.

If this line of strategy is implemented in a broad and brisk fashion, and if the point is reached where Southerners see not the standard NIEO reforms but a serious Northern set of counterproposals, a time of testing of both Southern and Northern objectives will at least have been reached. Will the South be satisfied to study and negotiate a range of proposals designed to ensure increased equality of opportunity in the present international system rather than proposals that focus on short-term redistributional devices? And will it exhibit enough concern with some of the longer-term, "world-order" issues (such as regime building in areas of serious interest to the South only in a 10–20-year time perspective) to welcome rather than repudiate such an agenda? If the agenda is all long-term in nature, one can easily predict repudiation; it will be a Northern responsibility to make the agenda balanced enough through proposals on trade liberalization, foreign economic assistance flows, and strengthened IMF and IBRD capacities to assist the developing countries to avoid what economists would refer to as a classical "time preference" conflict.

As for the North, will it demonstrate the capacity to move beyond the incremental graduation scenario? Is it prepared for "world-order politics"? Stanley Hoffmann has observed that four imperatives of state behavior are required to move in this direction: "(1) giving priority to what is collectively important in the long run over what is individually attractive in the short term; (2) being willing to commit certain resources in advance so as to decrease uncertainty; (3) reducing one's own and each other's vulnerabilities so as to make interdependence bearable; and (4) institutionalizing world politics."[16] Many of the types of reforms analyzed in this chapter would indeed require healthy doses of some or all of these four ingredients. Will Northern policy makers develop a consensus view that steps in this direction are required? If so, will they be able to overcome the formidable domestic constraints toward movement in this direction? In particular, will the United States be able to accept an approach to North-South relations which, despite the steady pace of international systemic change, is still perceived by many observers and practitioners as unduly accommodating in terms of traditional statecraft? As Hoffmann warns about United States foreign policy in general, every perceived failure to achieve something close to the theoretical best will be denounced domestically as "a failure of will."[17] In the North-South arena, where "the divorce between might and achievements"[18] may be perceived to be at its greatest, the domestic and legislative pressures opposing the global reform element of North-South relations may consequently be at their most formidable. Whether or not they can be overcome may depend upon the capacity of the final fundamental ingredient of North-South policy prescriptions in the 1980s—the basic-human-needs ingredient—to link otherwise disparate and often conflicting interest groups and perceptions, North and South, into a more homogeneous and unified source of support for an attempt to overcome the present stalemate system.

NOTES

[1]Mahbub ul Haq, *The Third World and the International Economic Order*, Development Paper No. 22 (Washington, D.C.: Overseas Development Council, 1976), p. 11. Emphasis added.

[2]Ibid. pp. 52–53.

[3]John G. Ruggie and Ernst B. Haas, "Environmental and Resource Interdependencies: Reorganizing for the Evolution of International Regimes," Appendix vol. 1, p. 223, Commission on the Organization of the Government for the Conduct of Foreign Policy (Washington, D.C.: U.S. Government Printing Office, 1975).

[4]Ibid, p. 225. Emphasis added.

[5]Ibid.

[6]Robert S. McNamara, Address to the Board of Governors of the World Bank, Washington, D.C., September 26, 1977, p. 16.

[7]For a discussion of several such possibilities, see John Williamson, "International Borrowing by Developing Countries," *International Finance and Development* (New York: McGraw-Hill for the Council on Foreign Relations 1980s Project, forthcoming), and Gordon W. Smith, *The External Debt Prospects of the Non-Oil-Exporting Developing Countries* (Washington, D.C.: Overseas Development Council, 1977).

[8]See, for example, the analysis by Albert Fishlow, "A New International Economic Order: What Kind?" in Fishlow et al., *Rich and Poor Nations in the World Economy* (New York: McGraw-Hill for the Council on Foreign Relations/1980s Project, 1978), pp. 9–83.

[9]Ruggie and Haas, op. cit., p. 218.

[10]National Research Council, *World Food and Nutrition Study* (Washington, D.C.: National Academy of Sciences, 1977).

[11]Lance Taylor et al., *Grain Reserves, Emergency Relief, and Food Aid* (Washington, D.C.: Overseas Development Council, 1977), pp. iv–v.

[12]National Research Council, op. cit., p. 53.

[13]Timothy King (ed.), *Population Policies and Economic Development*, published for the World Bank (Baltimore: Johns Hopkins University Press, 1974), p. 137.

[14]See Robert S. McNamara, *Address to the Massachusetts Institute of Technology*, April 28, 1977 (pamphlet published by the World Bank), passim.

[15]In 1977, for example, the House approved a provision in the foreign assistance bill banning "direct or indirect" United States assistance for the production or export of palm oil, citrus products, or sugar. The measure would have affected both United States bilateral assistance and United States funds allocated to international lending institutions. The provision was dropped only after President Carter pledged to instruct United States representatives to the lending institutions to vote against any loans that would increase the production of the three commodities.

[16]Stanley Hoffmann, "No Choice, No Illusions," *Foreign Policy*, no. 25, Winter 1976–77, p. 110.

[17]Ibid., p. 113.

[18]Ibid., p. 112.

Chapter 8
The Basic-Human-Needs Ingredient

I

The final basic ingredient adding policy space for North-South policy prescription in the 1980s is related to the concept of abolishing absolute poverty through the meeting of minimum basic human needs. The idea of "the meeting of the basic human needs of the absolute poor in both the poorest and the middle-income countries within a reasonable period of time, say by the end of the century,"[1] may at first glance appear to have burst upon the North-South (or the development economics) scene overnight. There is little question that within the past several years the concept of absolute poverty and the goal of its global abolition within a stated period of time have received a great deal of exposure within the so-called development community. Since the World Bank has played a major role in establishing the analytical underpinnings for the concept and the goal, it is not surprising that development economists should be quite familiar with them by this time.

What is remarkable, however, is the degree to which other individuals, groups, and institutions representing a wide range of countries, disciplines, and perspectives have independently arrived

245

at very similar concepts and goals during this same period of time. These concepts and goals lie at the very core of recent analysis and prescription by many Northern (and a few Southern) private organizations. They are prominent in the ILO Director General's report prepared for the 1976 World Employment Conference. Additionally, they are given substantial prominence by the international group of economists recently assembled by the Dutch economist Jan Tinbergen to present thoughts and proposals on North-South relations to the Club of Rome.

The ideas contained in these various reports have on many occasions captured the imagination of their audiences. Most notably, the World Employment Conference asserted that the meeting of basic human needs should become the core of the UN's Third Development Decade (DD III). Later UNGA resolutions accepted the idea that the concept should be given major emphasis in planning for DD III. And the U.S. House of Representatives, which had already begun to move in the basic-human-needs direction when it rewrote United States foreign aid legislation in 1973, added the following wording to a 1977 bill funding international financial institutions:

The Secretary of State and the Secretary of the Treasury shall initiate a wide consultation, designed to develop a viable standard for the meeting of basic human needs and the protection of human rights, and a mechanism of acting together to insure that the rewards of international economic cooperation are especially available to those who subscribe to such standards and are seen to be moving toward making them effective in their own systems of government.

No later than one year from the date of enactment of this action, the Secretary of State and the Secretary of the Treasury shall report . . . the progress being made in carrying out this section.

Finally, by mid-1977 both the U.S. AID Administrator and the U.S. Secretary of State had called for developed-country cooperation in examining the programmatic aspects of a basic-human-needs approach and developing proposals that might form the agenda for continuing North-South discussion. In requesting the OECD to design a "Program for Basic Human Needs," Secretary of State Vance made the following remarks:

The case for more concerted action is clear. Almost one billion people live in absolute poverty. The problem is growing. Increases in GNP for many developing countries have *not* meant increased benefits for the poor. For many, in fact, life is worse. Development has too often not "trickled down."

Knowledge about the development process and the ability to overcome poverty are now within our grasp. What we miss is the joint recognition by developed and developing nations that the North-South Dialogue is about *human beings*, and that "equality of opportunity" for a fuller life makes sense for *people*, not just states.[2]

It is highly unlikely that the concept of fulfilling basic human needs and all that it implies could have achieved such broad and high-level recognition without a great deal of empirical evidence substantiating the existence of a serious problem: the problem of absolute poverty. Nor could the concern with that problem have become so widespread and fundamental had it not been perceived as a normatively compelling issue. Both aspects of the emergence of the basic-human-needs theme suggest that it will, in a variety of ways, serve as a third fundamental ingredient in North-South relations and policy prescription in the coming decade.

Several questions concerning its capacity to moderate North-South conflict and produce an end to the present stalemate system are immediately apparent. Can it provide a response to the equity/distribution issues given such limited attention in the graduation scenario? Can one find in the basic-human-needs set of issues support for embryonic global reforms and for world-order politics? Because the normative element in this perspective on North-South relations is so predominant, it is very easy for some observers to envision it as the ingredient that can successfully bind together the best elements of all the other major policy approaches analyzed in this study. From the Northern perspective it might be seen as adding the missing equity ingredients; strengthening the building of regimes in the areas of food production, population stabilization, and health services; and finally, beginning the slow and arduous task of building global norms that might, over time, deflate the otherwise unassailable contention that at the present moment, "it would be ludicrous to attempt even the vaguest articulation of those values common to the participants in the struggle over a new distribution of wealth and power."[3]

But all these are Northern perceptions. Even if we assume that Northern domestic support for the basic-human-needs ingredient of North-South policies will be forthcoming—an assumption to be analyzed below—the issue of Southern perceptions presents an entirely different set of hurdles to be overcome. It is one of the great ironies of the present North-South relationship that, unless handled with utmost diplomatic finesse, the basic-human-needs ingredient may simply add to present levels of North-South conflict. But before a critique covering these and related issues is presented, we must examine the problem of absolute poverty and the emergence of the basic-human-needs approach to the resolution of that problem.

II

It is the very magnitude and the inherent dynamic of the absolute poverty problem that assure that basic-human-needs concerns represent much more than the latest in passing fashions within development economics. The extent of the absolute poverty problem is staggering, and in absolute numbers it is growing year by year. The best estimates available suggest that in the mid-1970s somewhere between 0.7 billion and 1.2 billion inhabitants of the developing countries were subsisting in extreme poverty. They were caught in a vicious circle in which their levels of food consumption and its nutritional value led to high levels of disease and infant mortality and to low levels of life expectancy.

Contributing to the syndrome of absolute poverty are inadequate infrastructures for appropriate health, sanitation, and basic education services. In most countries these infrastructures are heavily skewed in favor of the urban upper class (e.g., modern hospitals, college education) at the expense of far less costly and far more cost-effective rural services with an emphasis on preventive medicine and basic literacy. The end result in most cases is early death or, for those who survive, insufficient job opportunities to break out of the absolute poverty cycle. Often the lack of adequate nutrition impairs both the mental and physiological capabilities of those who do reach adulthood, limiting their capacity for productive employment even when such opportunities become available.

Generally the three areas thought to be most vital in overcoming the absolute poverty problem are those of food/nutrition, health care (including proper sanitation and clean drinking water), and basic education. As other elements, such as shelter and clothing, are added to the list of minimum needs, the number of people defined as living in absolute poverty expands. But in order to use the most reliable statistics available, this chapter will focus on the 0.7 billion to 1.2 billion people and the three most central aspects of the poverty syndrome: food/nutrition, health services, and basic educational services.

The one essential need itemized that is obviously more than physical in content is primary education. It is generally included in the minimum list of basic needs because it is envisioned as a critical element in the breaking of the absolute poverty cycle. The assumption is that a minimum level of literacy will generally be required to enable individuals to take advantage of the employment opportunities that must also be present if the problem of absolute poverty is to be overcome.

The following three tables illuminate certain aspects of the problem. Table 8-1, examining the unemployment problem in various regions of the South, suggests that a total of 283 million are unemployed or severely underemployed. Considering that two dependents per labor force member represents a fairly accurate average, these figures are consistent with the aggregate absolute poverty estimates found in Table 8-2. Finally, Table 8-3 confirms the partial evidence, from study after study at the individual country or regional level, that the absolute poverty problem is increasing year by year even if the percentage of total developing-country population involved is slowly declining.

The magnitude and the continued growth of the absolute poverty problem help us to place the basic-human-needs approach and its recent emergence as an international policy issue in the proper perspective. The development strategies of the 1950s and 1960s were dominated by the concept of rapid economic growth as the major criterion of development. Some economists supported the criterion because they felt that the benefits of rapid growth would quickly trickle down to the poor; other supporters of the rapid-growth approach were less certain that the workings of the marketplace would assure equitable sharing, but felt that corrective

**Table 8-1 Preliminary Estimates of Unemployment and
Underemployment in Developing Countries, by Region, 1975 (in Millions)**

	UNEMPLOYMENT*		UNDEREMPLOYMENT†		TOTAL	
	TOTAL	URBAN	TOTAL	URBAN	TOTAL	URBAN
REGION	NO. %	NO. %	NO. %	NO. %	NO. %	NO. %
Asia†	18 3.9	6 6.9	168 36.4	20 23.2	186 40.3	26 30.1
Africa	10 7.1	3 10.8	53 37.9	7 25.1	63 45.0	10 35.9
Latin America	5 5.1	5 6.5	28 28.9	14 22.8	33 34.0	19 29.3
Oceania	— —	— —	1 49.0	— —	1 49.0	— —
Total	33 4.7	14 8.0	250 35.7	41 23.3	283 40.4	55 31.3

*Defined as "persons without a job and looking for work."

†Defined as "persons who are in employment of less than normal duration and who are seeking or would accept additional work" and "persons with a job yielding inadequate income."

‡Excluding China and other Asian centrally planned economies.

Source: Employment, Growth and Basic Needs, Report of the Director-General of the International Labour Office (Geneva, 1976), p. 18.

government policies could achieve an appropriate degree of redistribution. Finally, there were those who focused on rapid growth as the primary developmental target in the belief that a growing degree of domestic inequality was essential for economic development. Only through this process, they argued, would the productive base for an eventual spread of the benefits of development emerge.

Against this general analytical background Northern economists (and governments) preached—and most Southern countries followed—development strategies that attempted to raise internal rates of savings and investment. Much of the investment took place in the protected "modern" sectors of the economy and also concentrated government spending on "economic overhead" projects, e.g., electrical power and transportation, at the expense of "social overhead" expenditures in rural education, health and sanitation programs, and traditional agriculture.

Table 8-2 Estimated Number of People in Developing Market
Economies Living in Poverty, 1972

REGION	TOTAL POPULATION	SERIOUSLY POOR	DESTITUTE	SERIOUSLY POOR	DESTITUTE
		(MILLIONS OF PEOPLE)		(PERCENTAGE OF POPULATION)	
Asia	1,196	853	499	71	42
Africa	345	239	134	69	39
Latin America	274	118	73	43	27
Total*	1,815	1,210	706	67	39

*Excluding developing countries in Europe and Oceania, with a total population of about 25 million.
Source: Employment, Growth and Basic Needs, p. 22.

In the past 25 years the costs to the poorest 40 percent of the population in most developing countries that followed the standard trickle-down strategy of growth have become clear. Not only have their relative incomes and standards of living decreased, sometimes markedly, but there is considerable evidence to suggest that the absolute standard of living of the bottom 20 percent has also fallen in a significant number of countries.

Thus two of the early judgments concerning the benign effects of a concentration on rapid growth have proved to be incorrect as

Table 8-3 Increase in Poverty, 1963–1972 (Millions of Persons)

REGION	TOTAL POPULATION	SERIOUSLY POOR	DESTITUTE
Asia	195	92	34
Africa	68	26	5
Latin America	62	1	4
Total	325	119	43

Source: Employment, Growth and Basic Needs, p. 23.

applied to a substantial majority of concrete developing-country cases. First, there has been no rapid trickle-down; in the extreme cases the effects have been negative in both relative and absolute terms. Second, governments have in most instances failed to alter the highly inegalitarian distributional results of the concentration on rapid growth.

The reasons for these particular distributional failings of the standard trickle-down strategy can be understood when one identifies the constituents of the so-called "forgotten 40 percent." The overwhelming majority of the absolute poverty group is rural in origin, composed of landless rural laborers and subsistence farm families. For the developing world in general, these rural groups represent over 70 percent of the poverty population. Obviously a strategy of economic development that concentrates tax structures, commercial policies, and public expenditures on the development of a modern, capital-intensive urban industrial sector does nothing of a *direct* nature to increase the development prospects of the rural poor. Trickle-down policies of this type will affect such groups only as increased employment in the new urban industrial sector absorbs surplus labor. If and when this point is reached, rural wages can be expected to rise, as will the demand for agricultural production. But even this eventual improvement is generally contingent on the use of labor-intensive modes of agricultural production. And in many developing countries where landholding remains relatively concentrated, the rapid introduction of capital-intensive modes of agricultural production has undermined still further the potential of trickle-down strategies of growth to benefit the landless laborer and the subsistence farmer.

The standard trickle-down strategy has produced similarly detrimental results for urban poverty groups: the unemployed, the underemployed, and the self-employed in the traditional service sector and in the traditional manufacturing sector. The concentrated rewards to both capital and labor in the protected modern industrial sector—resulting from limited competition, skewed factor prices favoring capital-intensive modes of production, and the development of a "labor aristocracy" within modern industries—have severely limited the capacity of the modern sector to perform the function required for trickle-down to benefit the entire population, i.e., to rapidly absorb the urban unemployed and to draw down excess labor reserves from the rural areas. Unemployment and underemployment figures in excess of 35 percent are not uncommon in many countries that have followed such growth practices for several decades, and no decline in these figures is projected for the coming decade.

Had Southern governments taken the corrective actions that many economists had assumed they would, the fruits of growth might have been more equitably distributed. And many Southern developmental "success stories" suggest that appropriate policies imposed upon a rapid-growth strategy can (and did) ease the equity problem implicit in the typical growth model of the 1950s and 1960s. In most countries, however, governments did not attempt— or failed in the attempt—to speed the trickle-down process. Typically, a symbiotic relationship developed between governing elites and new industrial elites which prevented attempts to spread the fruits of growth.[4] For reasons of political convenience and/or economic conviction, governments did not use tax and investment policies to offset growing inequalities. Indeed, most used those same policy tools and others as well (exchange-rate policies, tariff structures, and import licensing, for example) in a way that exaggerated the inegalitarian impact of the standard growth model. And when such policies were followed the rationale, always implicit in the model, was that policies that allowed capital accumulation on the part of the rich today were expanding the productive capacity to ease the poverty problem tomorrow.

Even in countries where this general policy approach succeeded in aggregate-growth terms, it generally failed in terms of equity measurements for three major reasons. First, rates of increased employment in the modern industrial and agricultural sectors have been unable to keep pace with a growing labor force. In many instances this problem could have been alleviated by the setting of appropriate factor prices, which would have led to increased use of labor in the aggregate.

Second, and in great part a reflection of that problem, living conditions for landless laborers and subsistence farmers in rural areas often deteriorated. Low rates of labor absorption in the modern industrial and agricultural sectors necessarily contributed to a steady deterioration of living standards for these two rural groups. A comprehensive strategy of rural development that might have supplied these groups with relatively inexpensive health and educational infrastructures (e.g., a health system that emphasized preventive rather than curative medicine), agricultural services, and rural industrial projects was seldom attempted because government investment remained concentrated in urban modern-sector activities. Yet without such a comprehensive rural strategy, conditions were bound to deteriorate for the poorest strata of rural society if only because population growth rates outpaced the expansion of rural productive employment opportunities.

Third, the urban poor suffered for similar reasons. Productive employment opportunities did not keep pace with their expanding numbers, and government health and educational infrastructure policies catered to the desires of the middle and upper classes.

The aggregate results of the trickle-down strategy as implemented in most developing countries over the last 25 years have led an increasing number of economists and others to question the fundamental assumption of the standard strategy and to consider a variety of alternatives that might address the growing problem of absolute poverty. Statistical measurements have demolished the idea that the benefits of rapid growth would rapidly trickle down to the "forgotten 40 percent" at the bottom of the income ladder; empirical evidence from country after country has confirmed that either the political will to control the distribution of growth gains was missing or the political constraints inherently produced by such growth models impaired the capacity of governing elites to implement policies aimed at limiting the inegalitarian impact of the growth pattern. Finally, analyses even began to suggest that an initial concentration of income in the upper 5 percent of a country's population was not a necessary condition for rapid savings, investment, and development of a productive economic base for further development.

This new analysis first focused on the supposed trade-off between a development strategy aimed at output maximization and one aimed at employment maximization. It is captured in the following commentary by Gustav Ranis, written in 1970:

What I am, in fact, suggesting is that the general experience of the '50s and '60s which indicates the existence of a severe conflict in terms of rising output and unemployment levels is entirely misleading because the very strategy which was followed in the pursuit of output maximization was erroneous while a different set of policies might well have given us more growth *and* more employment. As economists and perpetrators of the dismal science, we seem to have difficulty in accepting the notion that it is possible to have more of both, i.e., more output and more employment. It is an incontrovertible fact that a substantial part of the profession and an even larger majority of policy makers implicitly or explicitly assume the existence of a conflict and are proceeding to talk about employment strategies as a way to ameliorate or amend the "output only" policies of the past. They talk about dethroning the GNP on behalf of employment and distribution. My point is that it may well come to that, but it may also be true that we have not even begun to explore a set of policies and development strategies which would give us increased output as a direct consequence of utilizing our unemployed or underemployed labor more effectively.[5]

The ideas expressed by Ranis were a crucial ingredient in the search for alternatives to the prescriptions of the trickle-down approach—a search that eventually led to the mid-1970s efforts to conceptualize and "operationalize" a basic-human-needs approach to development.

The search began by focusing on strategies to limit unemployment. Low unemployment rates—or better, high rates of *productive* employment—were seen as the key to overcoming the absolute poverty problem. Continued research supported this emphasis in several different ways. First, the idea that only high-income families would save and invest at the levels needed for healthy aggregate growth rates was slowly brought into question. It was noted that the validity of this argument depended on fairly large differences in marginal savings rates between the rich and the poor. Yet a good deal of recent empirical evidence suggested that such differences had often been grossly exaggerated. There was apparently little if any trade-off between employment-oriented growth strategies and rates of savings.

Another example of evidence that confirmed the potential for the new employment-oriented emphasis concerned the effect of land reform measures on agricultural development. Numerous studies from different parts of the developing world began to suggest that the breakup of large estates into small family farms need not entail efficiency losses since per-acre yields did not increase with increasing farm size. In fact studies often suggested the opposite, that increased labor inputs to be expected on small family farms would be likely to induce per-acre production gains. It has been argued that policies of land redistribution to increase rural employment and reduce income inequality have far less room for application on the Indian subcontinent, where land-to-man ratios are extremely low in comparison to those in most of Latin America and Africa. But even there the argument remains unsubstantiated. The idea of an optimal farm size, while extremely popular, is simply inconsistent with a great deal of empirical evidence that indicates constant per-acre returns as well as more intensive utilization of available land as farm size diminishes.[6]

Such evidence suggested further policy innovations that might attack the absolute poverty problem—or, more broadly, the income-distribution problem—with good prospects of success. The first innovation concerned the need for infrastructure systems that could assure the distribution of the appropriate production inputs for small agricultural and manufacturing units. For there would be declines in productivity and savings unless the newly employed had access to appropriate economic, technological, educational, and other inputs. A second innovation concerned the appropriate balance between agriculture and manufacturing, particularly as part of an integrated strategy of rural development. If there was not enough land to guarantee full employment, the location of manufacturing activities in rural areas could provide significant alternative employment opportunities for rural laborers. This pattern had been employed so successfully in Taiwan that land reform and rural manufacturing are often cited as the two key ingredients of the extraordinary Taiwanese success in the process of economic development.

Finally, increased attention was given to the potential capacity for the export of domestically produced manufactured products after factor prices had been changed to encourage more labor-intensive production and exchange rates had been lowered to reflect more adequately the true international purchasing power of domestic currencies.

If these were the essential policy implications of a redirection of priority from rapid growth to high productive employment, they still fell one step short of what was finally considered essential to the "basic-human-needs" package. Those who focused their primary attention on the forgotten 40 percent were still concerned about two additional aspects of the absolute poverty problem. First, they worried about the lengthy period of time it would take to raise the near-starvation conditions of those 1 billion persons even if high-employment-oriented growth strategies were pursued with vigor. Justification for these concerns was at least partially supplied by a 1974 World Bank–sponsored study entitled *Redistribution with Growth*. The study suggested that even full-employment strategies with built-in asset transfers (mostly in the form of a redirection of annual government investment toward the infrastructure needs of the poorest) would require several decades to have much of a positive impact upon income shares of the poorest.

Second, there was concern about the degree to which strategies that did not design and implement specific programs to aid the poorest could actually affect their living conditions. On paper, a general program of increased and redirected rural infrastructure expenditures, for example, can look as if it will be of great benefit to the poor farmer. But so often in actual implementation what happens is that irrigation programs, feeder roads, and production credits end up aiding the rich farmers and never reaching the poor. The power structures at the regional and local levels are simply able to skew the best plans drawn up in capitals in ways that totally defeat the intent of the technocrats. This difficulty, which economists call the "leakage problem," was in the mind of one critic of the World Bank's "redistribution-with-growth" strategy when he offered the following assessment of it:

The problems of poverty in India remain intractable, not because redistribution objectives were inadequately considered in the planning models, nor because the general policies of the kind described in this volume were not attempted. . . . The major constraint is rooted in the power realities of a political system dominated by a complex constellation of forces representing rich farmers, big business, and the so-called petite bourgeoisie, including the unionized workers of the organized sector. *In such a context, it is touchingly naive not to anticipate the failure of asset distribution policies or the appropriation by the rich of a disproportionate share of the benefits of public investment.*[7]

Thus the final intellectual step was taken on the road to the articulation of a basic-human-needs program to overcome absolute poverty. It involved the proposition that a more direct and more rapid approach to the problem must be adopted. If the problems facing the 1 billion destitute people of the developing countries were to be eased with any rapidity, programs would be required which were specifically targeted upon their most basic needs—food/nutrition, health care, and basic education. This more narrow and specific focus on the basic needs of the world's destitute is not seen by those who endorse it as conflicting with the broader policy prescription for a high-employment-oriented development strategy that immediately preceded it as a major policy concern; indeed, the contrary is most often the case. Most of those who focus on the narrower, direct attack on the absolute poverty problem are the first to recognize that it is only through a successful strategy of high levels of productive employment that indestructible domestic foundations for the eradication of absolute poverty can be built. Otherwise a basic-human-needs program would in the long run be indistinguishable from a welfare program, which most Southern countries could not afford and most Northern states would not help to support. Therefore the basic-human-needs program is thought of as a necessary medium-term, supplementary measure to reduce present levels of destitution among the poorest billion in the context of an aggregate, high-employment-oriented set of development policies.

III

Perhaps the most appropriate way in which to analyze the various parameters of a basic-human-needs approach is once again to use a matrix that focuses attention on several specific though clearly linked aspects. Discussing the elements of the matrix should illuminate the problems and potential of the approach.

Most analysts and proponents of a basic-human-needs program explicitly recognize the four aspects of it noted in the matrix. They acknowledge that productive employment (box 1) is the only longer-term answer to the poverty problem. Therefore the apparent differences between those who stress the employment aspect and those who stress the direct distributional aspect are a matter of

Figure 8-1   A Basic-Human-Needs Program

	INDIRECT EMPLOYMENT EMPHASIS	DIRECT DISTRIBUTIONAL EMPHASIS
Domestic Financing	1	2
International Financing	3	4

degree, not kind, and are often much smaller than they are purported to be by opponents of the entire approach.

Perhaps we can make this point more concretely by focusing on a set of policy prescriptions made for India in the mid-1970s by John Mellor in his book *The New Economics of Growth*.[8] Mellor's analysis of India's economic development problems and its sociopolitical system led him to a set of prescriptions that emphasize a high-employment/increased-productivity approach to fulfilling basic human needs. He explicitly gears his prescriptions to a rural-oriented high-employment strategy because he concludes that a restructured growth model of this type contains great promise for indirectly resolving the absolute poverty problem and that the sociopolitical constraints on this set of changes are less formidable than those on a strategy emphasizing the direct distributional approach in the magnitudes required to significantly influence the absolute poverty problem in India.

His approach would place priority on increasing agricultural production through major investments in agricultural infrastructure, reduce the capital requirements for employees in the industrial sector, greatly expand small-scale manufacturing of a labor-intensive nature in rural areas, and increase both exports of labor-intensive goods and imports of capital-intensive goods.

His indirect approach to meeting basic human needs devotes priority to rapidly increased agricultural production. Crucial ingredients in this growth are the wider use of recently developed agricultural technology and improvements in present credit and marketing systems. All aspects of agricultural growth through the spread of technological change are based on expanding the number of rural supporting institutions to benefit the small farmer, who is, in Mellor's analysis, a crucial ingredient in the high-employment growth strategy.

Increased agricultural production of a labor-intensive nature will expand rural job opportunities and real income. The resulting increase in demand for manufactured consumer goods will be balanced by the growth of small, labor-intensive manufacturing capacity as part of an aggregate strategy of high-employment rural development. In detailing the changes needed to increase Indian growth rates at much lower levels of unemployment and with far greater infrastructure development to provide educational, health, and nutritional benefits for the rural-poverty population, Mellor suggests that many elements of the "Taiwan model" are not inappropriate if properly adapted to the Indian setting.

Mellor's approach lies at the indirect, high-employment-oriented end (boxes 1 and 3) of the basic-human-needs approach. He chooses it because, as noted above, he feels that sociopolitical constraints are less likely to undermine this approach than they are a more direct distributional alternative. This judgment leads to a concentration on the absolute poverty problem at one remove. His approach would attempt to diminish absolute poverty by initially raising the productive capacity of the rural smallholder. In turn, he would use a number of policy tools to ensure that the smallholder then contributed directly to ameliorating the poverty problem by hiring more landless laborers and expanding purchases of locally manufactured labor-intensive consumer products, thus creating additional job opportunities for the forgotten 40 percent in rural India.

The interested reader is encouraged to examine the Mellor book for all the details that inform this indirect policy approach to basic human needs via rapidly increased employment. The validity of each policy prescription is far less important than the overall conceptual approach to the problem.

At the other end of the spectrum are policies that would attack the absolute poverty problem far more directly. One can therefore think of the direct distributional half of the matrix as adding to the high-employment, poverty-oriented approach supplemental programs specifically designed to provide basic necessities to those persons not easily integrated into the development process.

It is at this point that the definitional, conceptual, and operational problems of the basic-human-needs concept are revealed to the analyst, admitted by the approach's proponents, and emphasized by its opponents. How are basic human needs to be defined and measured? Will they not vary from country to country, from culture to culture, from age group to age group? Once defined, there are problems with supply management. Should money or the actual ingredients of a basic-human-needs program itself be placed in the hands of the poorest? How much reliance can be placed on market forces, and how much direct governmental intervention is required? Equally important, can delivery systems be designed which assure that the ingredients of a basic-needs program reach the intended target population? In other words, can the leakage problem be minimized so that the benefits actually reach the absolute poor?

Supporters of the more direct distributional basic-needs approach believe that the problems posed by these questions can be resolved and argue that much of the information needed to develop appropriate policies already exists. All that remains to be done, they argue, is to pull the disparate pieces together from various pilot projects within numerous countries. Skeptics, who are most likely to emphasize the delivery problems, are far less certain that all the specific steps necessary to implement the approach are fully understood. While an enormous number of technical issues can always be raised unless and until such programs are actually implemented, what probably separates supporters from skeptics at this point is less the problem of "further analysis" than the probabilities each group assigns to the feasibility of such direct intervention.

In turn, the feasibility issue is intimately related to the (political and economic) questions of financing. The more emphasis that is put on supplemental programs that go beyond the introduction of a high-employment strategy in areas of concentrated poverty, the higher the economic (and sociopolitical) costs. A priori, it is reasonable to assume that the greater the degree of international financial support for these programs, the more relaxed will be the domestic constraints on attempts to implement them. The more the programs involve domestic redirection of future income flows (via tax reform, changing governmental investment patterns, etc.), the tighter the domestic constraints. Since the question of cost is an important aspect of the feasibility of the direct attack on absolute poverty—and thus of the feasibility of the entire basic-human-needs element in North-South policy prescription—the issue deserves exploration despite the "softness" of all cost estimates made to date. The analysis also allows a more detailed examination of the issue of domestic versus international financing.

The first published figures on eliminating absolute poverty suggested that a total expenditure of $125 billion (1974 dollars) spread over a 10-year period could achieve the goal.[9] The author admitted that these figures were crude estimates, as have all others who have since attempted such calculations. But estimates that have appeared more recently suggest that the order of magnitude is likely to be substantially higher than the first calculations. The most recent World Bank estimates suggest that a basic-human-needs program that would make available to the poorest billion minimum acceptable diets, drinking water, sewage facilities, public health services, and basic education might require an annual investment of $10 billion (1975 dollars) for a 20-year period above and beyond investments in these program areas implicit in present developing-country expenditure trends.[10] In quantifying the potential cost of eliminating absolute poverty in 20 years, those working on the World Bank estimates are quick to point out that they have been forced to make a host of assumptions concerning the problems of definition, conceptualization, and implementation referred to above, thus reminding the reader of the potential margin for error in the calculations.

They have also emphasized an aspect of the cost problem overlooked in earlier presentations, namely, the recurrent expenditures on wages, supplies, repairs, and other noninvestment costs that will necessarily accompany any successful investment program to meet basic human needs. They suggest that these recurrent costs, for which no reliable analysis yet exists, could run at an annual level that approximated actual investment costs. Should recurrent costs run this high, total expenditures for a global basic-human-needs program might have to approximate $20 billion per year over a 20-year period in order to establish a firm and rising "floor under poverty."

Let us assume that at least 50 percent of the recurrent expenditures can be financed over the course of a 20-year period by the developing countries themselves. We are then talking about a 20-year program at a total annual cost of $15 billion per year (1975 dollars), for which additional financing must be found. What major observations should be made about the possibilities of funding such a program?

The first is that this figure is less than total official development assistance given to the developing countries by the North and the OPEC countries in 1975. One could therefore infer that Northern financing alone, at present low foreign assistance levels, could almost cover the cost; any additional OPEC assistance would assure that the $15 billion figure was exceeded. But there are two obvious flaws in this inference. The first is that it ignores the country-by-country distribution of ODA funds; the second is that it ignores the purposes served by present ODA allocations. If allocation of ODA to finance a basic-human-needs program were followed, there would have to be a major shift of funds from countries like Israel, Egypt, and others where allocations reflect security concerns to India, Bangladesh, and sub-Saharan African countries where the great portion of the globe's absolute poverty population is located. And such shifts would mean that Northern ODA would no longer be used in such large quantities for political and strategic purposes, such as attempts to "balance" forces in the Middle East and limit Soviet influence. Thus one can only suggest that present levels of official development assistance alone *could* finance a global basic-human-needs program if it were assumed that the funds would henceforth be concentrated on this single goal and that the new goal would for all practical purposes determine country allocations.

The second major observation about the $15 billion figure, however, is more heartening. If the DAC countries of the North were achieving the 0.7 percent of GNP foreign assistance target rather than the 1976 0.33 percent figure, and if the additional amount were allocated to basic-human-needs programs, then it would be possible for the DAC countries once again to cover the entire cost of the new set of programs out of the *increase*, if they chose to do so. While nobody expects the DAC countries to reach the 0.7 percent of GNP figure, there are many policy makers who feel that a target of approximately 0.5 percent of GNP may well be reached early in Development Decade III. With the United States pledged as of 1977 to press for major increases in foreign assistance for economic development, with Japan as of 1977 publicly pledged to double its ODA within 4 years, and with the ripple effect of these changes in policy on the rest of the DAC members, it may not be overly sanguine to think that the DAC countries as a whole could achieve a figure of between 0.45 and 0.5 percent GNP in official development assistance by 1982. If an increase of this order of magnitude takes place, an additional $8 billion to $10 billion (in constant dollars) will be available for development assistance from the DAC countries. These new funds, together with some reallocation of existing ODA funds to the basic-needs goal, could provide the required $15 billion.

The third major aspect of the costing problem which the figures highlight is that major international transfers would undoubtedly be needed to initiate a basic-human-needs program in the poorest countries, such as India and Bangladesh. For these countries, the investment costs alone of financing the direct distributional elements of a basic-human-needs program (as opposed to the more indirect high-employment elements) might consume over half of their government revenues. Not only would such a sharp reallocation lead to serious sociopolitical difficulties and probably fail for those reasons alone; it would also undoubtedly cause a major slowdown in the growth process for a significant number of years and thus raise the growth versus equity trade-off in a dramatic and serious manner. Some few countries might be prepared and able to undertake this shift and face the obvious sociopolitical challenges that would be entailed; most would not.

For many other Southern countries in the middle-income range —for instance Brazil—a substantial portion of the financing for a basic-human-needs approach might be raised domestically. The crucial variable here would be the strength and personal persuasion of governing elites. Would they be able to manage such a switch in investment priorities while maintaining power, and would they desire to do so even if they could? While the percentage of gov-

ernment revenues involved in such a reallocation in a country such
as Mexico might approximate 20 percent rather than 50–60 percent,
political instability and/or governing-elite hostility to such a switch
in emphasis might still combine to produce serious domestic
resistance.

In summary, the matrix introduced in Figure 8–1 reminds us
that there are two major spectrums involved in any discussion of
the basic-human-needs approach and that policy targets can be
chosen to meet individual circumstances with much more flexibility
than most of the more hortatory discussion of the basic-human-
needs approach suggests. The first spectrum ranges from a high-
employment set of policies that attempt as quickly (but indirectly)
as possible to overcome the absolute poverty problem to the much
more direct (supplementary) programs to reach the poverty population as quickly as the appropriate delivery systems can be designed with food, health, and educational facilities. There are obviously many stopping points along this spectrum which may be
influenced by specific needs and opportunities in given countries
and by the availability of financing.

The second spectrum involves the source of basic-needs financing. As noted, governments in some of the poorest countries will
be unable to mount the more direct attack on absolute poverty
without very substantial initial international assistance (or internal
revolution). Their domestic revenues are simply too limited to
undertake such an abrupt policy shift without causing very major
changes in all forms of economic and political life within their
countries. This is one of the reasons that the Mellor strategy for
India analyzed above emphasized the more indirect approach to
the fulfillment of basic human needs. Beyond the poorest countries,
much more of a domestic choice appears available. A substantial
(25–30 percent) shift in the investment of government revenues
might in many cases provide the funds necessary to implement a
basic-human-needs strategy. But the Northern perception that
countries such as Mexico and Brazil—both of which contain substantial and generally concentrated absolute poverty populations—
could overcome the problem in two or three decades without international assistance often demonstrates a very unsophisticated
understanding of the sociopolitical constraints operative in such

countries and the degree of instability and challenge to governing elites which lies just beneath the surface of such "stable authoritarian-technocratic-bureaucratic regimes." Even in those countries whose governing elites would consider favorably such policy shifts, political cost-benefit calculations may prevent the introduction of such reforms unless subtle international pressures and some international financing of the appropriate type strengthen the domestic position of such policy makers.

In the following critique of the basic-human-needs approach and in the continuing analysis of the potential merits of the approach as a fundamental ingredient in North-South relations in the 1980s, it is important to bear in mind the two spectrums involved. Current discussion of the approach at the policy-making levels of governments as well as in international institutions so often focuses on one end or the other of each spectrum that participants in such discussions pass each other like ships in the night. "Converts" to the approach are often so convinced by the normative (and sometimes the prudential) value of it that they rush to box 4 of the matrix and advocate immediate delivery of the full range of direct distributional policies supported entirely by international financing. Discussion that focuses solely on box 4 instantly evokes the "global welfare program" and "the North won't pay" criticisms by opponents. Both criticisms are purely rhetorical, since no competent analysts who endorse the basic-human-needs approach would ever deny that it must be built on the efforts captured in box 1: high-employment-oriented growth strategies undertaken at the initiative and the expense of the developing countries themselves. It is in fact in this area that thoughtful analysts begin to link new global-regime policies with the basic-human-needs approach. For example, they note that successful full-employment strategies may accelerate demand for food faster than increased domestic production can supply it. If an international food regime could monitor such problems and assist by timely allocation of food reserves in the early years of the policy changes suggested by box 1, there will be fewer possiblities that new patterns of high-employment growth would lead to food shortages and other debilitating constraints.

If the basic-human-needs approach were to be undertaken in isolation from global reform considerations and at the box 4 extreme, the probabilities that it would add anything more than further conflict to North-South relations are very low. But to associate the basic-human-needs approach with box 4 in isolation is to create a straw man rather than to engage in serious policy analysis and prescription.

IV

A critique of the basic-human-needs ingredient of a North-South strategy for the 1980s must be related to the four major normative and prudential concerns that have led to its dramatic emergence in recent years. First there is the concern that without a much more focused attack on absolute poverty, its dimensions will continue to grow. What will the absolute magnitude of the problem be by the time—if it ever comes—that more traditional development strategies begin to create enough productive employment and appropriate infrastructures to limit the growth of a group that now approximates one-fourth of the earth's population?

Second, there is the related concern with population stabilization. If, as suggested in Chapter 7, the most rapid road to falling birthrates is intimately linked to such factors as basic living standards, falling infant mortality, rising employment opportunities for women, and other socioeconomic indicators of a similar nature, isn't a basic-human-needs approach of substantial importance as a mechanism through which to slow population growth in the most sustained way?

Third, will it be possible to continue to retain Northern legislative support for any forms of foreign economic assistance without a major emphasis on the basic-human-needs approach? The goals implicit in the concept are already a part of United States law, and they are equally important as stipulated goals of foreign assistance programs in several other OECD countries. Throughout the 1970s these legislative pressures increased, though such trends are hard to predict. Nevertheless it is the case that as of 1977 it was only the concern for designing programs to reach the absolute poverty population that produced United States congressional support for the development aspects of foreign assistance.

Finally—and most important even if least measurable—there is the issue of the creation of some fundamental global norms and

values upon which to begin to build some of the world-order ma-
chinery so clearly needed for the 1980s. Put most simply for the
moment, if the North and South can't strike a bargain over an
approach to the assistance of those billion people living on the
razor's edge of existence, is there really a likely prospect that they
can begin the process of accommodation anywhere else?[11]

The critique of the basic-human-needs approach begins with
three economic issues, then moves quickly to a set of more complex
domestic and international political issues. The first economic issue
raised concerns the actual capacity to design and implement the
more direct and costly aspect of the approach, which extends well
beyond the adoption of a more labor-intensive, rural/agricultural-
oriented development strategy. Can the conceptual issues of definition and implementation be overcome? Can delivery systems be
designed which assure that target populations are reached? The
questions are serious, and most of the answers lie in the realm of
politics, not economics, Certainly the delivery mechanisms can be
designed. The real question is whether or not a country's sociopolitical system will support or defeat the objectives for which the
blueprints have been created. Thus this issue will be further analyzed as a part of the political aspect of the critique below.

A second economic issue is the need for an elaborate basic-human-needs program. Some economists continue to believe that no
such direct, interventionist attack on the problem of absolute poverty is necessary. They believe that trickle-down strategies, properly modified, can overcome the problem. But on the basis of
historical performance, skepticism would seem to be in order. If
the magnitude of the problem has increased during 25 to 30 years
of rapid aggregate growth rates and if the outlook for LDC growth
rates—particularly among the least developed countries—for the
coming decade is somewhat uncertain, modest reforms in development strategies would seem to be a weak reed to lean on. Most
current projections for employment trends in the 1980s confirm
this judgment. At a minimum a commitment to the major shifts
implied in the Mellor analysis of Indian development strategies
would seem to be needed if the absolute poverty problem is to be
stabilized and then reduced in size. And the more pessimistic one
is about the opportunities to restructure the international economic

system (given Northern neo-mercantilist pressures) in ways that would enhance LDC growth potential, the less confidence one can have in proposals that seek to resolve the absolute poverty problem through the use of much improved macromechanisms that count on global markets and international capital flows to produce rapid LDC growth rates.

The third economic issue is more important than the others and concerns the problem of financing any extensive basic-human-needs program. As noted, we are talking about sums that could easily reach $15 billion per year for a 20-year period if the objective of "eliminating absolute poverty in two decades" is taken seriously. Where will these funds come from, and with what assurances that they can be counted on for a lengthy enough period to energize developing countries to design and implement appropriate programs? As the Alliance for Progress experience reminds us, any country can generate 5-year development plans if they are thought to provide access to additional international financial support. But if the funds are marginal to the objectives or the objectives themselves are not really internalized, the elaborate plans serve as the ultimate mockery of the entire effort.

The following generalization can be made with some degree of assurance concerning the issue of financing. If individual developing countries are in the process of restructuring their development programs toward the high-employment model in the first place, then their own investment programs will tend to minimize the extra funding needed for the direct distributive basic-human-needs programs; there will be an as yet unmeasurable but potentially considerable infrastructure overlap and a mutual supportiveness in this set of country cases. The high-employment model will already be creating more purchasing power for the poorest and providing more "low-income" health and educational services.

Nevertheless, it is clear that with about 80 percent of the world's absolute poverty population living in the poorest developing countries, a great deal of international assistance will be needed, since the internal savings for added investment in these countries simply will not be available in the short-to-medium term. This suggests that at least $10 billion per year in the earlier years might be needed from international sources if all the major poorest countries chose

to implement a basic-human-needs approach of the direct distributional type. Finally, if the North were to encourage the middle-
range (Third World) countries to redirect certain development policies to meet the needs of their poverty populations, such as those
living in northeast Brazil and the central plateau regions of Mexico,
another $2 billion to $3 billion per year in international funding
could be used if most of the financial burden for the added direct
distributional elements of the approach were to be borne by the
North. In terms of the matrix, in this set of countries the North
might attempt to provide financing for box 4 expenditures while
domestic efforts (and finances) were focused on box 1 efforts. Thus,
if present estimates approximate correct orders of magnitude and
if the North were prepared to shoulder 75–80 percent of the financing of the new basic-human-needs programs, a total annual
cost might approximate $12 billion per year.

Though large, this figure is obviously feasible under two conditions: first, that the DAC countries do succeed in raising their
aid donations to a level of approximately 0.45–0.5 percent of GNP
by the early 1980s and second, that most of that increase is allocated
to the support of an international basic-human-needs regime. As
noted above, the raising of the ODA contributions to 0.45–0.5
percent of GNP would increase available funds by close to $10
billion in constant dollars. Furthermore, if executive branches of
Northern governments would follow the expressed desires of their
legislative branches and reallocate even a modest amount of present
aid funds to basic-human-needs programs, the $10 billion figure
could actually be surpassed with a comfortable margin for error.
Finally, it should be noted that if any additional financing is forthcoming from OPEC sources, funds that might be expected if the
UN's Development Decade III document does make the basic-
human-needs problem a "core" of development efforts in the 1980s,
then even greater international assistance will be available for the
funding of such a global effort.

Therefore this aspect of the problem of economic feasibility re-
solves itself into two distinct political issues. First, will the North
(and, one hopes, the more wealthy OPEC countries) make the political decision to commit funds that are not substantially greater
in percentage terms than they already spend on "economic assist-

ance" to the goal of eliminating absolute poverty over the coming two decades? And second, will the developing countries assist in promoting Northern support for such a commitment by accepting the domestic programmatic implications of a "global regime for the fulfillment of basic human needs"?

Examining these issues in turn, it should be recalled that the major Northern interest in the global equity question has focused for the most part on the absolute poverty problem. For over 40 years the problem of basic human needs has been discussed and debated as a domestic issue in the United States. The legitimacy of the right to fulfillment of such needs is unquestioned. As Arthur Okun noted in the mid-1970s, "While I am not persuaded by the arguments for many proposed new rights, the case for a right to survive is compelling. The assurance of dignity for every member of society requires a right to a decent existence—to some minimum standard of nutrition, health care, and other essentials of life. Starvation and dignity do not mix well."[12]

The debate in the United States concerns the scope of the definition of "basic needs." The domestic experiences in most Northern societies are quite similar, though the extension of the definition and the societal modes of fulfilling those needs vary significantly. Nevertheless, the point is that basic human needs are an issue to which all Northerners can relate with understanding, empathy, and a desire to assist. Legislatures reflect this fact, and there is little reason to think that they will not continue to do so if the developing countries will join in an international effort that guarantees that Northern funds voted in support of the approach reach the target populations in the South. This necessity raises two integral political feasibility issues that thus focus on the Southern half of a basic-human-needs "bargain." First, will most Southern countries be willing to undertake serious efforts to overcome the absolute poverty problem? And second, will they accept whatever forms of oversight are required to assure continued Northern financial support for a basic-human-needs regime? The first issue might be labeled the Southern-elite problem; the second, the intervention problem.

Will a set of policies that in the medium-to-long term raise the probability of reducing the political power, socioeconomic status, and relative economic position of most developing-country elite groups—even if these reductions are slow and generally incremental—ever be accepted and implemented in most developing countries? Many observers strongly doubt the possibility. This viewpoint has been neatly summarized by Mahbub ul Haq as follows:

Fundamental institutional reforms are, in fact, the essence of new development strategies. At the heart of these reforms is a change in the existing control over the means of production and access to key services. Normally, the rich exercise enormous economic power within these systems because they control most of the means of production in the society, such as land and capital. That is why land reforms and public ownership of major industries have become the key elements in any institutional reforms. But these reforms can easily become a whitewash, and have, in many societies. Unless there is the necessary political will, it is impossible to change the established relationship between the owners of the means of production and those who have been perpetually denied these resources. What normally happens in many societies is that the governments nationalize a number of industries, banks, and some key services, like education and health, and they place these industries and public services in the hands of the bureaucrats or the same interest groups as before. It is not surprising, therefore, that these reforms amount to mere tokenism and not any real restructuring of society. This is really what has happened in a good part of South Asia, where the bureaucracy or the landlords or the industrialists have readily and enthusiastically embraced all the symbols and slogans of socialism.[13]

Several points should be made about Haq's observation. The first is that it may state the problem in a slightly exaggerated form. Recalling the Mellor strategy suggested for India, the high-employment approach does not require a dramatic change in "existing control over the means of production." It rather requires a rapid shifting of governmental and private investment flows away from certain (often highly protected) forms of production and into others. For the government, it means a greater concentration of investment on new forms of (often rural) infrastructure expenditures. It means establishing sources of credit for those heretofore unable to obtain credit. And it means adopting price and other policies that alter market signals, thus reallocating private investment into new (and generally labor- and export-intensive) industries.

Each of these shifts will be opposed by entrenched bureaucratic and private-sector interest groups. Haq is absolutely correct in emphasizing that point. But returning to the matrix, we should note that a basic-human-needs policy surely does not of necessity require a set of policies that merits the label "a change in control of the means of production." For better or worse—and the characterization remains a personal choice—one is in the realm of examining, developing, and implementing policies that will gradually change the *structure* of production, the access to crucial production inputs, and eventually the distribution of a much larger base of real assets.[14] Much of this is an incremental process affecting future income flows and governmental expenditures. Except where significant land reform is needed, it does not depend upon redistribution of existing wealth.

Another factor that tends to counterbalance the sociopolitical forces ordinarily creating major obstacles to the introduction of new high-employment strategies and concomitant direct distributional basic-human-needs programs is the growing recognition on the part of many developing-country elite groups that the risk of opposition to such an approach may well be greater than the risk of the innovation itself. At what point does the danger of resistance to change outweigh that of domestic accommodation?

There is within many developing countries a growing awareness of the magnitude and seriousness of the absolute poverty problem. Until recently the view that trickle-down strategies of growth would eventually overcome these poverty conditions was seldom questioned. This is no longer the case. And as the problem grows, so do the political dangers to many Southern governing-elite groups that cannot find the sometime treacherous path between doing too little (leading to rural unrest, terrorism, and increasing outbreaks of anomic violence on the part of the destitute) and doing too much (leading economic elites to "invite" military forces to assume "temporary" power).

Facing this general dilemma, how would an "average" developing country respond to a major Northern initiative for a global basic-human-needs regime that included major new sources ($12 billion per annum in constant dollars) of long-term funding? Most governments of the poorest countries could not help being attracted by the prospects of significant new funding for an approach to what is, in their countries, a problem of enormous magnitude. Unless the "performance criteria" and the degree of international intervention tied to the regime caused major political problems, negotiations on such a regime might very well succeed rather quickly.

Circumstances will be quite different in middle-range developing countries where the absolute poverty problem is less acute. Nevertheless, governing elites in many of these countries are ruling with a very thin margin for error. Therefore, despite the fact that the resource transfer for them will be of a much smaller magnitude, on the margin it may still be attractive. Consider the case of a governing elite that has presided over 40 years of steady economic growth in a country that, among developing states, is highly industrialized. The elite group's politics are highly institutionalized, and it faces no serious *organized* political opposition. Despite this performance, the absolute poverty problem for the forgotten 40 percent is worse than it was four decades ago, whether measured by absolute living standards or by numbers existing in absolute poverty. Population growth rates have until recently approximated 3.5 percent per year, unemployment and underemployment exceed 35 percent, and for the first time in several decades the political system shows signs of fragility as leftist middle-class leadership finds a growing constituency among the urban and rural destitute and the economic elite woos the "apolitical" military in an increasingly open courtship. How would a governing group in this (actual) situation react to the possibility of international economic assistance that, though marginal from the viewpoint of its entire budget, is far more significant when thought of as discretionary funds that could be allocated to an attack on the absolute poverty problem?

The generalized answer for middle-range developing countries may run along the following lines. Where governing elites feel themselves to be in firm control and are far less concerned with potential forgotten 40 percent problems than they are with the demands of an emerging middle class (a typical situation), then a basic-human-needs strategy would indeed face a serious Southern-elite problem. Such a government would be likely to pay little more than lip service—if that—to the concept. But in the situation portrayed in the previous paragraph, where a governing elite is caught between conflicting sociopolitical demands and desires, a much more responsive look at a global basic-human-needs regime is likely to be taken.

Thus the ultimate question of the feasibility of a basic-human-needs regime for many developing countries may be decided by the "terms of the contract." Will the regime prove too interventionist to be acceptable to many? The dilemma is simple. Northern financial support for a major basic-human-needs effort—whether unilateral, via the OECD, or as part of a broader North-South agreement on the subject—will not last long unless the effort is administered in ways that assure that the target populations do receive the benefits consistent with the objectives of the program. The benefits may be individually tailored to fit the strategy mix chosen by each country, but continued financial support will in all probability be contingent upon some appropriate measure of performance. How can a monitoring system be devised which is mutually acceptable to donors and recipients? Without serious monitoring, the probability is that the leakage will be very substantial and very few benefits will ever reach target populations. But how many Southern states will agree to a serious form of program oversight? Critics argue that on the one hand a monitoring program capable of measuring performance will never be accepted and on the other a basic-human-needs effort without that ingredient will fail to achieve its objectives, undermine that Northern support for North-South cooperation which is linked to the equity issue, and further exacerbate North-South relations for the 1980s.

Citing many of the feasibility issues raised above but particularly emphasizing the feasibility problems related to the issue of intervention, critics caution against a strong emphasis on the basic-human-needs set of issues as one of the fundamental ingredients in North-South policy prescription in the coming decade. In doing so they often add two final notes of caution. The first warns that any emphasis on basic human needs is most likely to politicize the human rights issue, adding further fuel to the North-South conflict. The second questions whether the "high-risk," interventionist basic-human-needs approach shouldn't be muted in favor of more traditional, interstate concentration on world-order problems in the coming decade.

The often implicit and sometimes explicit linkage of the human rights and the basic-human-needs issues, conceptually unavoidable, is now a fact of international political life. From the Northern point of view, the interest in and support for a basic-human-needs approach is a reflection of norms and value patterns that are deeply implanted in Western culture. And when those influenced by this cultural strain focus on individuals, as they do when considering basic human needs, they also turn their attention to the broader issue of human rights as delineated in the evolution of Western civilization. Therefore it is not at all surprising that those governments, private organizations, and individuals most desirous of eradicating absolute poverty also support the global application of certain basic human rights standards.

If Southern cultures were consonant with their Western counterpart on the definition and the ordering of human rights in an aggregate values system, then the basic-human-needs approach would entail no additional difficulties. However, the present North-South conflict over the human rights issue is as deep as any other aspect of the present confrontation. The two parties cannot agree on even the empirical content of the term "human rights," let alone appropriate international standards and policies supportive of those standards. Thus the conclusion that any Northern initiatives that illuminate the fundamental differences between North and South on the human rights issue will, for the medium-term future, be more detrimental than beneficial to aggregate efforts to improve North-South relations.

This line of argument is generally accepted by those critics of the basic-human-needs approach who feel that progress toward world-order politics and a resolution of many global agenda items in the 1980s will demand abstention from the pursuit of policies that appear to intervene in the domestic affairs of other states. It is argued that cooperation at the interstate or multilateral level can be accomplished only if the norm of noninterference in what are considered to be the domestic affairs of states becomes an acceptable procedural norm of the evolving international system. This norm refers not to intervention in the traditional military or "internal subversion" sense, but to criticism of domestic policies of other states and attempts to effect the reformation of those policies through overt bilateral or multilateral diplomacy.

V

These final two criticisms of a Northern emphasis on basic human needs as one of the fundamental ingredients of North-South policy making for the 1980s raise three of the most difficult issues to be considered in analyzing North-South relationships in the coming years and attempting to prescribe policy. First, is it possible to evade the issues of human rights and basic-human-needs in North-South diplomacy and still manage to break out of the present stalemate system? Does the analysis in this and prior chapters attach a reasonable probability to an "evasion" approach?

Second, even if it appeared to be a reasonably feasible approach, what would be the probable costs and benefits when measured against the moderate-international-system objectives highlighted in Chapter 1? Does an examination of the inherent normative trade-offs simplify or complicate the strategic choice involved?

Finally, remembering that one of the fundamental goals of the basic-human-needs ingredient in North-South policy making in the coming decade is the attempt to isolate and nurture one or two embryonic global norms, does the critique suggest that the search for such substantive norms—even as basic as the right to survival—remains inappropriate to the international relations agenda of the 1980s?

A recent examination of world-order politics for the coming decade illuminates the issue but fails to provide an explicit answer to the question. In calling for a "cooling" of national dogmas and ideologies in order to achieve the necessary modicum of order, Stanley Hoffmann offered the following prescription:

The goal would be not to reproduce the conditions of domestic integration at a higher level, but to translate these conditions; no central power, but effective international institutions; *no social or political consensus on a broad range of values, but* a dense web of ties signifying the prevalence of mixed interests over adversary relationships and of *behavior corresponding to a minimum of common values.* Since actors tend to behave according to their beliefs and in response to internal pushes and pulls, *the emergence of such a code requires,* not merely the ideological erosion already called for, but *the observance of minimum standards in domestic affairs.* [15]

As the previous chapters suggest, any search for "social or political consensus on a broad range of values" between Northern and Southern states would be quixotic in the extreme. The issue, as Hoffmann defines it in its global implications, is much more modest but no less crucial. It is the need for "behavior corresponding to a *minimum* of common values," and for "the observance of *minimum* standards in domestic affairs." But in the North-South arena, of what is that minimum to consist? In wrestling with this problem, both Hoffmann and Ernst Haas have suggested that economic development (Haas) or "the race to welfare" (Hoffmann) may represent one of the very few initial global norms on which to build.

Yet it is the perceived inequity in the distributional implications of present economic development strategies and the race to welfare that are currently undermining the legitimacy of the norm of "developmentalism." The gradual emergence of interest in and support for a basic-human-needs strategy for development in general and for the absolute poverty problem in particular is a direct reflection of this increasingly dubious legitimacy. So the questions remain: Are there any embryonic substantive norms that can be developed to ease present levels of North-South conflict and serve as a bridge to more constructive relations in the 1980s? And if so, is the concept of fulfilling basic human needs—contentious as it first appears—one of them?

NOTES

[1]Robert S. McNamara, Address to the Board of Governors of the World Bank, 1976, p. 23.

[2]Statement of U.S. Secretary of State Cyrus Vance at the meeting of the OECD Council at the ministerial level, Paris, June 23, 1977.

[3]Robert W. Tucker, *The Inequality of Nations* (New York: Basic Books, 1977), p. 199.

[4]See Roger D. Hansen, *The Politics of Mexican Development* (Baltimore: The Johns Hopkins University Press, 1971), for a case study of this process.

[5]Gustav Ranis, "Output and Employment in the 1970s: Conflict or Complements," in Ronald G. Ridker and Harold Lubel (eds.), *Employment and Unemployment Problems of Southeast and South Asia* (New Delhi: Vikas Publications, 1971), vol. I, p. 61.

[6]See, for example, William R. Cline, "Policy Instruments for Rural Income Redistribution," paper delivered at the Conference on Income Distribution in the Developing Countries, Princeton University, September 1974.

[7]Pranab K. Bardhan in Hollis Chenery et al., *Redistribution with Growth* (New York: Oxford University Press for the World Bank, 1974), p. 261. Emphasis added.

[8]John W. Mellor, *The New Economics of Growth* (Ithaca, New York: Cornell University Press, 1976).

[9]Mahbub ul Haq, *The Poverty Curtain* (New York: Columbia University Press, 1976), p. 209.

[10] If housing were added to the basic-human-needs list, the cost of the program would almost double. It is not included in the package being analyzed in this chapter.

[11]Ridiculous as this question would have appeared in the age of cabinet diplomacy or even in the cold war years, the analysis of novel constraints on Northern governments presented in Chapter 5 suggests its relevance to North-South relations in the 1980s.

[12]Arthur Okun, *Equality and Efficiency: The Big Tradeoff* (Washington, D.C.: The Brookings Institution, 1975), pp. 17–19.

[13]ul Haq, op. cit., pp. 66–67.

[14]Despite these qualifications, Haq's characterization of the degree of change required by new development strategies retains more than enough validity— particularly as it relates to LDCs in which land tenure is markedly inegalitarian— to suggest how strong the resistance to a major basic-human-needs effort may be in many LDC socioeconomic settings. Thus the enhanced importance of political elites in the process—at least the enhanced importance attributed to their potential role by analysts who stress their capacity for autonomous behavior.

[15]Stanley Hoffmann, "The Uses of American Power," *Foreign Affairs*, October 1977, p. 30. Emphasis added.

Part V
CONCLUSION

Chapter 9
Beyond the Stalemate System: The Necessity for Choice

I

One analysis of the 18-month North-South CIEC debacle in Paris (1975–1977), which climaxed a frenetic and fruitless 4-year cycle in North-South diplomacy, asserted that "CIEC was the end of a beginning—the first step in a long and arduous journey to (one still hopes) a more peaceful, more prosperous and more equitable future for all."[1] As the parenthetical remark suggests, uncertainty is likely to mark both the pace and the direction of the journey.

The characterization may have been apt if the beginning is seen as a choice between confrontation and dialogue. On the other hand, the author also noted with approval a *New York Times* description of the Northern strategy at the CIEC meetings as one that was designed "to talk them [the South] to death."[2] Surely it is unlikely that the North will retreat from its late 1970s posture of dialogue to its early 1970s confrontationist stance. The only cost to the North of 2 years of dialogue was a promise of a $1 billion Special Action Program to meet the most urgent foreign-exchange needs of the least developed countries. And since Northern economic assistance bookkeeping practices will determine whether this $1 billion actually involves *additional* funds or simply a shifting of previously appropriated foreign aid expenditures, it is highly unlikely that anywhere near the full $1 billion will be, in the aid jargon, "additive."

Yet this dialogue brought with it 2 years of moderate-country control within the group of 77, less confrontation in many international venues, and increased bilateral and regional diplomatic exchange between Northern and Southern states on a broad range of issues. Given this cost-benefit ratio of the movement from confrontation to dialogue (or, more accurately, "talking them to death") any Northern diplomat who suggested a return to confrontation would probably be placed on an early retirement list. No matter— he could always find employment writing on North-South issues for *Commentary* or the *Wall Street Journal*.

But if the CIEC experience was truly thought to represent the first step in the journey to greater North-South understanding and multilateral cooperation, then there is little reason to think that the judgment was an accurate one. It is highly unlikely that the suggested forward motion will begin—except for continued movement along the post-1964 (UNCTAD) line of incremental change—unless and until both Northern and Southern states begin to examine seriously the fundamental international systemic contributions to the North-South stalemate system analyzed in Chapter 2 and make the conscious choice to alter their modes of diplomatic interaction accordingly. Until both sides view the North-South problem as the absence of a statecraft more congruent with the emerging constraints of the international system, there is little reason to expect serious change.

Unless Northern states recognize and attempt to calculate the debilitating effects on their capacity to achieve their international goals of such systemic changes as the diminishing utility of force in North-South relations, the growing constraints on Northern foreign policies linked to growing welfare state demands, and enhanced Southern capacities to use international organizations and linkage strategies to achieve their own goals, why should Northern policy makers choose to move beyond a talk-them-to-death strategy? Indeed, if this strategy bought 2 years of relative North-South calm and the possibility of more to come, why choose an alternative course of action?

As for the Southern states, why should they choose an alternative course of statecraft? "Stridency" and "confrontation" brought the North to the bargaining table when nothing else would; the moderates among the G-77 were then given an opportunity to negotiate on the list of Southern demands. After that negotiation failed, it might soon be time for recharged radical leadership to confront once again, probing Northern diplomatic perimeters for signs of weakness.

Thus, in the late 1970s there seemed nothing inevitable about the taking of the first steps toward a changing relationship. That is why Robert Tucker may be proved correct (in the short run) in his prediction that we will witness no systemic change, but merely a new hierarchy of states in a constant struggle for power and wealth. In the longer run his prediction will prove misleading because of the systemic changes that even Tucker can't entirely dismiss. Again, however, without a conscious choice by Northern and Southern leadership to alter statecraft, the systemic changes Keohane and Nye have summarized as "increase in complexity and decline in hierarchy" might simply result in what they themselves described as "the absence of any effective leadership in organizing international collective action."[3]

A major reason that making this initial and fundamental choice will be difficult is that it requires a joint commitment to rethink goals and alter diplomatic methods on the part of both Northern and Southern states. The constraints on change to which each party is subjected necessitate this joint commitment. In the North the constraints appear in the form of domestic pressure groups and legislatures that mirror private-interest concerns. Unless Southern demands; diplomacy, and domestic policies reflect an understanding of the domestic constraints on Northern governments, those governments will probably be unable to take any sort of leadership role in breaking out of the stalemate system. For as long as Northern private interests are able to effectively characterize Southern demands and diplomacy as zero-sum in nature, exhibiting little concern with collective global needs or internal Southern equity issues, executive branches of Northern governments will be faced with an extraordinarily difficult domestic battle to alter present strategies toward the South.

Likewise, Southern change in statecraft is in good part hostage to Northern behavior. Given the fragility of the Southern coalition, the LDC concern with the potential weakening of upper-tier Southern state support for Southern unity, and the (generally accurate) perception that all Northern "offers" conceal strategies to stall or fragment, only a suspension of all Northern efforts of this nature can slowly lower Southern suspicions of Northern motives and tactics. Yet if those suspicions are not lowered, it will be almost impossible to create an atmosphere conducive to less politicized and more flexible Southern bargaining strategies and diplomatic behavior which the growing differentiation in Southern political and economic structures might otherwise produce as a matter of course.

Thus the necessity for political choice in order to move beyond the stalemate system begins with one of the most difficult decisions of all: to recognize that rules that have governed the behavior of states in the international milieu for centuries are no longer congruent enough with the global system and the needs of Northern and Southern states to be followed except at a very high cost to all parties. *How much* change is needed is highly debatable in both prudential and normative terms, as Part IV of this study has suggested.

II

If the first choice to be made is resolved in favor of attempting to escape the stalemate system in ways that go well beyond the talk-them-to-death strategy or its rejectionist antecedent in the North, and if the South supports this attempt by expanding Northern opportunities to make such changes, the next choice will center upon the graduation scenario and its evolution.

The graduation scenario is clearly perceived to be—and in the short run may well be—the "soft option" for the North. Examining the behavior of most Northern states, it is already obvious that this scenario incorporates most if not all their initial, instinctive responses to the first choice analyzed above even if the necessity for that choice has not been rationally examined and made. The second choice therefore involves not whether to follow this strategy but how much emphasis to place on it and whether to emphasize the broad (continuous-graduation) end as well as the narrow (co-optation) end of the spectrum of policies potentially involved.

Of the three basic ingredients for North-South strategies and policies in the 1980s, this one probably involves the most serious hazards, and for two distinct reasons. First, the plausibility of its co-optation strain blinds many policy makers and analysts to its only slightly less obvious risks. Second, it contains an inherent dynamic that centers attention on short-term, system-maintenance issues to the general exclusion of the holistic frame of reference the 1980s will increasingly require. Together, these two weaknesses tend to produce a third: a strong probability that the graduation scenario will be overemphasized in relation to the other major ingredients of a strategy for improving North-South relations.

The plausibility of the co-optation approach lies in the dual fact that the target upper-tier countries *are* beginning to share an overlapping set of economic concerns and objectives with countries of the North and *do* have the potential to impair the working of the present international economic system. From this particular vantage point it does make eminent sense to increase their stake in the system on the assumption that this reform will produce behavior supportive of the system.

There are problems with both the assumption itself and issues the assumption altogether overlooks. As noted in Chapter 6, the assumption is that a greater stake will produce system acceptance. But why should this be so? A greater stake implies greater influence, and the longer-term goals of the graduating states will largely determine the degree to which that greater influence is used to maintain or alter the system. Further, the problem of what system we are talking about remains. Since economic, political, security, and normative aspects of the system are often discordant, it is not at all clear what effect the integration of an Iran or a Brazil into one system will have on the structure and processes within other systems. As noted earlier, the potential for a substantial degree of conflict inheres in this problem because "the system" loses so much of its clarity beyond the international economic realm. Yet a graduation scenario is one that focuses attention and inducements on those very countries whose strong economic potential will lead most of them to become major actors in all systems provided that they survive the many challenges to political stability facing them. Given the heterogeneity of values, goals, levels of development, and geopolitical positioning of these upper-tier states, graduation in the economic system appears to be a very unrefined instrument to use for such a complex and multifaceted operation.

The inherent tendency of the graduation scenario to focus on short-term, system-maintenance issues stems from its forthright concentration on countries that are (or soon will be) in a position to weaken the present international economic system. This perspective immediately excludes two crucial sources of concern to North-South relations in the 1980s:

1. Those countries that are *not* in such a short-term position, e.g., India, Bangladesh, most black African countries, and most countries of Southeast Asia and Latin America
2. Major economic (and economic institutional) reforms that envision a changed system to achieve a set of goals that go well beyond system maintenance as it is defined in 1978

Policy makers who concentrate on countries that can currently disrupt the system are forever committed to putting out fires after they have started. What they miss from a prudential perspective are opportunities to prevent fires; what they miss normatively are the cases of self-immolation. As noted in Chapter 4, present trends in the South suggest a very large and rapidly growing economic gap between countries in the South. At best the lower-income LDCs may grow at an annual per capita rate of 1.5–2.0 percent while their upper-income counterparts are very likely to grow twice as fast. When, before a Southern country at the lower end of the ladder is literally about to fall off, is it considered a problem for system maintenance?

The graduation approach will never suggest that high-level policy makers closely examine the developmental issues facing an India or a Bangladesh with the following question in mind: What reforms, if any, in international economic arrangements might be of greatest assistance to these countries? In other words, they would never examine an entire range of possibilities that would be integral to the global reform approach or the basic-human-needs approach. Such perspectives are simply not a part of the graduation scenario's internal dynamic.

This problem would not be so serious if proponents of the graduation scenario viewed it as but one of several major strands of an aggregate set of North-South policies. But here one confronts the most disturbing aspect represented by the scenario: its substantial potential to further strengthen the strong and further weaken the weak. Major governmental adherents of the graduation scenario are already worried, for example, that any public support given to the basic-human-needs approach will tend to limit the resources and the executive branch flexibility needed to co-opt the upper-tier developing countries of greatest concern. They tend to view the basic-needs approach as one that might hypothetically, at some future date and perhaps as a result of some congressional amendment, create a trade-off situation between the two approaches. And they do not want that trade-off point, however hypothetical, ever to be reached. Therefore from the very outset strong adherents of the graduation scenario exhibit a desire to sweep the field of all competing approaches to North-South issues in the 1980s.

Thus the second choice—this one mostly a Northern (and heavily a United States) choice—is in many ways as crucial as the first choice that must be made. The danger with the graduation ingredient is not that it is unnecessary, but that it may become overwhelming. That is the nature of its own behavioral dynamic.

And what do the 1980s hold for North-South relations if it does become the predominant Northern policy ingredient? Judged against the matrix of potential moderate-system goals presented in Chapter 1, not much. Judged from the perspective of global equity, not much. Judged from the perspective of absolute poverty, almost nothing. And measured against world-order/global agenda problems, one would expect a modest contribution at most. For this policy guideline carried to excess offers nothing more than a potentially new hierarchy of states with no guarantee that the graduates intend to accept the reciprocal obligations expected of them; it is potentially the Keohane-Nye "absence of any effective leadership in organizing international collective action."

Is this judgment unbalanced? Does not the addition of Saudi Arabia to the Group of 10 and the chairs for Mexico and Brazil at the OECD suggest an expanded and strengthened capacity for collective action?

There may be instances in international relations when greater participation of middle-range actors has eased the problem of organizing international collective action of the type increasingly needed in the North-South arena. It is doubtful that this will be one of those instances. As Chapter 5 suggests, the North itself is having great difficulty resolving collective action problems as they apply to the North's own "trilateral" affairs. And as Chapter 4 notes, the extraordinarily rapid process of differentiation now going on within the South—highlighted by the rapidly growing intra-Southern rich-poor gap—will only be speeded by the graduation scenario.

Mix these two trends together, stir them with a bit of co-optation, and whatever emerges is highly unlikely to be effective leadership in organizing international collective action. Therefore the second choice must be to sharply limit the demands placed on the graduation scenario alone to produce moderate and constructive North-South relations in the 1980s. Let this first basic ingredient be recognized for what it really is: a very traditional, very necessary, and very short-term response that provides far less by way of constructive building blocks themselves than of time to devise and implement a much more comprehensive and coherent set of North-South policies.

Even if the graduation approach as defined in its broadest terms (see Chapter 6) salvaged the present international economic system with little further reform, the economic price of system maintenance alone would be a continuous growth of the absolute poverty problem and the Fourth World relative gap problem. Increasing costs would be attached to the failures to achieve progress on related problems of the food production/population balance and international regimes for the regulation of a wide spectrum of economic activity (e.g., in and beneath the oceans) and its side effects (e.g., pollution, dwindling traditional energy supplies). Beyond the economic realm, the problems of nuclear proliferation, conventional arms buildups, Southern regional conflicts, massive human rights violations, and many others whose impact upon North-South relations and a moderate international order in the 1980s would remain totally unresolved, and quite possibly exacerbated, by an all-out attempt at co-optation of emerging Southern powers into the Northern club. When the price of economic stability is totaled across this broad spectrum of problems, the need for further basic North-South policy ingredients should be all too obvious.

III

As the plausibility of an overemphasized graduation scenario begins to tarnish, the conceptualization of North-South statecraft on the part of Northern states and nongraduate Southern states will turn to two other fundamental ingredients. Southern leaders and Northern technocrats will tend to emphasize what we have called the global reform element that can constructively inform North-South diplomacy, while Northern political leaders and private groups will tend to emphasize the basic-human-needs element. Present and predictable trends in North-South relations strongly suggest that only the melding of these two elements into a North-South set of policies can win enough converts—North and South— to produce the first steps toward a more positive and fruitful relationship which were missed throughout the mid-to-late 1970s.

The initial element—global reform—is crucial for several reasons. First, so much can potentially be accomplished at minimal cost that the beneficial results for world-order politics entailed in the effort simply should not be foregone. Second, this ingredient may well entail a dynamic of its own which actually supports the emergence of an embryonic capacity for collective action. Finally, it may result in the building of global process norms whose contribution to constructive North-South relations will, at least indirectly, be greater than the results of any single negotiation.

Chapter 7 illustrated through the examination of a series of potentially modest reforms how much might be accomplished for Southern economic development. In the field of trade liberalization, a mere holding of the line against neo-mercantilist pressures should, *ceteris paribus*, permit per capita growth rates in the middle-income LDCs of 4 percent per year, with exports of manufactured goods increasing at 11 percent per annum. A substantial cut in Northern tariff and nontariff barriers on LDC manufactures, together with improved LDC use of export potential, could increase the rate of export growth by at least another 3 percent per year.[4]

Likewise, modest reforms of present international financial institutions could greatly enhance the growth potential of the middle-income developing countries. Increases in IMF quotas, Compensatory Finance Facility funding, short-term assistance through the so-called Witteveen facility (if and when approved by national legislatures), and an expanded capital base to permit increasing rates of real lending on the part of the World Bank together provide increased sources of short-term foreign exchange and long-term investment funds. Furthermore, the added stability these reforms would lend to patterns of LDC growth should considerably enhance their access to private capital markets, a gain that has been a central element in developing-country demands for years.

Modest reforms in these two areas alone produce projections of middle-income LDC growth rates that equal and/or exceed the rapid per capita growth rates of the 1960s and early 1970s. If we begin to disaggregate the South once again, as in Chapter 4, it is obvious that continued trend-line reforms of this modest and traditional order could do much to ensure continued rapid middle-income LDC growth rates. With the graduation scenario and their own sources of wealth assuring rapid economic advances on the part of the high-income LDCs, this means that only the poorest LDCs would remain in a relatively unchanged and unenviable position.

But the global reform ingredient can in the longer run provide much more for North-South relations than the obvious economic benefits to be derived from such traditional reform proposals. As one thinks of the global agenda issues of the 1980s, it is really in the more novel areas where this strand of North-South policy prescription can make lasting contributions to constructive North-South and world-order efforts. As noted, the pressures of science and technology on the one hand and political perceptions and choices on the other will produce rapidly increasing demands for the constitution of new global rules and regimes in the coming decade to govern the economic and scientific activities of private-sector groups and nation-states.

In the environment of the late 1970s, the challenge to North-South statecraft will be great, since the relationship starts from such a conflicted base. It could, as we are constantly reminded, result in nothing more than a replay of the 1970s: a leaderless struggle for wealth and power. But Northern states are presented with the opportunity to adopt two potential "regime-construction rules" that, in combination with all the other elements of a North-South strategy, could immeasurably increase the probability that progress can be made in this arena of activity. Those rules are (1) where and when possible, give primary attention to the conceptualization, negotiation, and implementation of regimes of vital interest to major segments of the South and (2) when feasible, include automatic resource transfer mechanisms in such regimes so that the developing countries will be provided with a short-term rationale for accepting a long-term global collective good.

What would the first regime-construction rule suggest more concretely? First, that issues such as food production and distribution, energy production and distribution, and population stabilization be given priority consideration on the global agenda. Whenever the "scanning process" described in Chapter 7 identified problems of potential concern and/or interest to the South, they would be given priority attention by Northern governments.

Second, in giving such issues priority consideration, Southern perceptions, concerns, and needs—and they will not always overlap—must be among the primary factors in all Northern analysis and presentation of proposals. This point is crucial, but easily misunderstood. The rule would not call for regimes that sacrificed optimal solutions to (sometimes invalid) Southern perceptions; it would, however, demand that Northern presentations from the outset address themselves to Southern concerns and demonstrate how the proposals set forth would deal with them. A straightforward technocratic presentation will not suffice because global regimes may in fact embody elements of collective welfare functions in and across certain issue areas, and nothing could be less technocratic and more political than the negotiating of a global collective welfare function in the absence of a global community. Thus the manner of conceptualization and presentation will be as important as the proposals themselves, as the events of LOS III suggest.

The second regime rule would suggest that whenever an automatic resource transfer element can be built into a global regime that does not undermine its technical (or political) feasibility, the attempt to add the element be made. Perhaps the classic example produced by policy analysis in the 1970s is the transfer of taxes that might be collected as part of a globally optimal fisheries regime to Southern development efforts. As suggested in Chapter 7, the 1980s are likely to provide a significant number of opportunities to combine optimal regimes (which Northern states, legislatures, and private groups should support out of self-interest) with additional funds for Southern development (which should ease the task of moderate Southern leadership of such institutions as the Group of 77).

If such a pattern can be established, the process of "global norm" creation and "collective action" will have begun. It will be a slow and difficult learning process, and the present LOS III negotiations suggest that some of the most difficult aspects of the process may result as much from intra-Southern disputes as from North-South disputes. But the bias for hope in this general global reform policy prescription is that a LOS III negotiation in the environmental setting created by all three of the fundamental policy ingredients advocated in this study would have produced a substantially different internal dynamic, both within the G-77 and within the North-South arena at that conference. Among the many reasons that might be cited to support this line of argumentation, two are particularly obvious. First, the G-77 would have had less reason to reject initial United States proposals out of hand, suspecting that any proposal tabled by the United States was not what it appeared to be. Second, if a basic-human-needs program were a fundamental element of the 1980s Development Decade III strategy receiving major Northern financial support—thus assuring greater assistance to many of the poorest landlocked and shelf-locked states of the South—the intra-Southern splits at the present conference over the distribution of potential gains from a LOS treaty would be unlikely to have become as intense and debilitating to the conference as they now are.

As noted in Chapter 7, the global reform approach will face serious challenges in both the negotiation and the implementation stages, challenges that may prove insurmountable unless the first two choices noted in this chapter lay the groundwork for the reform effort. If those choices have been made, then the positive-sum nature of the reforms to be considered should allow for progress that can win domestic support in both Northern and Southern states.

There will be no difficulty in demonstrating that such reforms are in the longer-term interest of all states. As the case of trade liberalization suggests, this does not imply that strong private-sector opposition (from business and/or organized labor) to each potential reform will not develop. It simply means that the reforms themselves will be highly defensible analytically, and will thus be capable of developing support within a well-reasoned national-interest perspective. Whether or not national-interest argumentation will generally defeat concentrated special-interest opposition will depend to a great extent upon the evolution of Northern domestic and international trends analyzed in Chapter 5. Again using trade liberalization as an example, the evolution of IMF "rules of behavior" with regard to the new exchange-rate regime and balance-of-payments policies may well determine whether or not neo-mercantilism spreads widely or is held in check over the coming 5 years. The general levels of global economic activity may also strongly influence this particular trend. For neo-mercantilism is a reflection not only of domestic demands of the welfare state, but of the added economic problems caused by a breakdown in the monetary regime, the OPEC trade surpluses, and stagflation. Thus while optimism concerning the evolution of the global reform scenario would be inappropriate given present Northern domestic trends and weakened global economic norms and institutions, the possibilities of cumulatively positive negotiations should not be overly discounted.

Finally, a note might be added by way of explanation and defense of the regime-construction rule encouraging the search for resource transfers for development. First, as noted in Chapter 7, the mechanism should be adopted only in the case of regimes that generate revenues as a result of their inherent operation. Thus they would not need to be defended continuously before Northern legislatures and publics in the same manner that aid appropriations must. Second, thought should be given to allowing developing countries to have the determining voice in the allocation of such transfers. This judgment reflects the hope that a very significant percentage of Northern Official Development Assistance funds will by the mid-1980s be allocated to a global basic-human-needs regime. If such a program has developed, and if an institutional mechanism has been created to allocate and oversee the expenditure of these funds, then the North might well be pushing the intervention issue too far if it demanded, as part of the global reform element, that all potential transfers from new regimes also be subject to joint North-South agreement on allocation and use.[5]

Despite the analytically defensible nature of a major global reform

ingredient in North-South strategies of the 1980s, the approach
suggests the unleashing of technocrats to find optimal solutions to
mutually identified problems after basic political commitments have
been made creating an international "community" that will share
the benefits of the approach. Without a mutual North-South political commitment to make such an approach work, does it not
simply represent another desperate wager that a global "functional"
approach to growing technical problems will itself produce the
political "community?" At the very time analysts of Northern domestic societies are wondering whether those centuries-old communities "may be near the limit of explicit social organization
possible without a supporting social morality,"[6] and analysts of
Southern societies predict continued if not growing conflict over
the content of domestic legitimacy, how can the search for fragments
of a "global welfare function" meet with anything but failure?

IV

Without the addition of the basic-human-needs ingredient to the
fundamental elements of North-South strategies in the 1980s, and
without Southern willingness to work with Northern states to develop this protean concept into a set of policies developing countries
can support, the failure of the global reform approach may indeed
be unavoidable. For the closer one examines the various political,
economic, and diplomatic pieces of the North-South puzzle, the
more compelling becomes the notion that only a joint North-South
effort of very considerable magnitude to overcome the problem of
absolute poverty can provide the initial ingredients of a "supporting
social morality" upon which further cooperative efforts can slowly
be constructed.

Of all the "fragile flickerings of 'universal consciousness'"[7] that
might be looked to for this purpose, the absolute poverty problem
and the basic-human-needs approach to its resolution merit priority
consideration for many reasons, all of them potentially supportive
of a constructive evolution of North-South relations. Of major importance is the potential support for this ingredient within Northern
societies.

As noted throughout this study, Northerners constantly return
to the intra-societal equity theme in their analysis of North-South

issues. If they did so in an egalitarian sense, one that actually sought specific degrees of income equality, then this aspect of North-South relations would have extremely adverse consequences for improved North-South relations. But when most Northerners raise the intrasocietal equity issue, they are not primarily concerned with Gini coefficients of income inequality, but rather with the existence of absolute poverty. Recall Robert Lampman's statement that Americans "don't really seek any particular degree of income equality, but rather seek a system of sharing that recognizes human needs, restrains certain arbitrary or capricious inequalities and serves social purposes."[8] This view is consonant with that of James Tobin who, in his 1970 essay, "On Limiting the Domain of Inequality," suggested that the American ethos regarding income inequality was one favoring slowly increasing resource transfers from rich to poor to meet the latter's needs for a limited but expanding number of "essential" goods—including food/nutrition, health care, education, and housing.[9] It is thus part of the basic American—and more generally, Northern—domestic experience to increase the allocation of what economists refer to as *merit wants* on a subsidized basis to the poor, thus directly easing the absolute poverty problem and, by providing better health and educational services and more food, raising the potential earning power of the poorest in the future.

All the definitional and conceptual dilemmas of the term *equality of opportunity* notwithstanding, it seems a fair characterization to conclude that there is broad general agreement that absolute poverty and deprivation must be eliminated. That is why Northern societies have set and are meeting very concrete goals of this nature. As Arthur Okun recently observed, "The society that stresses equality and mutual respect in the domain of rights must face up to the implications of these principles in the domain of dollars." And in calling for continued support for those governmental programs established to overcome the problem of absolute poverty within the United States, Okun stressed "the urgency of assisting the bottom fifth on the income scale and helping them into the mainstream. . . .If those at the bottom receive [help] and are granted greater equality of opportunity, most will get on their own two feet."[10]

Okun is among the first to realize that many social scientists do not share his viewpoint. But for our more specific purposes, the issue is not the nuances that currently inform the debate over equality of opportunity in the North but the widespread Northern acceptance of the (ambiguous) concept. As noted in Chapter 5, that faith may be weakening—more rapidly in some societies than in others—but it nevertheless remains a belief and a value that may well be used with success as part of an effort to overcome the present North-South stalemate system.

As the analysis in the last chapter suggested, there is much support—existing and potential—for the basic-human-needs approach within the South. The reasons may vary widely, including such diverse sources as normative commitment, governing-elite concern with its power base, and longer-term concerns about population growth and unemployment. In terms of beginning a process of cooperation in confronting the basic-human-needs issues, background motives matter less than the potentially congruent implications of those motives.

Yet another reason for Southern countries to support such an approach is the need to balance the interests of their own coalition. If even the most modest global reforms noted above are adopted, the middle-income developing countries will substantially profit thereby. But the poorest countries could well be left with literally nothing of significance unless it is to appear in the form of a globally supported effort to overcome the problem of absolute poverty. Therefore, as long as Northern states are willing to implement aspects of both a global reform approach and a basic-human-needs strategy, it is in the best interest of continued intra-Southern cohesion for the developing countries to respond affirmatively to both sets of initiatives.

Yet Chapter 8 closed with a strong critique of the basic-human-needs touchstone. What problems must be resolved if the general approach is to marshal consensus rather than conflict, and with what risks entailed if the problems fail to be resolved? First there is the problem of funding. If the currently discussed cost figures are of any validity whatsoever as orders-of-magnitude guidelines, they suggest that an annual Northern contribution of $12 billion to $15 billion per year would provide enough financing to cover all the investment costs and approximately one-half the annual maintenance costs of a global attack on absolute poverty.

Is the figure itself feasible, given the present state of Northern domestic "public household" problems? Three assumptions based upon present evidence suggest that it is. First, it remains the one element of a foreign economic assistance program for which the U.S. Congress and other Northern legislative bodies have shown ever increasing support since the problem of the forgotten 40 percent was identified early in the decade of the 1970s. Second, if the United States—which has constantly undermined rather than supported the concept of an ODA target—were to commit itself to seek yearly contributions at the 0.5 percent GNP level and were to come within striking distances of that figure by the early 1980s (at minimum, 0.45 percent), an increment in ODA funds of approximately $8 billion would be available on an annual basis for the financing of a basic-human-needs program. This calculation assumes that with the United States finally adopting a positive attitude toward such a target, other DAC countries still below the 0.5 percent level would also increase their assistance. Finally, if approximately $5 billion of the $14.8 billion of ODA being distributed in the latter 1970s were also targeted (or reallocated) to this purpose, a $12 billion annual figure could be reached within the North with ease. Any OPEC contributions would then push the annual funding available close to the $15 billion per year range.

This series of "ifs" is quite obviously listed not as compelling evidence but as a suggestion of how plausible the financial target of the basic-human-needs element is if the program and the Southern support it receives are capable of convincing a somewhat skeptical but sympathetic Northern public that the attempt to overcome absolute poverty would be properly targeted on the needs of the poorest and would be implemented in a way that provided a reasonable hope for success.

Attention then focuses on the issues of program development and implementation. Can the program be embodied in a concrete "basic-human-needs regime" whose organizational focus and rules of behavior balance Northern needs for program monitoring with Southern sensitivities concerning external intervention? If a basic-human-needs commitment were to become a central feature of the

UN Development Decade III strategy, then the prospects for resolving the institutional and implementational issues would be very
substantially increased. For the basic-human-needs ingredient in
North-South relations would then have the legitimizing blessing
of the organization that has been the stage for the most dramatic
North-South conflicts of the past decade. And with that blessing
would come the potential prospects of using all relevant elements
of the UN system (including the World Bank and regional development banks) in program development and implementation. Psychologically, the UN endorsement could prove to be a very
significant first step to an effective resolution of the intervention
problem in Southern states.

However, it is still probable that a basic-human-needs regime
would require the creation of a new technical and decision-making
institution of its own. The institution, which would not involve any
country-representation element, would have three purposes: first,
to receive financial contributions from the North (pledged on a
multiyear basis that would be needed to strengthen the program's
probabilities of success); second, to make allocative decisions (based
on Southern-member program performance and yearly budgetary
needs); and third, to monitor program performance to assure that
the regime's funds were being used in accordance with previously
negotiated program guidelines. The advantages of such a new institution would be several. First, it would serve as an apolitical,
technical agency with decision-making powers to receive Northern
financial assistance and disburse it to those Southern countries that
voluntarily decided to become members of the regime.[11] Second,
the institution would be staffed to contain a very high degree of
economic developmental expertise, with leadership chosen on the
basis of "neutrality" in the North-South conflict and commitment
to the success of a basic-human-needs approach to economic development. Third, the expertise and integrity of this new institution
would ease Northern countries' concerns about program monitoring, assuring them through annual evaluation procedures that funds
were being used for the implementation of jointly agreed goals.
Fourth, the institution's monitoring of developing-country members' programs would be far less interventionist than the same
degree of monitoring carried out by representatives of individual

Northern countries. In sum, every effort would be made to negotiate the political issues—Northern financial commitments and
their duration, the elements of a basic-human-needs program, and
a set of indicators that the institution would use to measure performance standards—between Northern and Southern states party
to the basic-human-needs regime prior to the formation of the new
institution that would then become a central element in it. All
countries, North and South, would be free to join the regime if
they accepted the reciprocal commitments central to its purposes.
From that point forward all decisions on financial allocations would
be left to the institution itself, which would make them on the basis
of technical judgments concerning performance standards and annual budgetary needs. The implicit Northern assurance that the
use of funding would be well-monitored would lie in the fact that
a failure in monitoring by the new institution would ultimately lead
to a withdrawal of Northern financial support.

The scheme might seem unnecessary to many observers even
if the basic-human-needs touchstone were to become a central focus
of Development Decade III activities. Why not simply continue
with bilateral or World Bank assistance at higher financial levels
and with more specific targets?

The answer lies in the somewhat more revolutionary nature of
the scheme being proposed. If it is to have a modest probability
of success, the scheme will call for two crucial ingredients: (1) long-
term, high levels of Northern funding and (2) a developing-country
willingness to commit those funds to an altered development strategy that will call for significant and often politically difficult domestic
reforms. Neither set of commitments has the faintest chance of
being generated by a simple increase in bilateral aid levels or
increased World Bank/IDA disbursements. A new regime, symbol-
ized by the new institution, would signal not only a novel reciprocal
commitment but also the establishment of a technically capable
institution whose sole objective would be the effective implementation of a basic-human-needs program. It would thus be as "depoliticized" an institution as could possibly be created and it would
be in the institution's own vital self-interest to see that it managed
the regime with the best possible results measured solely in terms
of eliminating absolute poverty. For that measurement would, over

the years, determine whether or not the regime succeeded and whether the abolition of absolute poverty truly became accepted as a global norm. Neither bilateral aid programs nor multilateral programs would have such a singularity of objectives and focus; both are highly infused by other objectives, concerns, and political pressures. This is not to say that bilateral and multilateral aid disbursements could not be used in support of a basic-human-needs effort. But it should be recognized from the outset what a second best approach they would entail except as a contributing element to the basic regime approach advocated here.

In the proposed regime there would be ample room for assistance from such specialized agencies as the World Food Council, the International Fund for Agricultural Development, the UN Industrial Development Organization, and especially the World Bank in the development and implementation of the regime's program in the aggregate and individual countries' programs more specifically. It has already been noted that the conceptual efforts of the World Bank have provided the intellectual impetus to much of the work now being undertaken in this general area. The purpose of the new regime and a new organization would be to serve as the official embodiment of the new North-South commitment to the basic-human-needs approach. The new institution would be the ultimate locus of responsibility for the receipt, allocation, and accounting of the program's finances and for the adaptation of conceptual and operational refinements to ongoing programs as the learning process in the basic-human-needs arena progresses.

Two final supporting arguments for a new regime should be noted. The first concerns the advantages that would accrue to advocates of the basic-human-needs approach from both North and South. Each group could use the new regime to strengthen supportive arguments. In the North, it could accurately be argued that such a regime would "lever" more funds from more Northern (and potentially OPEC) countries for the program than would increased bilateral efforts. It could also be persuasively argued that the existence of a new technical institution, with its oversight functions, would assure less leakage of funds to non-poverty-oriented expenditures than would bilateral and multilateral programs, for the simple reason that the basic-human-needs program would be its sole raison d'être. Thus countries with little or no intention of implementing such programs would either not join the regime in the first place or soon be denied funding since the longer-term success of the entire regime (and the institution) would be jeopardized by continued financial allocations to countries that couldn't demonstrate a pattern of expenditures in conformity with regime norms. And in the South, the same logic would apply. Those groups interested in a successful basic-human-needs effort would need the promise of long-term Northern financial support which a new regime would provide. Additionally, they would not want such prospects jeopardized by the actions of Southern states intent on using program funds for non-basic-human-needs objectives.

The final argument for a new regime and institution concerns the attempt to nurture embryonic global norms to support world-order politics in the 1980s. The norm at issue here concerns an attempt to universalize the notion that within the next several decades no human being should have to live on the razor's edge of existence; all should have that minimum of food/nutrition, health care, and basic education that would begin to narrow the gap between the richest and poorest peoples (not states) as measured by infant mortality, life expectancy, and literacy rates. Among others, these indicators might be used to determine on a regional basis whether participant countries were investing their basic-human-needs funding appropriately.

As noted earlier, it is difficult to imagine another norm around which to begin to build toward anything we might call an emerging community of values relevant to both North and South. If that is to be one of the major purposes of the basic-human-needs ingredient of North-South policies in the 1980s, then an unequivocal statement of the goal and its institutional embodiment seem far more appropriate than incremental increases in bilateral and World Bank/IDA lending.

Those who disagree will argue that a basic-human-needs effort at this level of salience would be a potentially more costly approach than we need risk and therefore will continue to propose an incremental approach. Their arguments raise two questions the answers to which are decisive in making the final choice in the field of North-South relations: how much support to give to a global attack on absolute poverty. First, what are the potential costs of an incremental approach itself? Second, how do these potential costs compare with those of a more outspoken Northern commitment to a North-South "bargain" in behalf of a global basic-human-needs strategy?

The potential costs of a more incremental, bilateral (and partially multilateral) approach are a function of the probabilities one attaches to the following outcomes. First, the incremental approach gradually drains what is left of Northern support for foreign economic assistance. The rhetorical question, why should the poor in the rich countries be taxed to support the rich in the poor countries? increases the difficulties of mustering legislative support for what looks very much like more of the same.

Second, the internal dynamic of the graduation scenario successfully undermines any serious northern initiative in the arena of basic human needs. Policy makers concerned with the day-to-day problems of system maintenance successfully deflate any executive branch initiative to spell out and seek Northern legislative support for a new policy emphasis that might at some unspecified point in the future impinge upon Northern freedom of action to work with the Brazils, the Irans, and other graduates.

Third, the failure to build the basic-human-needs normative core into the Third Development Decade effort limits Northern interest in the spectrum of global reform proposals that might otherwise be forthcoming. As noted, this general set of reform proposals will be of considerable value to the middle-income developing countries but of relatively minor short-to-medium-term assistance to the poorest countries. If the widespread but diffuse Northern support for the equity concerns in North-South relations is not focused and reinforced by a significant and forthrightly articulated attack on the absolute poverty problem, legislative support for a series of "world-order" or "global agenda" reforms of a far less visceral, more technocratic nature will be very difficult to achieve. For each reform proposal will ignite the opposition of specific domestic interest groups; if the general North-South environment within which debates on global reforms take place is not improved, private interests will have a far greater opportunity to defeat many items constituting the global reform element in North-South relations.

These prospects will be of little concern to those who share neither the goals of a moderate international system presented in Figure 1-1 nor the analytical implications concerning the present stalemate system examined in Chapter 2. In the latter chapter it was suggested that one of the major challenges facing North-South relations in the 1980s will be to determine appropriate objectives and policies affecting those relations that are congruent with the emerging changes in the international system. Measured against the goals of a moderate international order in the next decade—in terms of lost global reform opportunities and the opportunity to push forward with the one global issue that might contribute more to eventual constructive accommodation than to a continuing pattern of diplomatic divisiveness—the cautious and incremental approach to the establishment of a basic-human-needs set of policies appears potentially far more costly in both normative and prudential terms than does the more prominent regime approach.

The more visible effort, i.e., Northern financing of $12 billion to $15 billion each year for a basic-human-needs regime that is a core ingredient of Development Decade III, may not succeed in its avowed purposes. The major hurdles were analyzed in the last chapter. But the probabilities of success certainly seem higher if the concept is approached directly in the processes of intra-Northern and North-South discussions and negotiations than if efforts are made to increase aid flows and World Bank lending to support the same goals *without* any attempt at a broad international commitment.

First, the probabilities are increased that Northern financing will become available in significantly greater amounts if international agreement can be reached. Northern legislatures are very rapidly tiring of the old approaches, are insisting on this genre of shift, but can hardly be expected to do more than signal the changes they desire. They have neither the expertise to write the actual language nor the authority to carry out the appropriate negotiations.

Second, the probabilities are that the South would find this approach far more satisfactory than the present, scatter-gun approach to the use of aid funds, which follows no logical pattern, is often cluttered by legislative riders requiring monitoring and reporting procedures that serve no valid purpose, raises the human rights issue in a unilateral Northern manner, and leaves each party to the aid giving-and-receiving game uncertain as to current rules and norms.

If agreement could be negotiated as part of Development Decade III on the broad outlines and policy choices within a basic-human-needs approach that included the wide spectrum of objectives and goals analyzed as part of Figure 8-1, Southern countries would recognize that basic-human-needs policies could be shaped according to individual countries' needs and factor endowments. The only firm constraint would be the necessity that development strategies in general and the expenditure of the new institution's funds in particular were designed to increase the standards of living of a country's absolute poverty population as rapidly as feasible. Where that result can be most effectively achieved through policies emphasizing what was labeled in Chapter 8 as the more indirect, high-employment approach, such policy choices would be wholly appropriate to a basic-human-needs regime. The obvious need for specific, country-by-country analysis and policy planning confirms the need for a new institution that incorporates both high standards of technical expertise and the neutrality necessary to make binding decisions concerning allocations of funding.

Southern states would also recognize that the middle-income countries who decided to join the regime could draw upon the available funding for support in efforts to overcome their more regional, localized absolute poverty problems (e.g., in the northeast of Brazil or the central plateau regions of Mexico) without radically reversing their aggregate development strategies. In other words, through joint attempts to codify the conceptual and technical ingredients of a basic-human-needs approach, the South would come to recognize that it was *not* simply a program that would allocate all funds to the Indian subcontinent and sub-Saharan Africa, but one that could be used by all developing countries in which the absolute poverty problem encompassed a significant percentage of the population (e.g., 20 percent).

In sum, the very process of North-South discussions preceding the agreement on such an approach—an approach the U.S. Secretary of State has already asked the OECD to examine in considerable preliminary detail—would greatly enhance the probabilities that the regime forthcoming would be one committed to overcoming the absolute poverty problem with enough country-by-country flexibility to attract rather than repel Southern participation. At present much Southern skepticism results from the absolute lack of North-South discussion about the objectives and programmatic implications of a basic-human-needs approach. But it is that very discussion, which would develop the details of a program, that no interested groups or World Bank analysts have yet produced. These international discussions, which would be a crucial element in the evolution of the basic-human-needs concept, would never even be undertaken in a less formal, exclusively Northern move toward incrementally increased assistance targeted on absolute poverty.

The final reason that the more salient, international effort to establish the fulfilling of basic human needs as a globally legitimized goal in the 1980s is proposed concerns the growing North-South conflict over human rights and the prospects for narrowing this particular "value gap" through North-South discussions about and negotiations over a basic-human-needs regime.

At the present time most developing countries are united against Northern (particularly United States) intervention on the issue of human rights. Many fear that the issue will simply be used as another Northern perspective from which to attempt to influence domestic LDC affairs. But this issue masks another more fundamental problem: differing definitions of human rights. Precisely what do human rights include? For most Northerners, they incorporate the classical civil liberties and political rights enshrined in the first half of the Universal Declaration of Human Rights. Included are such concepts as freedom of expression, information, association, religious beliefs and practices; equality before the law; and a judicial process that protects individual rights.

For many Southerners, these concepts have less value than do those emphasized in the second half of the same Declaration. In this section one finds the following concepts: the right to a standard of living adequate for the health and well-being of individuals; the right to security in the event of unemployment, sickness, or disability; and access to economic, social, and cultural rights perceived as indispensable for dignity and the free development of personality.

The perceptual and value gap between these two sets of concepts, both embodied in the Universal Declaration of Human Rights, have not been bridged since the document was written three decades ago. The first set continues to reflect the cultural values and norms of Western civilization and receives the support of all Northern countries. The second set, emphasized by the South, reflects the desires of societies and ethnic groups at far lower standards of living to raise those standards.

Unless a serious discussion is joined on this amalgam of issues quite shortly, the North and the South may well continue to drift even further apart on human rights issues, and the cost, measured in terms of negative impact on other joint endeavors, could mount yearly. Several events of the mid-to-late 1970s are suggestive of this trend, including U.S. congressional insistence that governments involved in flagrant violations of human rights as defined by Western civilization be made ineligible for United States foreign aid other than aid clearly marked for the poor. In the mid-1970s, the World Bank experienced two split votes on loan proposals—two of the very few in its 30-year history—over the issue of human rights. In both cases the recipient country was Pinochet's Chile, and highest among the reasons listed by those countries opposing the loans was the Chilean government's human rights practices. In both cases almost all European countries voted against the loans or abstained, while the United States and almost all developing countries supported the loan proposals.

Two further fragments of evidence suggest that this aspect of North-South relations has the potential for greatly increased conflict and confusion in the coming decade. The first concerns the Carter administration's attempts in the late 1970s to use foreign aid (both economic and military) to signal its approval or disapproval of the human rights policies of Southern recipients. The ad hoc methods used to determine the behavior being measured and the signals being sent had, by late 1977, reduced the United States policy initiatives to utter confusion. An autumn 1977 administration decision to grant Somoza's dictatorial regime in Nicaragua military aid while temporarily withholding an economic loan "for the poor" sent conflicting signals to all parties concerned, split the staff of the National Security Council, angered Congress, and created a general sense of dismay among all interested observers and participants.

Second, as one reviews the evidence concerning the probable evolution of Southern societies set forth in Chapter 4, it is clear that the human rights issue will have more potential for North-South conflict in the 1980s than it does at present. The probable trends (with cyclical variations) toward increasing authoritarianism in Africa and Southeast Asia and the substantial potential for major ethnic conflicts in Africa over the coming decade suggest that human rights problems will dominate the global media. How governments respond to each significant new problem will be a function of the basic understanding they are able to share concerning appropriate forms of interstate behavior on human rights issues.

Given this potential for ever-growing conflict on the human rights issue, given developing-country demands for Northern assistance in accelerating economic development, and given all the other North-South concerns and problems captured in the phrase world-order politics, it is quite probable that a serious effort at a North-South exploration of the human rights issue is a better course of action than is an attempt to skirt the problem in order to minimize sensitive issues of interference in domestic affairs. For better or worse, we have reached the point in international relations when the real challenge is to work to legitimize certain forms and pro-cedures of "interference" rather than to issue inoperable pledges of abstention in domestic affairs preferred by latter-day Metternichs who yearn for the halcyon days of cabinet diplomacy. Foreign aid legislation, World Bank votes, and many other aspects of the North-ern domestic legislative process confirm this reality—fortunate or otherwise—of interdependence.

Since Southern demands (focused on interstate equity issues) and Northern responses (focused on intrastate equity issues) inev-itably illuminate and politicize the issue of human rights, the ne-cessity to search for minimal substantive and procedural norms will become increasingly pressing. As the global absolute poverty prob-lem becomes increasingly visible, it will trigger two reactions on the part of many Northerners: first, a humanitarian instinct to assist in easing the problem; and second, a tendency to criticize devel-oping-country governments for "failing" to meet the basic needs of their own populations. And that criticism, combined with criti-cism of human rights violations, will inevitably be reflected in amendments to major pieces of "North-South legislation" that will further politicize these issues and exacerbate North-South relations.

What must be recognized in the North is that it is our own system of cultural values and norms that creates this politicization problem. We are expressing our own value system when we concentrate on absolute poverty and human rights. There is no reason why we shouldn't, so long as we also realize what we are thus adding to the North-South set of problems and respond with the recognition that constructive steps to begin to resolve these problems are an objective that we desire and should therefore be prepared to pay a price for. To attempt to impose our own ordering of values and norms on developing countries without a recognition of what we are actually trying to accomplish is a typical example of our own ethnocentrism carried to the extreme. On the other hand, to suggest that we must view these value preferences as a constraint that will be reflected in Northern responses to Southern desires and that we must attempt to make these preferences a basis for constructive policy formulation is something quite different.

Thus the suggestion that North-South discussions be undertaken on a potential basic-human-needs regime and on the manner in which human rights issues can be managed in ways that relax Northern legislative constraints on the functioning of such a regime. There is, after all, much more room for serious North-South consideration of the human rights issue if the North is at the same time preparing to cooperate in a substantial manner in the financing of a basic-human-needs program. For the first time since the Universal Declaration of Human Rights was written, the North would be explicitly recognizing the legitimacy of the concepts in the second half of the Declaration, namely, the right to a material standard of living without which other forms of human rights lose most of their meaning. Thus a search for human rights norms that would ease North-South tensions and allow for more constructive relationships would be undertaken in a novel environment: one in which the North had ex ante accepted the legitimacy of some basic Southern concerns about the very content of human rights and had broadened the definition of the term to cover basic economic rights.

Would that Northern commitment be enough to open a fruitful North-South dialogue on a mutually acceptable mix and ranking of human "rights" and human "needs"? Could it produce embryonic forms of mutually acceptable international norms on human rights performance standards and acceptable international responses to derogation from those standards? The analysis in Chapter 4 suggests what a high fence this particular objective is to ride at, as does any familiarity with the state of North-South conflict over the human rights issue during the late 1970s. But even if little progress is made toward mutually acceptable and mutually supported international human rights standards, the operative policy question is whether or not North-South relations will be more conflictual for having made the attempt.

The answer would surely seem to be no. Those who urge that the issue of human rights not be raised are at best guilty of misrepresenting the problem. The issue *has* been raised, and long before the advent of the Carter administration in Washington. The relevant question is how best to handle the issue now that it has been raised and written into statute after statute. It is against this background and in the context of an attempt to constitute a global basic-human-needs regime that the proposal for serious North-South discussions of the human rights issue is made. For without such discussions, that issue could plague the institutionalization and operation of a basic-human-needs regime—most probably through Northern threats to withhold funding if Southern "human rights violators" received any assistance—just as it is now plaguing so many other aspects of North-South relations (e.g., bilateral aid, multilateral aid, military security assistance, and trade policy). At minimum—and this may be all that can be achieved on this complex subject—what will be needed is a de facto North-South understanding concerning the relationship between human rights issues and a basic-human-needs regime. The nature of the understanding is less important than the existence of one. For without it, all the efforts to construct a new human-needs regime and institution could be negated by an all too predictable chain of human rights–related policy linkages during the coming decade.

V

A slowly changing international system, a part of which is a growing Southern capacity to confront the North with both demands (e.g., the NIEO proposals) and problems (e.g., lack of progress on major global agenda issues), is gradually forcing four choices upon the OECD countries. First, should an attempt be made to break the present North-South stalemate system of diplomatic interaction, or should a steady course be held in the belief that present degrees of Southern unity will slowly disintegrate? Second, if an attempt to break the stalemate system is made, how much reliance should be placed on the classical co-optation approach? Third, will the capacity of Northern states to achieve foreign policy objectives in the 1980s, including particularly the novel objective of managing global agenda problems, necessitate a much more serious and comprehensive examination of the potential of systemic reforms in such arenas as population stabilization, food production and distribution, nuclear proliferation and related energy problems, and international commons regimes? And finally, how much emphasis should be placed on an effort to establish a basic-human-needs regime to overcome the global problem of absolute poverty? Is such an effort likely to be too interventionist in international relations of the 1980s? Or is it better characterized as the most appropriate centerpiece of an effort to narrow the present conflict in values, goals, and objectives between North and South, thus increasing the opportunities to move toward goals set forth at the beginning of this study?

Few analysts will give identical responses to these four choices. But the prospects for the development of more constructive North-South relations in the 1980s—a development whose necessity should become more obvious with each passing year—will ultimately depend upon the seriousness with which each of these four choices is analyzed.

NOTES

[1]Jahangir Amuzegar, "A Requiem for the North-South Conference," *Foreign Affairs*, October 1977, p. 155.

[2]Ibid., p. 151.

[3]Robert O. Keohane and Joseph S. Nye, *Power and Interdependence: World Politics in Transition* (Boston: Little, Brown & Co., 1977), p. 229.

[4]It may well be that continued "trend-line" Northern trade liberalization will no longer be possible in the 1980s, as much of the evidence in Chapter 5 suggests. However, even under altered trade rules and norms—for example, those that might emerge with the adoption of more explicit "industrial policies" in the North or major changes in present GATT "safeguard" rules—explicit opportunities for expanding LDC industrial production could be made an integral part of such alterations.

[5]One of the major reasons the Southern countries fought so arduously throughout the 1970s for the integrated commodity program and a common fund to finance the program was the intense desire to assert autonomous control over an operational international institution that would control significant financial resources. The above suggestion seeks to respond affirmatively to this developing-country desire. Since the source of the funds would be negotiated regimes of which the North approved, it should be easier to negotiate an arrangement that, with very few limitations, gave the South the predominant voice in revenue allocation decisions.

[6]Fred Hirsch, *Social Limits to Growth* (Cambridge, Mass.: Harvard University Press, 1976), p. 190.

[7]Stanley Hoffmann, "The Uses of American Power," *Foreign Affairs*, October 1977, p. 29.

[8]Robert J. Lampman, "Measured Inequality of Income: What Does It Mean and What Can It Tell Us?" *The Annals of the American Academy of Political and Social Science*, September 1973, p. 91.

[9]James Tobin, "On Limiting the Domain of Inequality," *Journal of Law and Economics*, vol. 13, October 1970, pp. 263–277.

[10]Arthur M. Okun, *Equality and Efficiency: The Big Tradeoff* (Washington, D.C.: The Brookings Institution, 1977), p. 118.

[11]This optional membership element would be crucial to both the successful negotiation and the implementation of the regime. Predictable Southern opponents (e.g., Argentina) would be under no pressure to join. And if such countries "opted out," their absence would diminish considerably the potential implementation problems their membership would almost certainly cause.

Selected Bibliography

Aspen Institute for Humanistic Studies, Program in International Affairs: *The Planetary Bargain: Proposals for a New International Economic Order to Meet Human Needs*, Report of an International Workshop Convened in Aspen, Colorado, July 7–August 1, 1975.

Bell, Daniel: *The Cultural Contradictions of Capitalism* (New York: Basic Books, 1976).

Chenery, Hollis, et al.: *Redistribution with Growth* (Oxford: Oxford University Press, 1977).

Dag Hammarskjöld Foundation: "What Now?: Another Development," *Development Dialogue*, nos. 1/2, 1975.

Fishlow, Albert, et al.: *Rich and Poor Nations in the World Economy* (New York: McGraw-Hill for the Council on Foreign Relations/1980s Project, 1978).

Gosovic, Branislav: *UNCTAD: Conflict and Compromise* (Leiden, Holland: A. W. Sijthoff, 1972).

Haq, Mahbub ul: *The Poverty Curtain* (New York: Columbia University Press, 1976).

Hirsch, Fred: *Social Limits to Growth* (Cambridge, Mass.: Harvard University Press, 1976).

Hoffmann, Stanley: *Primacy or World Order: American Foreign Policy Since the Cold War* (New York: McGraw-Hill, 1978).

Huntington, Samuel P., et al.: *The Crisis of Democracy* (New York: New York University Press, 1975).

International Labor Organization: *Employment, Growth and Basic Needs: A One-World Problem*, Geneva: ILO, 1976.

Jansen, G. H.: *Nonalignment and the Afro-Asian States* (New York: Praeger, 1966).

Keohane, Robert O., and Joseph S. Nye: *Power and Interdependence: World Politics in Transition* (Boston: Little, Brown & Co., 1977).

Kimche, David: *The Afro-Asian Movement: Ideology and Foreign Policy of the Third World* (New York: Halsted Press, 1973).

Mellor, John W.: *The New Economics of Growth* (Ithaca, N.Y.: Cornell University Press, 1976).

Morse, Edward L.: *Modernization and the Transformation of International Relations* (New York: The Free Press, 1976).

Tucker, Robert W.: *The Inequality of Nations* (New York: Basic Books, 1977).

Index of Names

Index of Subjects

About the Author

ROGER D. HANSEN is the Jacob Blaustein Professor of International Organization at the Johns Hopkins School of Advanced International Studies. He was formerly a senior fellow of the 1980s Project at the Council on Foreign Relations. He has also been a senior staff member of the National Security Council and a senior fellow of the Overseas Development Council. His publications include books on Mexican and Central American economic development and numerous articles on global distribution of income, North-South relations, and relations between the United States and Latin America.